W9-BSP-598

Doctrines of Religious Communities

WILLIAM A. CHRISTIAN, SR.

Doctrines of Religious Communities
A Philosophical Study

Yale University Press
New Haven and London

Designed by Nancy Ovedovitz and set in Bembo type by
David E. Seham Associates Inc. Printed in the United States
of America by Edwards Brothers, Inc., Ann Arbor,
Michigan.

Library of Congress Cataloging-in-Publication Data

Christian, William, A., 1905–
    Doctrines of religious communities.
    Includes index.
    1.Dogma.   2. Religions.   I. Title.
BL85.C48   1987   291.2'01   87–2027
ISBN 0–300–03795–3 (alk. paper)

The paper in this book meets the guidelines for permanence
and durability of the Committee on Production Guidelines
for Book Longevity of the Council on Library Resources.

10   9   8   7   6   5   4   3   2   1

Contents

Acknowledgments

William H. Austin, William A. Christian, Jr., Richard Fern, Hans Frei, and Ninian Smart read the manuscript. Norvin Hein, George Lindbeck, Joseph A. DiNoia, Rulon Wells, Victor Hapuarachchi, Ellison Findly, and Bruce Mullin responded to calls for help. The Yale Department of Religious Studies sheltered the project in Jedediah Morse's old home. Rebecca Clouse did much to put the manuscript into shape. Nancy R. Woodington of the Yale University Press went through it with a sharp eye and a good ear. I thank them all.

Doctrines of Religious Communities

CHAPTER ONE
Introduction

If we think of religion as a kind of human activity about which something can be learned, and survey the scene from that point of view, a striking fact is the existence of a number of massive and enduring communities with non-overlapping memberships, each with its own body of doctrines. Indeed, the history of religion is to a very large extent the history of religious communities.

Historical studies shed light on the bodies of doctrines of religious communities. So do anthropological and sociological studies. Along with these there is room for philosophical studies, and the question which has prompted the investigation we begin here is: What can philosophers learn by studying doctrines of religious communities?

Among the topics philosophers can investigate with a reasonable hope of learning something are the structural features of bodies of doctrines and the positions a community might take on claims which arise outside its bounds. We deal with the first of these topics by studying some types of principles and rules which communities build into their bodies of doctrines. Then we shall see how such principles and rules would affect the position of a community on alien claims.

The doctrines a community brings with it into the world are mainly doctrines about the setting of human life and the conduct of life in this setting. These are the doctrines the community exists to promote and to nurture in the lives of its members. We can speak of these as primary doctrines of a community. They propose beliefs about the settings of human activities; they propose courses of inward and outward action to be undertaken in these settings; and they propose valuations of various features of these settings, valuations of human intentions and dispositions, and valuations of the consequences of courses of action.

Often philosophers who study doctrines of religious communities concentrate on their primary doctrines, for example, on their teachings about the constitution of the world in general and about human nature in particular, or on their precepts for human conduct, or on the arguments given by teachers of religious communities in support of their primary doctrines.

1

Such studies are often thought of as contributions to metaphysics or ethics or logic.

Primary doctrines are not the only feature of bodies of doctrines which deserves the attention of philosophers. As a community enters upon its teaching activities, and especially as it reflects on its body of doctrines, it comes to hold and teach doctrines of another sort also. Along with its doctrines about the setting of human life and the conduct of life in that setting, a community works out principles and rules to govern the formation and development of its body of doctrines. These norms are doctrines about its doctrines; they are the community's governing doctrines.

We could say that the primary doctrines of a community, taken together, are what the community has to say to the world. And we could say, by way of contrast, that a community's norms for its doctrines, taken together, are what the community has to say to itself about its doctrines. This simplifies a complex contrast, but it reminds us that a community has an active and important part to play in the formation and development of its body of doctrines.

Doctrines about doctrines apply to the primary doctrines of a community, but not only to them, for they apply throughout the community's body of doctrines and hence also to themselves. For example, a doctrine which would yield criteria of authenticity for doctrines of a community would have to satisfy these criteria to be acceptable as an authentic doctrine. Again, a doctrine which says that authentic doctrines of the community are consistent with one another would have to be consistent with authentic doctrines of the community if it is to be acceptable as authentic.

It is with doctrines of this latter sort, doctrines of religious communities about their doctrines, that this study is mainly concerned, though as we go along various connections between doctrines about doctrines and primary doctrines will be noticed. The aim is to explore some types of governing doctrines which one community or another might adopt and to trace out some consequences for the community's body of doctrines.

A community's governing doctrines are not likely to be noticed or studied unless the community's problems in shaping and maintaining its body of doctrines are attended to. In the first place, as a community develops from its origins, disputes among its members about its doctrines often occur. Is what is said in some sentence an authentic doctrine of the community or not? So a community needs principles and rules to guide judgments on such questions. It needs to be able to identify its doctrines. We study some types of such principles and rules in chapter 2.

Questions also arise in a community about relations of its authentic doctrines with one another, about priorities in importance among doctrines, and about the consistency of doctrines with one another. In chapter 3 we consider some types of principles and rules which bear on these questions.

Other principles and rules connect claims that doctrines are authentic with claims that they are true or (for practical doctrines) right. We study these, and along with them some types of principles and rules for deriving and arguing for doctrines, in chapters 4 and 5.

Chapter 6 takes a different tack. There we study some types of connections between doctrines of different religious communities. This will give us some background for dealing with doctrines and alien claims in chapters 7 and 8, and incidentally some distinctions which will prove to be essential in those later chapters.

So bodies of doctrines will not be taken up one by one and expounded as wholes. Instead the object is to bring out some structural features of bodies of doctrines, especially such principles and rules as those mentioned.

In doing so we keep foremost in mind the bodies of doctrines of the Hindu community, the Buddhist community, the Judaic community, the Christian community, the Muslim community, and sometimes subcommunities of these. These communities are notable because of their historical importance or the extent of their geographical spread, but mainly because of the degree to which their doctrines have been reflectively developed.

In the course of the study a number of cases are introduced for the sake of advancing the argument. Often a passage is drawn from the literature of one or another of the major religious communities. Some of these passages are fairly lengthy, so that readers may work their own way into the movement of thought in the passage.

Ordinarily a passage drawn from the literature of some community is chosen because what is said has some plausibility as a doctrine of the community. The plausibility comes from the apparent status in the community of the text from which the passage is drawn or from the apparent standing of the author as a teacher of the community. So what is said can be taken as a prima facie doctrine of the community. But it is not a part of our program to claim or argue that what is said in such a passage is indeed an authentic doctrine of the community in question. That is one way this investigation is different from some of the inquiries undertaken by teachers of religious communities, for example by theologians of theistic communities and by comparable teachers in nontheistic communities. In some of those inquiries it is essential to ask, and if possible to determine, whether what is said in some sentence or other is indeed an authentic doctrine of the community to which, and for which, the teacher undertakes to speak. For those teachers do not aim to speak just for themselves as individuals. They mean to speak as Hindus or Buddhists or members of the Judaic community or Christians or Muslims. Furthermore, their judgments on such questions are respected by members of their communities for the acuteness and the depth of their understanding of the sources of the community's doctrines, for their knowledge of its history, and for their devotion to its welfare.

But in our own inquiry decisions on such questions are not necessary for reaching the conclusions at which the argument is aimed, though the principles and rules which seem to guide those teachers in their decisions are an important part of our subject matter. That is one reason for refraining from characterizing or expounding particular bodies of doctrines as wholes.

So the cases where passages from the literatures of religious communities are introduced are hypothetical cases. We can learn something to our purpose from a passage without undertaking to decide whether what is said is indeed an authentic doctrine of the community in question. But the argument does aim at conclusions which have important bearings on the bodies of doctrines of the major religious communities. For that reason we need passages where there is at least a likelihood that what is said is a doctrine of the community in question. We need some respectable candidates for authenticity, but we do not need more than that. Indeed, at some points we can do with less than that. Implausible cases, cases where it is implausible that what is said is an authentic doctrine of some community, can be instructive also.

This limitation on the range of the argument, and some reasons for it, will be discussed further in the next chapter. One fairly obvious reason can be mentioned here. If each passage drawn from the literature of a religious community had to be accompanied by arguments to show that what is said is an authentic doctrine of the community, we would have on our hands an extremely complicated enterprise. But something can be learned about bodies of doctrines of religious communities without that. So this study is hypothetical with respect to the authenticity of what is said in the passages drawn from the literatures of religious communities.

The argument is hypothetical in another way also. The types of principles and rules which will be discussed are introduced for the sake of exploring some issues for religious communities. A particular community may or may not be in a position to accept doctrines of those types as authentic, depending on the sources of its doctrines and its criteria of authenticity. Here again it is not necessary, in order to reach the conclusions at which the argument is aimed, to claim that any particular community has adopted, or should adopt, a certain principle or rule as an authentic doctrine about the doctrines of that community, much less to claim that all communities do so or should do so. It is true that I venture some generalizations about doctrines of the major religious communities at some points. But the main argument is aimed at showing some consequences for the doctrines of a community if it should adopt the principle or rule in question. (So "if" and "suppose" will occur frequently as the main argument gets under way.) In this way we can learn something about bodies of doctrines without having to settle whether or not some particular community accepts the principle or rule and without having to settle whether some particular community ought to accept it.

Another way of putting this general point is to say that the main argument deals in abstractions. But if abstractions are well designed they can be as useful in studies of doctrines as they are in inquiries of other sorts. How indeed could we do without them? Especially, how could philosophical studies do without them?

If this study had taken as its subject matter the reflections of religious individuals, as many essays in the philosophy of religion have done, a general theory of religion as a feature of human experience might have been needed to demarcate the topic. As it happened, in the beginnings of this study a two-part investigation was projected, one part to deal with the reflections of religious individuals and a second part to deal with doctrines of religious communities. In spite of considerable cultivation, the topic of the projected first part yielded only meager returns. So the topic of the projected second part became the topic of the whole. This brought with it a number of unexpected challenges and some rewarding surprises.

Though a general theory of religion would be relevant to a study of doctrines of religious communities, I have tried to do without one. For the purpose of the argument it may be enough to focus on some well-known communities which are generally recognized as religious communities. Indeed it might be said that if the Hindu community, the Buddhist community, the Judaic community, the Christian community, and the Muslim community are not good examples of religious communities, we would be at a loss to give one. The case studies and analyses which will appear in what follows will also mitigate the absence of a full-blown theory of religion.

With a view to getting a sense of the shape and proportions of a body of doctrines, let us develop a perspective on the primary doctrines of a community. This will help by way of a contrast to put in their own places the principles and rules of communities for governing their bodies of doctrines that will occupy us hereafter. Without a perspective on the primary doctrines of a community we would be likely to have a distorted perspective on its norms for its doctrines.

It seems a fair generalization to say that each of the major religious communities teaches its members to live in a certain way, in accord with a certain pattern of life, and that it teaches them how to live in that way. It nurtures them in that pattern of life. The beliefs, valuations, and courses of action which are proposed in its primary doctrines are constituents of the pattern. By way of precepts, backed by accounts of how the world is, by way of examples, pointing to individuals whose lives have manifested and defined the pattern concretely, and by way of direct induction of its members into certain practices and habituation in those practices, a community aims at shaping the lives of its members. It instils habits of appreciation, of overt behavior, and of thought, which hang together as a more or less coherent pattern of life.

So, to live in accord with such a pattern of life it is not enough to have certain beliefs about the world, nor even to have certain valuations of various objects and events and ideals for human life. Living as a Hindu, a Buddhist, a Jew, a Christian, or a Muslim means something more than having a philosophy of life. It involves, among other requirements, carrying out various inward and outward courses of action. Some of these are distinctive of the community in their outward forms as well as in their motives and intentions, for example studying certain scriptures, carrying on disciplined meditation or engaging in prayers, participating with other members of the community in worship or meditation and in celebrations of solemn or festive occasions, and supporting and promoting the institutions of the community. Other courses of action are less distinctive except with respect to the motives and intentions with which they are to be carried out, for example giving alms to the needy, avoiding harm to other beings, telling the truth, and acting justly in various sorts of situations.

Thus some of the primary doctrines of religious communities have the force of proposing courses of action. To accept such a doctrine is to undertake to carry out the course of action. We can speak of these doctrines as practical doctrines.

It is unfortunate that in the study of religion, and indeed also to some extent in religious literature, the term *doctrine* tends to be restricted to a certain range of teachings, teachings which have the force of asserting that something is the case. This is unfortunate because the full range of what is taught, in the patterns of life proposed by religious communities, includes *agenda* as well as *credenda*. It is true that "doctrine" contrasts with "practice" when what is taught is being contrasted with what is actually being done, as shown in Richard H. Gombrich's study of contemporary Buddhism in rural Sri Lanka, *Precept and Practice*. The point here is that precepts are doctrines. The doctrines of religious communities include precepts as well as assertions. If we should take doctrines which have the force of assertions as paradigmatic for understanding the doctrines of religious communities, we would distort our subject matter grievously.

Indeed, if in studies of doctrines we had to choose between beginning with proposals for belief and proposals of valuations, in which assertions are made, and on the other hand beginning with proposals of courses of action, practical doctrines, there is something to be said for the latter option. In either case we would have to go on to say that doctrines of all these types are built into the pattern of life a community teaches and in which it nurtures its members. Proposals of courses of action are complemented by proposals of beliefs and valuations which generate motives and intentions.

For evidence of the importance of practical doctrines consider the Shorter Catechism of the Westminster Assembly, one of the doctrinal standards of Protestant churches in the Reformed tradition. There are 107 Questions in the catechism. Of these, forty-one are on the Ten Commandments and twenty-nine are on the preaching and hearing of the word of God, on the sacraments, and on prayer. Thus nearly two-thirds of the Questions in the catechism introduce practical doctrines; the answers given propose various courses of inward or outward action as requirements of the Christian life.

Along with practical doctrines there are doctrines with a different force. They propose valuations as constituents of the pattern of life taught by the community, positive or negative valuations of various features of the setting of human life and of human dispositions and actions. Something is said to be good or bad in a certain way and for some reason or other. Accepting a doctrine of this sort means coming to the point of making the judgment proposed in the doctrine.

Consider the following as explicit or implicit proposals of positive or negative valuations.

Also in the matter of worship, austerity, and giving,
  Steadfastness is called *Sat;*
And action for such purposes as those
  Is likewise called *Sat* (good).

Even the gods envy him whose senses are subdued like horses well tamed
  by the charioteer, who is free from pride and free from taints.

Better is little, with the fear of the Lord,
Than great treasure and trouble therewith.

Now abideth faith, hope, charity, these three; and the greatest of these is
  charity.

Muhammad is the most excellent of men.

Beware of cursing anything that God most high has created, whether animal or food or man himself.

Judgments that something is good or bad in some certain way are con-
nected with the courses of action proposed in practical doctrines. Some courses of action cannot be carried out without making appropriate val-uations. For example, sincerely and earnestly repenting of one's sins cannot be carried out without making judgments about the goodness or badness of past conduct and present dispositions. Further, if reasons are given for undertaking courses of action, these reasons have to include valuations of the courses of action and their consequences.

Along with courses of action and valuations, beliefs are constituents of the pattern of life taught by a religious community. So some primary doc-trines have the force of proposing that in the setting of human life there is, or that there is not, a being of a certain description, or proposing that there are, or that there are not, beings of a certain sort, or proposing that some or all existents are conditioned in certain ways, or proposing that cer-tain events have or have not occurred.

Consider the following as proposals for belief:

The world is a manifestation of Brahman.

There is no permanent substantial self.

All persons are subject to rebirth unless they attain nirvana.

All objects and persons are transient aggregates of phenomena.

God is the creator of the world.

God acts in every event.

All men are of one blood.

Muhammad recited the verses of the Qur'ān.

All the qualities of Allah are different from those of the creatures.

In utterances of sentences such as these something is asserted as to what existents there are and what the conditions of existence are. To accept a doctrine which has the force of such an assertion is to take what is asserted as true, but a further point needs to be brought out about doctrines which have this force.

The point can be led up to by considering first a distinction between different kinds of proposals of courses of action, between commands and recommendations. If a speaker issues a command, he is not thereby required to give the hearer good reasons for undertaking the commanded course of action, though he may add threats or promises. But a speaker recommending a course of action ought to be ready and willing to offer the hearer good reasons, reasons which are not just threats or promises, for undertaking the course of action.

Similarly we can distinguish between two kinds of existential assertions, informative utterances and proposals for belief. Informative utterances occur in situations where (1) it is taken for granted that the speaker is in a position to tell the hearer what is the case on some point and (2) questions about the truthfulness of the speaker do not arise. It is supposed that the speaker is both competent and truthful. Further it is supposed (3) that the speaker has not misspoken, that he has not accidentally said something other than what he meant to say. Hence in these situations there is no immediate occasion for arguments in support of what the speaker says. There are many such situations in the course of everyday life. In the case of proposals for belief it is otherwise. If a speaker makes a proposal for belief he ought to be ready and willing to offer reasons for accepting what he says as true.

So different responses are being called for. Commands and informative utterances call for simple acceptance. But recommendations of courses of action and proposals for belief (and, we could add, proposals of valuations) call for reflection and judgment. Of course situations of the first kind often turn into situations of the second kind when questions about what is said arise in the mind of the hearer.

I believe that in the actual situations in which teachers of the major religious communities put forward practical doctrines on behalf of the community these doctrines have the force, though not always the form, of recommendations of courses of action. Recommendations vary in strength, from mild advice to urgent advocacy. And I believe that when such teachers, speaking for their communities, make existential assertions, these doctrines have the force of proposals for belief. On the whole the major religious communities do not seem to be content with unthinking acceptance of their doctrines by their members. Characteristically they give reasons of one sort or another for accepting their doctrines.

I am speaking here of the teaching activities of religious communities, not of their juridical and administrative activities. Also a distinction is needed between (1) the kind of authority a community may ascribe to some individual in its past, such as its founder, or to God, and (2) the way the community itself carries on its teaching. A community might say that no reasons have to be given (though reasons may be, and often are, given) by the founder or by God in support of some prescription or some assertion. But it would not follow from this that no reasons need to be given by the community in its teaching activity for its doctrines, including doctrines about the founder or about God.

We have noticed connections between practical doctrines and valuational doctrines. There are also connections between doctrines of both those sorts and doctrines which propose beliefs. A proposal of a course of action supposes that general conditions of existence and the particular situation of the proposed course of action permit that course of action. It supposes that the course of action is a real possibility, a possibility permitted by real conditions, not just an abstract possibility. So propositions advanced in proposals for belief are supposed by practical doctrines. Further, propositions are often given as reasons for undertaking courses of action.

Similarly, valuational doctrines suppose the actuality or the real possibility of what is to be valued as good or bad in some way. Assertions of the form "——— is good [or bad]" and of the form "——— would be good [or bad]" call for references to fill in the blanks. Also, propositions are advanced as reasons for judging that something is good or bad in a certain way.

Some of the forms of teaching in religious communities do not seem at first sight to fit into the perspective we have been developing. Consider stories, which abound in the literatures of religious communities and seem to be important vehicles of their teachings. If the point of telling a story is to assert that some sequence of events actually took place, then it is clear that the story conveys a proposal for belief, in this case a historical assertion. The story of the enlightenment of Gautama under the bo tree, the story of the giving of the law on Mt. Sinai, and the story of the death and resurrection of Christ seem to have functioned in this way in Buddhism, Judaism, and Christianity respectively, and other important doctrines of those communities have been thought to depend on those historical assertions.

The main point of some stories seems to be a different one. A number of stories in the New Testament gospels are said to be parables, for example the parable of the Sower, and there are many stories in Buddhist scriptures with similar features. Though the sequences of events they relate are often of an ordinary kind, it seems that the main point of telling the story is not to assert that a certain event of that kind did actually take place. Typically, definite names, places, and dates are not given in the course of the story. It seems that the stories are not meant to be accepted in the same way historical assertions are meant to be accepted. How then do these stories convey doctrines of a community, and how are they meant to be accepted? Consider the parable of the Sower.

> "The sower went forth to sow his seed: and as he sowed, some fell by the way side; and it was trodden under foot, and the birds of the heaven devoured it. And other fell on the rock; and as soon as it grew, it withered away, because it had no moisture. And other fell amidst the thorns; and the thorns grew with it, and choked it. And other fell into the good ground, and grew, and brought forth fruit a hundredfold." As he said these things, he cried, "He that hath ears to hear, let him hear."   [Luke 8:5–8]

It seems that this story is meant to be taken as an analogy. Indeed, this intention is made explicit later on when the disciples asked Jesus "what this parable might be." He said, "The seed is the word of God" (Luke 8:11). Sometimes, however, a story is told without explanation, but in a context in which the point of the story can be discerned. The story suggests its point to those who are spiritually alert and are familiar both with the setting the teacher supposes and with what he has said in the past. So coming to accept the story as a vehicle of the teaching of the community would involve coming to discern its point. In this way the hearer's own powers of discernment are aroused and enlisted. "He that hath ears to hear, let him hear."

For a different kind of case consider the following verses from a Buddhist scripture:

> Look upon the world as a bubble: look upon it as a mirage. Him who looks thus upon the world the king of death does not see.
>   Come, look at this world resembling a painted royal chariot. The foolish are sunk in it; for the wise there is no attachment for it.[1]

Let us venture to take these verses together with what is said elsewhere in Buddhist literature, and let us place what is said in the perspective on primary doctrines developed above. A course of action is being recommended. Hearers should look upon the world in a certain way, as a bubble, as a mirage, as a painted royal chariot. Not just once, or just now and then, we may suppose, but steadily. Keep in mind that a bubble is empty

1. *The Dhammapada*, trans. S. Radhakrishnan (London: Oxford University Press, 1950), chap. 13, 4–5 (pp. 116–17).

and that it bursts; remember that a mirage is not what it seems to be and that it vanishes; think how a painted royal chariot, for all its splendor, is a composite of parts and is destructible. So this is a way of thinking about the world as one keeps these images in mind. The recommendation is to cultivate a steady habit of looking at the world in this way.

This course of action involves certain valuations of the world or, we might say, a turning away from those valuations which would attach one to the world. If one judges that the world is good in itself or that it is bad in itself, adversions or aversions are generated which would tie one to it one way or the other. But a steady habit of looking on the world as a bubble, as a mirage, as a royal painted chariot, will have the effect of blocking off attachments of either kind. The world has the value of a bubble, a mirage, a royal painted chariot, no more and no less.

Why should this course of action be undertaken and carried out? Why should the imagination be trained in this way? And why should the world be valued in this way? A reason is given in a doctrine about the constitution of the world. It is proposed for belief that all the objects and processes which go into the makeup of the world are subject to conditioned origination *(pratityasamutpāda)*. Nothing whatever exists in itself. Every existent, including both things and persons, is conditioned in its origin and in its passing away by other existents. Nothing is independent of all other things; hence nothing is permanent. So training oneself to look on the world as a bubble, as a mirage, as a painted royal chariot, and to value it as one would value such things is in accord with the way the world is.

Now, turning back from this perspective on the primary doctrines of religious communities to the principles and rules which are our main target, what functions do those governing doctrines have in a body of doctrines? At this point the best answer may be, "Wait and see," for as yet hardly anything has been said about them. But certainly it would be misleading to say that they are parts of a superstructure which is added on more or less arbitrarily to the primary doctrines of a community. It would be less misleading to say that they condition and regulate various sorts of decisions a community makes about its body of doctrines. It would be better still to say that they express a community's understanding of the structure of its body of doctrines. For these, as well as its primary doctrines, are doctrines of the community. But first we should look for piecemeal answers as we take up various types of principles and rules.

CHAPTER TWO

Authenticity

Consider what Irenaeus, bishop of Lyons in the second century, has to say in his treatise *Against Heresies*. Irenaeus has much to say about the setting of human life. He speaks of the creation of the world and of the history of its redemption. And he has a good deal to say about how human beings should conduct their lives in this setting. But along with propositions about the world and proposals of courses of action, Irenaeus brings in considerations of a different order.

He must do this because he wants to argue that certain doctrines taught by various gnostics are not authentically Christian. So he cannot be content with ridicule and invectives, though he descends to these at times. And he cannot be content to argue against these doctrines from general standards of truth or from general standards of moral rightness, though he argues in those ways at times. To make his point, he has to appeal to more specific standards. For his direct object is to show that these gnostics have gone astray from the authentic teachings of the Christian church.

So he needs a framework for arguments on questions of the form: Is *s* a Christian doctrine? These questions cannot be argued unless there is some non-arbitrary way of dealing with them. They call for principles and rules to guide arguments and judgments. The following are some of the parts of the framework Irenaeus develops for dealing with such questions:

s is not a Christian doctrine unless it is in accord with the Scriptures.
Passages in the Scriptures, like passages in Homer, ought to be interpreted
    in their contexts. [I, ix, 4]
Apostolic tradition confirms and amplifies what the Scriptures say.
Bishops can be relied on to preserve apostolic tradition.

Now in *Against Heresies* it is clear that Irenaeus means to speak not just for himself but for his community. So he must be putting forward these principles and rules as Christian doctrines. And, since their function in the situation in which he speaks is to guide judgments as to whether something is a Christian doctrine or not, we might say of the framework as a whole that it is being proposed as a Christian doctrine about Christian doctrines.

Similar situations with comparable requirements occur in the histories of other religious communities. So we have here a characteristic of bodies of doctrines of religious communities when these communities become reflective and articulate. Along with doctrines about the setting of human life and doctrines which propose courses of action in that setting, doctrines about their doctrines are required. This feature of the bodies of doctrines of religious communities, that they include governing doctrines, is by no means a new discovery, but it might well attract the attention of philosophers and prompt them to study some of its occurrences.

Later on we shall study some doctrinal principles and rules which have other functions and are required for other reasons than those we have noticed in the case of Irenaeus. For example, developed religious communities have something to say about the relations their doctrines bear to one another, about the consistency and the ordering of their doctrines. But the best place to begin is with those doctrines which serve as principles and rules for identifying doctrines of a community. Such principles and rules are necessary to guide judgments on questions of the form: Is s a doctrine of R? that is, questions which ask whether some sentence can be used to express, well and truly, an authentic doctrine of the community in question.

"IS s A DOCTRINE OF R?"

It is not hard to see that such questions are very likely to arise when we consider the vast bodies of literature which have accumulated over many centuries in the case of each of the major religions. These include canonical scriptures, commentaries on scriptures, and commentaries on commentaries; liturgies and rules for ceremonial observances; legal codes; catechisms and other aids to education; chronicles of the community's past; stories told in celebration of prophets, revered teachers, saints, and martyrs; guides for personal meditation or prayer; apologetic and polemical treatises; expressions of mystical experiences and speculations; and writings of various other sorts. These elements of the literature of a religious community derive from various periods in its history, and they reflect various social environments in which the community has from time to time put down its roots. Yet they all purport to express the teachings of the community, and it has preserved them as parts of its heritage. When we are confronted with a body of literature of such range and variety it is not surprising that questions of the form Is s a doctrine of R? should arise about some of the things that are said.

Furthermore, the histories of various religious communities show that from their beginnings their teachings have included contrasting strands of thought and practice and that sometimes it has been problematical how to weave these strands together into a more or less coherent body of doctrines. Also, none of the major religious communities has developed in isolation from alien patterns of life, religious or secular, which have impinged on the lives of their members. Thus the ancient Israelite community had to take account of Canaanite beliefs and practices; the early Buddhist community had to take account of Brahmanism; the early Christian community had to place itself in relation to Judaism, to Graeco-Roman culture, and to the Roman empire; and the early Muslims had to deal with traditional Bedouin religion, with Judaism, and with Christianity. To maintain its own identity a religious community has to define its stance toward alien patterns of life. One result is that in such situations its doctrines have to be pointed up more sharply than might otherwise be the case.

Questions of the form Is s a doctrine of R? suppose that the teachings of a community can be taken as a multiplicity. They ask whether what is said in some sentence can be identified as a member of that multiplicity. And it is true that religious communities often list some of their doctrines one by one for purposes of instruction. There are ten commandments; there are four noble truths; there are five pillars (of Islam); there are thirty-nine (Anglican) articles of religion.

It is also true that religious communities often speak of their teachings as more or less ordered wholes. This is suggested by uses of singular terms, for example in the history of Judaism certain uses of "the Torah," beginning in the rabbinical period, to refer not just to the five books of Moses, and not just to what is said in the Hebrew Bible, but to all the instruction God has given his people, Israel. Another case in point is the use of "the Dharma" in Buddhist literature for all that the Buddha taught about the way to enlightenment, as in "I take refuge in the Dharma."

So taking the doctrines of a religion as a multiplicity, for the purpose of asking whether what is said in some particular sentence belongs to that multiplicity, does not suppose that the doctrines of a religion are unrelated to one another. The point is that two sorts of questions can be asked. One is whether what is said in some sentence is a doctrine of the community; the other is how doctrines of the community are related to one another, in general and in particular. In neither case can questions of the other sort be ignored.

Questions of the form Is s a doctrine of R? often arise outside a community, when individuals who are not members of the community want to know for some reason or other what it teaches on some particular point. For example, such questions are asked by historians, anthropologists, sociologists, psychologists, or philosophers in the course of their studies. They are asked also by attorneys, judges, and legal scholars when legal issues have arisen, and by politicians and public administrators in the interest of shaping public policy. Consider a British governor of Buddhist Ceylon, or a court deliberating on the case of a conscientious objector, or a candidate for election to Congress from a district which includes a number of Catholics or Mormons. In these cases we can speak of external questions about doctrines.

On the other hand, questions about doctrines often originate within a religious community. Members of the community want to know what their membership in the community commits them to on some point at issue. Teachers in the community want to know what they should teach. Or there are disagreements within the community on some point, and it has become important to settle them. For some reason or other it has become problematical whether some sentence expresses a doctrine of the community or not. In such cases we can speak of the questions as internal questions.

Now consider some of the differences between external questions and internal questions. In both kinds of cases information is needed, and judgments are called for. But there is a difference in the contexts of the judgments called for and hence in the force of the questions. To bring out this difference, suppose that some scholar is an expert in the study of some religious community of which he is not a member. For example, Etienne Lamotte and Edward J. Thomas do not speak as Buddhists, though they are experts in Buddhist studies, and Ignaz Goldziher and A. J. Wensinck do not speak as Muslims, though they are experts in Islamic studies. Such a scholar may know more about his subject than many or even most of the members of the community he is studying, but his position in relation to a question of the form Is s a doctrine of R? is different from the position of a member of that community who asks a question of that form.

In the first place, if the scholar should conclude that s is a doctrine of that community, he is not placed thereby under any obligation to accept s or to propose it. That is to say, if an utterance of s has the force of an assertion, then he has no obligation to believe s or to assert it, and if s has the force of a precept he has no obligation to undertake the course of action it proposes or to propose that course of action to others. But if a member of that community should come to a parallel conclusion, he would have an obligation to accept s, even if for some reason or other he should also have obligations which run counter to this one. Also, under certain circumstances he would be obligated to propose s to others.

This difference makes another difference. Since a member of the community has thus a moral stake in the question whether s is a doctrine of the community, he has an obligation to consider whether s is acceptable. That is to say, if s has the force of an assertion, he has an obligation to consider whether what is asserted in s is true, and if in s some course of action is proposed, he has an obligation to consider whether that course of action is right. But the scholar who is not a member of the community he studies is not placed, by his conclusion that s is a doctrine of the community, under any obligation to consider whether s is acceptable, though he may consider this and though he may be obligated for other reasons to do so.

This suggests that our scholar is not in a position to speak for the community on the point at issue in the way a member of the community, who might be equally learned, would be. The scholar might well agree. He might acknowledge that his responsibility is to speak of the community he studies but not to speak for it, in spite perhaps of occasional temptations to do so. What he can do, he might say, is to show what has been said in the past, including the recent past, on the point at issue and how the past activities of the community bear on the point. He may even allow himself to speculate on what is likely to be said in the community in the future. But all this is different from speaking for it on the point at issue.

The case of dead religions is relevant here. If no members of a community now exist, there is no one to speak for it except in a hypothetical way. Questions of the form Is *s* a doctrine of *R?* must be transposed into the past tense. Hence all such questions about that community must be external questions. But if it is a living and developing community, there are voices which can speak for it now, and they have a right to be heard.

It seems that the internal questions cannot be settled just by determining what members of the community have happened to believe or practice at some past time. For it is often argued within religious communities that some belief or practice which was prevalent in the community at some past time is not an authentic teaching of the community. Its prevalence was due, it may be argued, to assumptions or customs which were common in the general society within which the community existed at that time, for example Ptolemaic astronomy or slavery.

Also, it seems that these questions are not to be settled by polls to discover current opinions or by surveys of present practices of members of the community. For it is often argued within religious communities that the present state of the community is a degenerate one. Indeed, a Buddhist doctrine predicts a historical decline in the clarity and purity of the teaching of the Dharma.

The fact that such arguments as these are relevant shows that we must reflect further on what is at issue when internal questions about doctrines arise. No doubt studies of the prevalence of various beliefs and practices in a community at some past time or at present can yield important facts of which a community ought to take account. Further, these studies might be sufficient to warrant some judgments about the doctrines of the community by nonmembers of it, for example in cases where legal or political considerations are preponderant. But they could not be sufficient to settle internal questions about doctrines. The reason is that these questions have a normative flavor. This can be explained in either of two ways.

When members of a religious community, speaking as members of it, ask whether some sentence expresses a doctrine of the community, we could say (1) that they are asking whether the community *should* teach what is said in the sentence. They are not just asking whether it is being taught in the community at the time or whether it is generally accepted in the community. They are asking whether the community ought to teach this, in view of certain sorts of considerations we shall explore further.

Or we could say (2) that they are asking what the true community does in fact teach on the point in question. Here the initial focus shifts from (a) the notion of a community which, in some temporal segment of its existence, may or may not teach what it ought to teach to (b) the notion of a community which is not to be strictly identified with any one of its temporal segments but which persists with an enduring character through various temporal segments and continues to teach what it ought to teach. In this case the corollary question arises: How is this true community to be identified? And it may be asked further: To what extent is the teaching of the true community effective in some temporal segment of its existence?

For example, consider the following *hadīth* (i.e., a saying or account of an exemplary action ascribed to Muhammad and handed down through a chain of reporters): "My people [*umma*] will never agree in an error."[1] Now in the history of Islam it seems clear that many opposed claims about Muslim doctrines have been made by speakers who regarded themselves as Muslims and who furthermore had some standing as Muslim teachers. From this it would seem possible for Muslim teachers to agree that some errors about doctrines have occurred among those who have regarded themselves as Muslims. So it seems there must be a distinction between Muhammad's "my people" and the community made up of people who regard themselves as Muslims, and that the former notion functions as a norm. In the true community, the community of those who are faithful to what Muhammad taught, errors will be weeded out.

Or these different manners of speaking can be combined by saying that the community ought to teach what is said in some sentence because in doing so it would be faithful to that enduring character which constitutes its own identity throughout the successions of its temporal states. It ought to teach this because it ought to be true to itself.

Thus it seems that, to answer internal questions of the form Is *s* a doctrine of *R?* criteria of authenticity are needed, and that these criteria must be different from criteria of the prevalence of some teaching. One function of a community's principles and rules for identifying its doctrines is to yield criteria of authenticity which can guide decisions about what the doctrines of the community are.

So if someone who is not a member of the community sets out to decide a question of this type, it seems that two courses are open to him. He may undertake to speak only at second hand, strictly as a historian, let us say. But he may find that the historical facts are not clear. Or he may find that a strictly historical answer is not sufficient, since he is studying a living community which is still in the course of developing its doctrines on the point at issue.

1. H. A. R. Gibb and J. H. Kramers, eds., *Shorter Encyclopaedia of Islam* (Ithaca: Cornell University Press, 1953), s.v. "Idjmā'," 157b.

If so, and if he still undertakes to say whether some sentence expresses a doctrine of that community or not, then he must shape his judgment in accord with that community's own framework for such judgments. We could say that he would be speaking as a self-appointed surrogate for spokesmen of the community. He would have to do something like what a member of that community would have to do. He would have to accept, for the purpose of his inquiry (though only for that purpose), those of its norms for its doctrines which are relevant to his question. His inquiry would commit him to accepting as a framework for argument the community's criteria of authenticity. But he would not be committed thereby to accepting the community's primary doctrines about the world and about conduct in the world, or any of its norms for its doctrines which are not relevant to his inquiry.

There are other considerations. Suppose that a historian who is not a Muslim is approached by two of his friends who are Muslims. The two Muslims have been engaged in a dispute on some point in Muslim theology or in Muslim law. The disputed question is whether or not what is said in some sentence is an authentic doctrine of the Muslim community. Now they ask the historian for his opinion on that point. He makes various comments on relevant matters in the history of Muslim theology and law. But his Muslim friends continue to press him. Perhaps they are as learned in Muslim history as he is; hence they are already familiar with the matters he calls to their attention. So the historian begins to see that they want from him something more. They are inviting him to cast his vote, so to speak, on the disputed issue.

It would not be strange if the historian should decline this invitation. Since he is not a Muslim, he would not have to live with the consequences of a decision on the disputed issue in the way his Muslim friends would have to live with them. So, he thinks, he would not be acting responsibly if he should take an active part in the decision. It would be wrong for him to go beyond the bounds of his own responsibility. Perhaps he thinks it would even be in some way absurd.

Notice that the point on which the Muslim disputants are asking the historian to cast his vote is whether the disputed sentence expresses an authentic doctrine of the Muslim community. The historian's reaction would be different if the disputed point was whether what is said in the sentence is true or right. In that case the historian might have no scruple against casting his vote.

These considerations about the relation of historical studies to questions of the form Is s a doctrine of R? have consequences also for philosophers who undertake to study doctrines of religious communities. Suppose a philosopher thinks that he is not called upon by his own religious community, if he has one, to speak for it in the course of his enterprise and, on the other hand, does not wish to speak for other religious communities. Even so he could study the logic of questions of the form Is *s* a doctrine of *R?*, and of answers to such questions without undertaking to answer them.

CONSENSUS

The normative flavor of internal questions about doctrines and the answers they call for may be brought out further by considering some doctrines which advance consensus as a criterion of authenticity. For example, when Roman Catholic Christians ask whether some sentence has been accepted as a teaching of the church everywhere, always, and by all, applying the rule of St. Vincent of Lerins, the scope of the question is often narrowed to focus on the fathers and doctors of the church. Similarly, when Sunni Muslims ask whether what is said in some sentence is a part of the *ijmā'* (consensus) of the Muslim community, attention is focused on the *mujtahids*, those who have a right, in virtue of knowledge, to form a judgment of their own on the question at issue.

In these cases it seems that a consensus of the community is not to be determined statistically by an unweighted count of the opinions of all the members. Of course there would be practical difficulties in making such a count, increasing with the number of members and the geographical spread of the community. Even in the case of small, compact communities the principle that silence gives consent might have to be relied on. Also, how could the opinions and practices of individual members in the distant past be included in the count? The more important consideration is the one mentioned above, that on a doctrinal issue the judgments of some members of the community are given more weight than the judgments of other members.

So the qualifications for being respected in this way would have to be considered. It seems that judgments of those who are known to have thought deeply on the issue would have more weight than judgments of others. Also, judgments of those who have shown concern for the welfare of the community as a whole would have more weight than judgments of those who have evinced strong personal or sectarian interests. Both intellectual and moral qualities would be taken into account.

Whatever the scope of a consensus is taken to be, it seems implausible that a religious community could teach and continue to teach that the authenticity of some doctrine can be determined from historical and sociological considerations alone. Suppose it is said that some practical doctrine, for example a prescription of the use of a certain prayer in the course of a liturgy, is authentic because it has been the general practice of the community, perhaps even for so long that the memory of man runneth not to the contrary. It may be that the universality of the practice is taken as evidence that it originated in a divine command. But let us leave out explanations of that sort and consider the claim about the general practice itself.

Any community, whether a family or a trade association or a learned society or a nation, has to take account of long-standing habits of thought and practice. It cannot admit innovations indiscriminately if it is to survive. This applies to religious communities also, and perhaps especially to them. So it would not be surprising if a consensus in practice should count toward authentication of a practical doctrine. But arguments for the authenticity of a doctrine would probably have to include considerations other than historical or sociological assertions about past or present states of the community. To survive, a community must have a life of its own. That is to say, it must have reasons for existing which go beyond saying that it has happened to exist, and reasons for teaching what it teaches which go beyond assertions that some or all of its members have happened to believe and act in certain ways.

This brings us back to the point that internal questions about doctrines call for assertions which have a normative force. They ask whether the community ought to teach what is said in some sentence. And it suggests a further point, that the ground of some such obligation must be rooted in the community's own conception of itself. This may be illustrated in the following way.

The *Constitutum Constantini* is a document in which the emperor Constantine I is represented as conferring temporal sovereignty over the western part of the empire on Pope Sylvester I and his successors. For a number of centuries the document was generally accepted as genuine in the Christian church and in other quarters, and the Donation of Constantine was asserted by various church authorities including popes, though not as a dogma essential to the Christian faith. In the fifteenth century Lorenzo Valla showed that the document was spurious.

It seems that this historical discovery imposed an obligation on the teaching of the church, namely, that it should no longer teach that the document was genuine. And it seems that the ground of this obligation is external. The obligation does not seem to stem from any distinctively Christian principles.

This obligation is negative; it specifies something which the church should not teach. But does there follow from Valla's discovery a positive obligation on the church, namely, to teach that the *Constitutum Constantini* is spurious? Certainly a conditional positive obligation seems to follow from Valla's discovery, namely this: if in the course of the teaching activity of the church the Donation of Constantine is mentioned, then the speaker should say that the document is spurious, or at least be ready and willing to say so if necessary, if for example the speaker cannot take it for granted that his hearers are familiar with the fact.

This conditional positive obligation, it might be argued, does follow from a principle which is internal to the Christian community. The argument would run as follows. The Christian community claims that the assertions it makes in the course of its teaching are true. Hence it is bound not to assert as part of its teaching anything it knows to be untrue. But it seems that this argument is not strong enough to support a claim that there is an unconditional positive obligation on the community to make the spuriousness of the document a part of its teaching.

From the principle that a religious community should not assert anything that it knows to be false, it does not necessarily follow that the community should teach everything that happens to be true. A community would have to consider the reason for its existence and estimate the range of its competence in the course of deciding whether some assertion should be included in its teaching activity. Certainly various religious communities have had to learn from bitter experiences in their histories to reflect on this point.

Here we verge on a topic that will be explored in later chapters; relations between the teachings of a religious community and those historical, scientific, and other claims which have their origins in secular inquiries. (We shall recur to Valla's discovery in chapter 7, where this topic will be introduced.) The immediate point here is to suggest that there are certain limits on what can be said from an external point of view about what a particular religious community ought to teach. It seems we could say that in certain respects what a religious community ought to teach is its own business. And this could be said without thereby ruling out external criticism of what the community does teach.

Before moving on to some other types of criteria of authenticity, notice some further points about appeals to a consensus of a community. The historian Ignaz Goldziher, in "Reaction against the Fabrication of Hadīths," says:

> The most enduring result was achieved by that form of reaction which arose in the circle of the traditionists themselves against the overwhelming growth of traditions and manifested itself in the development of a kind of criticism of true tradition.
> . . . The theologians themselves appear to have extended the theory of the *ijmā'* [consensus] to the credibility of the hadīth at an early date and to have accepted the general feeling of the community as supreme judge of the truth of traditional sayings. Ibn 'Abbās is made to say: "If you hear from me a communication in the name of the Prophet and you find that it does not agree with the book of God or is not liked by people. . . , know that I have reported a lie about the Prophet." In other words: also in respect of the credibility of words and actions ascribed to the Prophet the *ijmā'*, the general feeling of the community, is decisive. What the *umma* [community] considers to be true is really true.

Goldziher gives in a footnote an assemblage of hadīths by al-Khatib al-

Baghdādi from which, he says, "It is evident that authenticity or rejection of the prophetic tradition is made conditional on the impression that it made upon the community." This assemblage of sayings ascribed to Muhammad is as follows:

> If you hear my name in a communication which is agreeable to your heart, which makes your hair and flesh tender . . . and about which you feel that it is close to you, then none of you is as close to it as I am. But if you hear a communication in my name which is against your heart and from which your hair and flesh shrink and which repels you, then none of you are so far removed from it as I am.

Then Goldziher's text continues:

> Conscientious students of tradition did not allow themselves to be guided by this easy way of deciding the authenticity of the vast accumulation of material and, in view of the danger which threatened the orthodox community from the masses of tendentious hadīths, they asked for other proof of credibility than the acceptance of the community.[2]

Some comments on these passages may be hazarded.

1. The saying attributed to Ibn 'Abbās, a cousin and a Companion of the Prophet, does seem to make the general feeling of the community a decisive determinant of the falsity of a hadīth. But it does not seem to make the general feeling of the community a sufficient determinant of the truth of a hadīth. For that, it seems, agreement with "the book of God" (the Qur'ān) would be required also.

2. A distinction seems to be needed between a general feeling, if this means something that is liked or not liked by the people, and what the *umma* considers to be true. To discover what the people consider to be true one would have to take account of reflections as well as of impressions.

3. It is not hard to understand how a religious community might wish to consider seriously the immediate impact on its members of what is said in some sentence. The ideal unity aimed at might be not only that its members may be of one mind, but also that they may be one in heart.

It was not only conscientious specialists in hadīth study in the Muslim community who wished to limit the efficacy of consensus as a criterion of the authenticity of doctrines. The highly respected theologian al-Ghazzālī says, in a legal judgment on the status of certain sectarians:

> We do not deny the dangerous nature of this opposition to the consensus, . . . but we do not go so far as to declare them in unbelief. This is because it is not clear to us that one who goes against the consensus is (necessarily) an

2. Ignaz Goldziher, "Reaction against the Fabrication of Hadīths," in S. M. Stern, ed., *Muslim Studies,* trans. C. H. Barber and S. M. Stern (London: George Allen & Unwin, 1971) 2:133. I omit two Arabic clauses which are given in parentheses in the text.

unbeliever. Indeed there is difference of opinion among the Muslims as to whether proof (of a doctrine) can rest on consensus alone.[3]

Finally it can be said that religious communities differ from one another (1) in the amount of attention they give to the topic of consensus in their literatures, (2) in their conceptions of the scope of a consensus, (3) in their procedures for determining a consensus on some point of doctrine, and (4) in the weight they assign to consensus relative to other criteria of the authenticity of doctrines.

THE *MAHĀPARINIBBĀNASUTTA*

Now we come to a case in which criteria of authenticity of a different sort are advanced. This case and similar cases developed elsewhere are meant to show something about functions which various types of principles and rules seem to have in the teaching activities of religious communities. I have not offered arguments to show that the doctrines proposed in these passages are indeed authentic doctrines of the communities in question, though the speakers seem to have considerable standing in their communities. Also not much has been said about historical contexts. So these cases are brought in as abstractions useful for the purpose of philosophical investigation.

Consider the following passage from a Buddhist scripture, the *Mahāparinibbānasutta* (IV, 7–11):[4]

Now there at Bhoga-nagara the Exalted One stayed at the Ānanda Shrine. There the Exalted One addressed the brethren and said:—"I will teach you, O brethren, these four Great Authorities. Listen thereto, and give good heed, and I will speak."

"Even so, lord!" said the brethren, in assent, to the Exalted One, and the Exalted One spoke as follows:—

"In the first place, brethren, a brother may say thus:—'From the mouth of the Exalted One himself have I heard, from his own mouth have I received it. This is the truth, this the law, this the teaching of the Master.' The word spoken, brethren, by that brother should neither be received with praise nor treated with scorn. Without praise and without scorn every word and syllable should be carefully understood and then put beside the Suttas (the stock paragraphs learnt by heart in the community) and compared with the Vinaya (the rules of the Order). If when so compared they do not harmonize with the Suttas, and do not fit in with the rules of the Order, then you may come to the conclusion:—'Verily, this is not the word of the Exalted One, and has

3. "A *Fatwā* of al-Ghazzālī against the Esoteric Sects," in *A Reader in Islam,* ed. Arthur Jeffery (The Hague: Mouton, 1962), p. 256.

4. *Dialogues of the Buddha,* Part 2, trans. T. W. Rhys Davids and C. A. F. Rhys Davids (London: Oxford University Press [1910], 1959), pp. 133–36. Translated from the *Dīgha-nikāya.* Bracketed phrases are the translators'. Victor Hapuarachchi and Ellison Findly were helpful on the Pali text.

been wrongly grasped by that brother.' Therefore, brethren, you should reject
it. But if they harmonize with the Suttas and fit in with the rules of the Order,
then you may come to the conclusion:—'Verily, this is the word of the Exalted One, and has been well grasped by that brother.' This, brethren, you
should receive as the first Great Authority."

The other three Great Authorities deal with cases where some monk
reports having heard claims to a Buddha-word from "a company of the
brethren with their elders and leaders," from a group of "many elders of
the Order, deeply read, holding the faith as handed down by tradition,
versed in the truths, versed in the regulations of the Order, versed in the
summaries of the doctrines and the law," or from a single elder, "deeply
read, . . . and the law." The responses to these cases have the same pattern
as in the first Great Authority.

Notice several points about this passage.

In each of the four Great Authorities the claim under consideration is
that some reported saying is the truth, the law, the teaching of the master.
The question at issue is whether the reported saying is indeed the word of
the Exalted One, so that the teaching of the Buddha has been well grasped,
or whether the reported saying is not the word of the blessed one, so that
the teaching of the Buddha has been wrongly grasped.

It seems there are threshold conditions to be satisfied before any such
claim can be taken seriously, before it can be brought to court, so to speak.
The only reports mentioned in the passage are reports made by monks,
members of the order. Reports made by nonmembers of the order are not
mentioned. Further, the sayings reported are claimed to be from, we might
say, Buddhist sources: from the Buddha himself, from a fully constituted
company of monks with their elders and leaders, from a group of learned
and faithful elders in the order, or from a single such elder. It seems that
claims said to emanate from other sources, for example from a single monk
who is not an elder or from someone who is not a member of the order,
would not deserve the same respectful and careful attention. So we have
here a situation where questions of the form Is s a doctrine of R? arise as
internal questions.

The phrases "harmonize with the Suttas" and "fit in with the rules of
the Order" state conditions which have to be satisfied before the conclusion
can be drawn that the reported saying is indeed a word of the Buddha.
These conditions hold even if the saying is claimed to have been heard from
the mouth of the Buddha himself. Let us consider some possible explications of these conditions. My object in developing these explications is
not to settle questions about the meaning of the passage but to develop
some distinctions which will be useful later on.

(A) The reported saying (let us say s) must itself be found in the suttas or in the rules of the order, i.e., *s* and some sentence in the existing corpus must be tokens of the same type.

But "harmonize with" and "fit in with" would seem to have no point if *s* is the same as some sentence in the existing corpus. Also, if this were so, would the question whether *s* is indeed a Buddha-word have arisen at all? Perhaps so, if the monks to whom the report is brought are not themselves well versed in the suttas and in the rules of the order. However, the passage seems to suppose that monks who bring such reports may indeed have heard Buddha-words which were not already included in the suttas and the rules of the order. It sounds as though this possibility had to be considered seriously in each case. For these reasons, (A) seems too strong as a necessary condition for concluding that some sentence is a Buddha-word. So let us try another formulation:

(B) *s* must be consistent with everything in the suttas and the rules of the order; it cannot be opposed to anything which is said by the Buddha in them.

While it is clear enough that this would have to hold, it is not clear straight off that this explication would be strong enough. For, one might think, many sentences might be consistent with what the Buddha is known to have taught and yet have nothing to do with what he is known to have taught. For example, "the willow is green" seems to have nothing to do with "the ratio of the circumference of a circle to its diameter is 3.1416," though the two sentences are consistent. They could stand together without conflicting with each other. So, if some reported saying should have no apparent connection with the sayings in the existing corpus of Buddha-words, it might still be consistent with what is said in the corpus. So it would not be ruled out from being a Buddha-word by (B).

Consider the point about relevance further. The objection was that the rule of consistency is not strong enough. It does not rule out as Buddha-words sentences which are irrelevant to sentences the Buddha is already known to have said (the existing corpus). The objection supposes that such sentences *should* be ruled out. But what are the criteria of relevance? It is not always easy to say. Would it be unreasonable to say that if the Buddha did in fact say something, then what he said would be somehow relevant to what he is already known to have said? Would the Buddha have said something entirely irrelevant to what is said in the existing corpus?

If we do not see the relevance, perhaps that is because either the new sentence, or some of the sentences in the existing corpus, or both, have not been rightly understood. Reconsideration may lead to a better understanding of the existing corpus and of the new sentence itself. Many times in the history of human thought new advances have been made when something which seemed irrelevant has turned out to be relevant. This might be true of some of the historical developments of doctrines of religious communities.

Still, there are probably cases where the appearance of irrelevance is so strong that it might count against a claim that a sentence is indeed a word of the Buddha, whether decisively or not. And it seems that the possibility of such cases would count against interpreting the rule in the sutta as in explication (B).

Another tack might be taken to strengthen the case for (B). Suppose that the rule of consistency could be extended to cover not only assertions but utterances which recommend, or approve or disapprove of, attitudes and courses of action. Then the requirement of consistency would rule out a great deal more than might appear at first sight. A case in point is the Buddha's policy of refusing to answer certain sorts of questions, for example whether the world is eternal or not. So if some reported saying proposes an answer to a question of one of those sorts, this saying could be said to be inconsistent with his known policy. In this case we would have an inconsistency, not between one assertion and another, but between a reported assertion on some question and a known policy of not making assertions on that question.

Or suppose that in the reported saying, which is being claimed to be a Buddha-word, a course of action is recommended which is incompatible with some course of action taught in the existing corpus. That is to say, it would be impossible to carry out both courses of action; hence it would be absurd to undertake both courses of action. Then the reported saying would be inconsistent with something in the existing corpus. And, on the supposition that the teachings of the Buddha are not inconsistent with one another, this would discredit the reported saying as a genuine Buddha-word.

It is not clear, however, whether these and other extensions of the concept of consistency would resolve all problematical cases. A stronger requirement than consistency might still seem to be called for. So perhaps, along with (B), something more needs to be added, for example:

(C) s must enhance what is said in the suttas and the rules of the order. It must put more clearly, forcefully, or vividly what is said there. Or it must apply what is said there to different cases. Or it must otherwise draw out the meaning of what the Buddha is already known to have said.

Then the rule would be: s can be concluded to be a Buddha-word if it is found in the existing corpus, *or* if it is both consistent with *and* enhances what is said in the existing corpus. There are problems about conditions of this sort. They might seem to leave too much latitude for interpretation.

Now, leaving aside these problems about the explication of "harmonize with" and "fit in with," we can schematize the rule which seems to be exhibited in the passage from the sutta in the following way:

It may be concluded that *s* is a saying of the Buddha if
  i. *s* is found as a saying of the Buddha in the suttas or in the rules of the order, *or if*
  ii. *s* is reported by a monk as having been heard from the mouth of the Buddha himself *or* heard to be a Buddha-word from a fully constituted company of monks with their elders and leaders *or* from a group of learned and faithful elders *or* from a single learned and faithful elder, *and*
  iii. *s* harmonizes with the suttas and fits in with the rules of the order.

One lesson we can learn from the passage is this: the principles and rules a community develops for identifying its doctrines, that is to say its criteria of authenticity and its procedures for applying them, can be complex. Though a community may present, as a doctrine of this sort, an apparently simple rule or principle, for example, "if *s* is taught by the Buddha, *s* is a doctrine of the Buddhist community" or "if *s* is taught in the Bible, *s* is a doctrine of the Christian community," circumstances may make it necessary to include conjunctions, alternatives, qualifications, provisos, and even perhaps exceptions.

The complexities of the rule we are considering arise from the possibility that some Buddha-word might be found which is not included in the existing corpus of his teachings. When in the next chapter we study some norms for doctrines which deal with the consistency of the doctrines of a community, we shall see some other ways in which complexities arise. For example, problems of interpretation posed by apparent inconsistencies among doctrines have an important bearing on principles and rules for determining authenticity. So principles and rules of interpretation generate complexities in principles and rules for determining authenticity.

FRAMEWORKS FOR CRITERIA OF AUTHENTICITY

Here are some types of conditions which might be advanced by a religious community as criteria for saying that some sentence *s* expresses an authentic doctrine of the community (henceforth letting *s* stand for "what is proposed in utterances of *s*"):

s has been believed (or practiced) by all faithful members of the community everywhere and at all times.

s was taught by all the Tannaim (or the fathers and doctors of the church or the mujtahids, etc.).

s has not been denied by any of the Tannaim, etc.

s was taught by Muhammad (or by the Buddha or by Christ, etc.).

s is a clear teaching of the scriptures of the community (e.g., the Vedas or the Torah or the suttas and the vinaya or the Bible or the Qur'ān).

s has been declared an authentic doctrine of the community by a competent authority (e.g., by a duly constituted council).

s is a supposition of essential practices of the community.

s follows from authentic doctrines of the community.

Such conditions would be elements in a framework for identifying doctrines of the community in question. They would be substitutable for the three dots in one or another of the following schemas or in a combination of some of these schemas:

s is an authentic doctrine of the community if . . .

s is an authentic doctrine of the community if . . . or . . .

s is an authentic doctrine of the community if . . . and . . .

s is an authentic doctrine of the community if . . . unless . . .

s is an authentic doctrine of the community only if . . .

A statement of such a framework, in which the dots would be replaced by some such conditions as those listed above, would express a doctrinal principle of the community in question. In some cases rules for applying the principle would be needed, for example a rule for concluding that what is said in some sentence is a saying of the Buddha. The set of conditions a community builds into its frameworks for identifying its doctrines would constitute its criteria of authenticity.

It is highly plausible that conditions of some of these types are included in the frameworks of the major religious communities for identifying their doctrines. But the list is constructed only for the sake of giving examples of such conditions; none of these conditions is being prescribed here as a requirement for all religious communities or for any religious community.

Furthermore, the list is not meant to be complete; it could be extended. For instance, there is no reason for us to exclude other conditions which are defensible on general logical or epistemological grounds and thus are not dependent on the distinctive doctrines of a community. Recall that Irenaeus introduced the principle that a passage in a text should be interpreted by reference to its context and applied this principle to the Christian Scriptures as well as to Homer. Is that principle dependent on distinctively Christian doctrines? Or is it a general principle which is independent of distinctively Christian doctrines?

It will be argued in chapter 4 that a religious community needs some distinctive criteria for identifying its doctrines. That is why each religious community has to develop its own criteria of authenticity. But we should not rule out conditions which do not depend on its distinctive doctrines, which a community might include along with those which do depend on its distinctive doctrines.

In this connection consider further the last item in the list set out above. In the Anglican *Articles of Religion* ("The Thirty-Nine Articles"), Article VI, "Of the Sufficiency of the Holy Scriptures for Salvation," reads in part as follows:

> HOLY Scripture containeth all things necessary to salvation: so that whatsoever is not read therein, *nor may be proved thereby,* is not to be required of any man, that it should be believed as an article of the Faith, or be thought requisite or necessary to salvation. In the name of the Holy Scripture we do understand those canonical Books of the Old and New Testament, of whose authority was never any doubt in the Church. [Emphasis mine.]

And paragraph VI of the first chapter of the *Westminster Confession of Faith* reads in part as follows:

> The whole counsel of God, concerning all things necessary for his own glory, man's salvation, faith and life, is either expressly set down in Scripture, *or by good and necessary consequence may be deduced from Scripture:* unto which nothing at any time is to be added, whether by new revelations of the Spirit, or traditions of men. [Emphasis mine; Biblical references omitted.]

Now from the italicized clauses in these passages it seems that the following schema of a criterion of authenticity might be derived.

For any pair of sentences *(s1, s2)*, if what is said in *s1* is an authentic doctrine of *R*, and if what is said in *s2* follows from what is said in *s1*, then what is said in *s2* is an authentic doctrine of *R*.

And it seems that if a religious community has a criterion of authenticity which fits this schema, and if it should turn out that the authenticity of *s1* is somehow inconsistent with the authenticity of *s2*, then the community would have to say either (1) that *s1* is not really an authentic doctrine of *R*, or (2) that *s2* does not really follow from *s1*, or (3) that both (1) and (2) hold.

The immediate interest of the schema is this: it seems that, if a criterion of authenticity which fits this schema is to be effective, principles and rules are needed to determine whether what is said in some sentence does indeed follow from what is said in some other sentence. There needs to be some way of telling whether what is said in some sentence "may be proved" by what is said in the Scripture, some way of telling whether what is said in some sentence may "by good and necessary consequence" be "deduced" from Scripture. Further, it seems that some of these principles and rules must be general, not peculiar to some particular body of doctrines, unless the terms "prove," "consequence," and "deduce" are being used in an idiosyncratic way. The effectiveness of a criterion of authenticity which fits the schema depends, it seems, on some general principles or rules of deduction.

The moral to be drawn for our own investigation is only this: we should not rule out the possibility that a community may adopt criteria of authenticity which embody or depend on general principles and rules, principles and rules which are not distinctive of its own body of doctrines. A comment by William Austin may be added here: a conservative might want to include only such general conditions as are necessary for the explication or application of conditions that are dependent on distinctive doctrines of the community. For instance, Irenaeus' point about context might be justified as necessary for the application of "*s* is a clear teaching of the Scriptures." The question whether some community should or should not adopt such criteria is not for us to decide.

If a community has more than one criterion of authenticity, which seems likely, it may need ordering principles which would yield rankings of criteria of authenticity.

Earlier we noticed tendencies for a community to give more weight to the judgments of some of its members on what it ought to teach than to judgments of others. Also, the judgments of some of its recognized teachers are given more weight than the judgments of other teachers. On various points of doctrine, or more generally, some of its teachers are thought to be better qualified to speak to and for the community than others are.

Similarly, there seem to be rankings of various scriptures, or various parts of a scripture. On certain points of doctrine some texts are thought to have more to say on the point than other texts do; some are clearer on the point than others are; some give a better perspective on the point in relation to the teachings of the community as a whole.

Such ordering principles could be brought into use when a community has to decide what it ought to teach on some topic and more than one criterion of authenticity is applicable.

ARE RULES FOR AUTHENTICITY SYNTACTICAL?

It has been suggested by J. M. Bochenski[5] that the rules of the major religious communities for identifying doctrinal sentences, which he calls heuristic rules, are "usually syntactical." Our discussion of the passage in the Mahāparinibbānasutta gives an opportunity to consider this. For the sake of argument let us take it that "syntactical" means "pertaining to the formal characteristics and arrangements of the symbols in abstraction from their meanings," in distinction from "semantical."[6] And let us ask whether

5. Joseph M. Bochenski, O.P., *The Logic of Religion* (New York: New York University Press, 1965), pp. 60–61. The Cambridge University Press permitted use of parts of "Bochenski on the Structure of Schemes of Doctrines," *Religious Studies* 13 (1977): 203–19, in the present chapter.

6. Irving M. Copi, *Symbolic Logic* (New York: Macmillan, 1954), p. 184. Bochenski's own explanation of "syntactic" seems consistent with this, in his *The Methods of Contemporary Thought*, trans. Peter Caws (Dordrecht: Reidel, 1965), pp. 32–33.

the rule exhibited in the passage from the sutta could be characterized as syntactical in this sense.

It seems clear enough that if the hypothetical explication (A) were a satisfactory explication of the requirement that a reported saying must "harmonize with the Suttas" and "fit in with the rules of the Order," then we could say that the requirement is syntactical. It would be sufficient to see whether some reported saying has the same pattern of sounds or inscribed characters as some sentence in the existing corpus of doctrines. The meaning of the reported saying would not have to be considered.

But, as we have noticed, explication (A) seems too strong, for more than one reason. An additional consideration which counts against the adequacy of explication (A), and more generally against construing the rule in the sutta as syntactical, is the following. The syntax of the context of the sentence in the existing corpus would have to be taken account of to see whether there are syntactical features in the context, for example expressions of the form ". . . Māra said. . . ," which would disqualify an identification of the sentence in the corpus with the reported sentence *as a Buddha-word*. What makes some sentence in the existing corpus a Buddha-word is not just that a token of that type occurs in the corpus; what counts is whether an utterance of the sentence is ascribed there to the Buddha. Furthermore, in the suttas many sentences are ascribed to the Buddha which he did not teach. He is represented there as uttering many sentences, as examples of errors arising from ignorance, which he himself was not asserting. Again, if one should set out to handle these features of the texts syntactically, how is one to know how much of the context of the sentence in the existing corpus one ought to consider?

Next, can the requirement formulated in (B), the requirement of consistency, be tested syntactically? This seems doubtful. For it seems that, in some cases, to know whether sentences are consistent with one another we have to consider their meanings. It is true that some cases can be decided syntactically, for example the following pair of sentences:

Brahmā Sahampati appeared to Sakyamuni.
Brahmā Sahampati did not appear to Sakyamuni.

We can say that these sentences are inconsistent with each other without knowing the referents of the names they use and without knowing what it means to appear. But there are other cases where this is not possible, for example:

Peter is the one who denied Christ in the court of the high priest.
Cephas is the one who denied Christ in the court of the high priest.

Unless we know whether "Peter" and "Cephas" refer to the same person, we do not know whether the sentences are consistent with one another.

If, as in (C), "harmonize with" and "fit in with" are taken to express a stronger requirement than consistency, then it would be quite clear that this is not a syntactical test. In fact the passage says, "Every word and every syllable [of the problematical saying] should be carefully understood." This seems to say that the meaning of the saying must be understood before it is put beside the suttas and compared with the rules of the order. (The mention of syllables may be just a conventional way of emphasizing the need for care.) If the considerations introduced in (C) are admitted as part of the rule, then formal considerations would not be decisive. For though agreement can be reached often on whether some utterance genuinely clarifies, or applies, what is said in some other utterance, counterarguments are not excluded.

It is true that the rules used in the major religious communities for identifying their doctrines are rules for assigning a certain status to sentences or sayings. They are meant to guide decisions as to whether what is said in some sentence is or is not an authentic doctrine of the community. They do not directly refer to those objects referred to in primary doctrines of the community, and they do not directly enjoin those courses of action which primary practical doctrines enjoin. They are doctrines about the community's doctrines. Further, usually they require reference to sentences located in certain bodies or collections of sentences preserved in writing or in oral tradition, in the Bible, for example. These bodies of sentences must be taken into account in deciding whether some saying is a doctrine or not. So it is true enough to say that there are syntactical elements in the frameworks for these decisions. But it would come as a shock to traditional commentators on the Vedas or the Nikayas or the Bible or the Talmud or the Qur'ān to be told that, when they try to discern and formulate the doctrines taught in these scriptures, syntactical rules are sufficient.

We noticed that the judgments of some members of a community are more respected than the judgments of other members of the community. We may suppose that the qualifications of the elders mentioned in the third and fourth Great Authorities, namely that they must be "deeply read, holding the faith as handed down by tradition, versed in the truths, versed in the regulations of the Order, versed in the summaries of the doctrines and the law," are in effect reasons for having respect for their judgments. So reports that such people as these have claimed that something is a Buddha-word deserve careful consideration. Here an analogy with legal systems would be better than the analogies with logistic systems which Bochenski suggests. Opinions of some judges and legal scholars have more weight than those of others.

To be useful an analogy does not have to hold at all points. One might say that both the question whether some formula is a theorem of a logistic system and the question whether some saying is a doctrine of some religious community are internal questions, though not in the same way. In the former case the question is an internal one in the sense that, to be a theorem, a formula must be derivable from the axioms of the system. Whether or not it is derivable from other axioms is not to the immediate point. In the latter case one might say that whether or not some saying expresses a doctrine of the community depends on internal considerations also, as we have seen. These considerations are not easy to sum up, but the main point can be suggested in the following way: it would be anomalous, if not absurd, for the World Council of Churches of Christ, or any other non-Islamic body, to have a responsible part in making a normative decision on whether or not some statement or some prescription is a doctrine of Islam; or to ask a Buddhist council, or any other non-Christian body, to put on its agenda the normative question whether infant baptism, for example, should be taught by the Christian church.

AN ANALOGY WITH LEGAL SYSTEMS

Here again an analogy with legal systems would be useful. The distinction between the primary doctrines of a religious community and its doctrines for identifying its doctrines is comparable with H. L. A. Hart's distinction between the primary rules of obligation in a society (e.g., rules against theft) and the society's "rules of recognition" for identifying its primary rules. The doctrines we have been studying are principles and rules for answering questions of the form Is s a doctrine of R? with respect to the teachings of a religious community; Hart's rules of recognition are rules for answering questions of the form Is s a law of N? with respect to the legal system of a society, for example a nation ("Is s constitutional?"). Hart says:

> The use of unstated rules of recognition, by courts and others, in identifying particular rules of the system is characteristic of the internal point of view. Those who use them in this way thereby manifest their own acceptance of them as guiding rules and with this attitude there goes a characteristic vocabulary different from the natural expressions of the external point of view.[7]

Similarly, questions of the form Is s a doctrine of R? have to be answered by applying a religious community's own principles and rules for identifying its doctrines. And those who use the rules in this way manifest their own acceptance of them for the purpose at hand.

Ronald M. Dworkin in "Is Law a System of Rules?", commenting on Hart's rules of recognition, argued that principles as well as rules are required to determine primary rules of obligation, and that principles, unlike rules, do not dictate results, come what may. They "incline a decision one way, though not conclusively, and they survive intact when they do not prevail."[8]

7. H. L. A. Hart, *The Concept of Law* (Oxford: Clarendon, 1961), p. 99.
8. In Robert S. Summers, ed., *Essays in Legal Philosophy* (Berkeley: University of California Press, 1968), p. 49.

In an earlier article Dworkin gave as examples of "standards other than rules" the following: "No man shall profit by his own wrong" and "Infants are the wards of the law."[9]

Whether or not Dworkin's point holds for legal systems, it seems clear enough that rules for identifying doctrines, as these operate in religious communities, are supplemented by principles or, we might say, have principles built into them. Thus for example the framework Irenaeus developed for judging the authenticity of a doctrine included a principle for interpreting the scriptures, that a passage should be interpreted in its context, and the principle that bishops can be relied on to preserve apostolic tradition. And the rule in the Mahāparinibbānasutta leans on the principle that the teachings of the Buddha are not inconsistent with one another.

The object of this chapter has been to introduce one type of norms for doctrines, those principles and rules of religious communities which yield criteria of authenticity. It may suggest a larger project. That project would survey criteria of authenticity in the major religious communities, or some of them, one by one. It would focus on similarities and contrasts among them, studying these in depth. Our own program calls for study of other norms for bodies of doctrines as well. But as we go along we will pay attention to connections among norms of various types and throughout the study criteria of authenticity will continue to have an important place.

9. "Judicial Discretion," *The Journal of Philosophy* 60 (1963): 634–35.

CHAPTER THREE

Ordering and Consistency

A religious community needs principles and rules to guide judgments as to whether some sentence expresses an authentic doctrine of that community. It needs criteria for identifying its doctrines, in response to the question Is *s* an authentic doctrine of *R*?

Doctrines about doctrines of a different sort are needed by a community when questions arise about relations of its doctrines to one another. Some topics of these latter doctrines about doctrines are the ordering of doctrines in importance and the consistency of doctrines with one another. Most of this chapter deals with doctrines bearing on consistency, but we should notice some examples of doctrines which would bear on orderings of doctrines.

ORDERINGS OF DOCTRINES

Suppose as a contrast case a community which treats its doctrines as items on an unweighted list. The list includes primary doctrines of various types and governing doctrines of various types. This hypothetical body of doctrines gives no indication that some item on the list is intrinsically more important than some other item on the list. In a particular presentation of the body of doctrines there would be an ordering suitable to the occasion. But it would be understood that no order of listing would be intrinsically better than some other order. If this understanding is made explicit (that is, if it is taught), then it would amount to a doctrine of the community about ordering its doctrines, a doctrine saying that no authentic doctrine of the community is more important than another.

Though such a body of doctrines might be accepted unreflectively as a matter of custom, arguments for it could be given in a reflective stage of a community's history. It simplifies instruction. It counters tendencies to play down some doctrines and thus to relax some of the requirements of the community. It tends to maintain evenly the force of the community's teachings. A more direct argument would be that the community has no right to pick and choose among the doctrines it ought to teach.

Tendencies to think of a body of doctrines as an unweighted list appear at various points in the histories of religious communities. Unweighted lists of doctrines are included in bodies of doctrines fairly often, for example the four noble truths of Buddhism and the last six of the ten commandments. But the point of introducing the notion of a body of doctrines as an unweighted list is to throw into relief those doctrines about doctrines which do permit or require rankings of some doctrines as more important than some others. Doctrines of this latter sort are not uncommon in the literatures and teaching practices of the major religious communities.

It is not uncommon to find it said that some doctrine sums up the point of a whole set of doctrines, or that some doctrine or set of doctrines is more central to a body of doctrines than some other doctrine or set of doctrines is. Such doctrines also seem to be supposed by some of the teaching practices of religious communities. By reiteration and emphasis a community usually gives more prominence to some doctrines than to others. Also, relaxations or reformulations of some doctrines are resisted more firmly than in the case of others.

Reasons of various sorts are given for such rankings of doctrines in importance, and the principles introduced in these arguments specify various modes of importance. One sort of reason is that a certain ordering in importance is found in the sources of the community's doctrines. For example, it is argued that in the Nikayas the instructions of the Buddha for attaining insight (wisdom) are ranked over his injunctions to "mere morality," though without nullifying them. This could be construed as a teleological ordering. The moral precepts lead up to the precepts for gaining wisdom; they are steps on the path to wisdom. Moral practice is for the sake of wisdom. For another example, it is argued that Moses and the prophets taught that injunctions to justice and mercy may override, though they do not abrogate, certain ceremonial precepts.

Another sort of reason for giving more weight to some doctrines than to others is that some doctrines are more clearly and certainly authentic than others. This principle seems to be implicit in distinctions among the different theological qualifications or "notes" and corresponding censures which appear in Roman Catholic theological literature.

To some doctrines the note *de fide* is attached because these doctrines are truths which (1) are immediately revealed and which (2) have been explicitly defined by the church. These doctrines are dogmas. If some teaching is directly opposed to a dogma it deserves censure as *haeresis*. If circumstantial evidence warrants a probable judgment that some teaching is heretical, then that teaching would incur the milder censure *haeresim sapiens,* smacking of heresy.

If a teaching is a strict theological conclusion, that is to say, if it is necessarily connected with an immediately revealed truth, it is said to be me-

diately revealed and *theologice certa*. Teachings directly opposed to theologically certain doctrines incur the censure of *error*. If circumstantial evidence warrants a probable judgment that some teaching is in error, then
that teaching incurs the censure of *errorem sapiens,* smacking of error.

If a teaching is (1) connected with a revealed truth by highly probable,
but not demonstrative, reasoning and is (2) accepted by the majority of
theologians, then it is said to be *valde probabilis* or *moraliter certa*. Acceptance
of a teaching contrary to highly probable or morally certain teachings is
censured as *temerarius* (rash).

Further qualifications and corresponding censures are developed in the
literature, but these are sufficient for the purpose at hand. They show the
character of a set of principles and rules for ordering the doctrines of a
community in a certain way.

Another reason for ranking some doctrines over others is that some have
more important consequences than others. For example, the Presbyterian
theologian Benjamin Breckinridge Warfield (1851–1921) says, in the course
of a defense of the doctrine of the plenary inspiration of the Bible:

> Let it not be said that thus we found the whole Christian system upon the
> doctrine of plenary inspiration. We found the whole Christian system on the
> doctrine of plenary inspiration as little as we found it upon the doctrine of
> angelic existences. Were there no such thing as inspiration, Christianity would
> be true, and all its essential doctrines would be credibly witnessed to us in
> the generally trustworthy reports of the teaching of our Lord and of His au-
> thoritative agents in founding the Church, preserved in the writings of the
> apostles and their first followers, and in the historical witness of the living
> Church.[1]

As Warfield goes on to explain, he is not saying that the doctrine that
the Bible is fully inspired in all its parts is less authentic than other doctrines
taught in the Bible such as the incarnation or the atonement. Instead he
claims that since plenary inspiration is clearly taught in the Bible (which
he argues at length), there is as much to be said for the authenticity of
plenary inspiration as for the authenticity of any other doctrine taught in
the Bible. His principle is that plenary inspiration is less important than
the trustworthiness of the Bible not in respect of its authenticity as a
Christian doctrine but in respect of its consequences. Plenary inspiration
depends on the trustworthiness of the Bible; the trustworthiness of the Bible
does not depend on plenary inspiration.

This suggests that the rule Warfield would propose is this: if one Christian doctrine depends on some other Christian doctrine, and if the second
doctrine is independent of the first, then the second is more important than

1.   Benjamin Breckinridge Warfield, *Revelation and Inspiration* (New York: Oxford University Press, 1927), pp. 209–10.

the first, though both are authentic. If this rule were adopted by the Christian community it would have the function of a Christian doctrine about the ordering of Christian doctrines.

The following seems to express a similar principle for ordering doctrines: "It is true that there exists an order and as it were a hierarchy of the Church's dogmas, as a result of their varying relationship to the foundation of the faith. This hierarchy means that some dogmas are founded on other dogmas which are the principal ones, and are illuminated by these latter. But all dogmas, since they are revealed, must be believed with the same divine faith."[2]

AN ORDERING OF CANONICAL TEXTS: JODO SHINSHU

For a case which bears on the ordering of doctrines in a different way, consider a passage from *An Introduction to Shin Buddhism* by Kosho Yamamoto.[3] He is speaking as a teacher of the Jodo Shinshu school of Mahayana Buddhism, and he is discussing the relation of Shinran (1173–1262), the founder of the school, to Shinran's teacher Honen, the founder of the Jodo school. The passage occurs in a section titled "The Canon of Shinshu."

> Honen named in his *"Senjakushu"* the three sutras of the *Muryojukyo*, the *Kammuryojukyo*, and the *Amidakyo*, and one treatise the *Jodoron* of Vasubandhu as the canons of the Jodo sect. This tradition is generally handed down to Shinshu in spirit. But Shinran, though he regards these as important, states in his *Kyogyoshinsho*, his chief work dealing with the doctrine of Shinshu from academic standpoints, that his teaching rests on the *Muryojukyo*. Thus started Shinran's Hangyo, *i.e.,* the 'classification of the Buddha's teachings' from a sectarian standpoint. The elimination thus worked out meant also a declaration of independence of Shinran's teaching, because to select out the *Muryojukyo* as the most important will also carry the inference that others are less so. The affixing of grades to the three sutras is also accompanied by the view held of the grade of importance in regard to the three vows of the Nineteenth, the Twentieth, and the Eighteenth, . . .

First a word about the vows. Eons ago a number of vows were made by a bodhisattva before he became the Buddha Amida. Those who rely on those vows will be reborn in the Pure Land, the western paradise, and will attain enlightenment there. Both the Jodo school and the Shinshu school are Pure Land schools, differing as to which of the three vows mentioned by Yamamoto is more important, and on other points.

Now as to the hangyo. Various schools of Mahayana Buddhism rely on some of the Mahayana sutras ascribed to the Buddha more than on oth-

2. Sacred Congregation for the Doctrine of the Faith, *Declaration in defence of the Catholic doctrine on the Church against certain errors of the day* (Vatican City, 1973), p. 12.

3. Kosho Yamamoto, *An Introduction to Shin Buddhism* (Oyama, Japan: The Karinbunko, 1963), pp. 103–04.

ers for the distinctive teachings of the school. The Kegon school relies principally on the Avatāmsaka Sūtra, and the Tendai school relies principally on the Lotus Sūtra. Each school has its own canonical ordering of the sutras. The object of such a classification of the Buddha's teachings, the hangyo of a particular school, is not to rule out altogether any of the sutras as a source of doctrines. In that respect the position of a school is unlike that of the second-century Christian heretic Marcion, who left the Old Testament and three of the gospels out of his own canon. When Yamamoto speaks of Shinran's "elimination" of certain sutras, he means only that they were left out of the top rank of sources of doctrines, where Honen had placed them.

Instead of eliminating some sutras from the canon altogether, the object of a hangyo of a Mahayana school is to rank various sutras as to their importance for developing the distinctive doctrines of the school, the doctrines which in the judgment of the teachers of the school are central to Buddhism. So in ranking various sutras in importance a school is in effect ranking the distinctive doctrines of those sutras in their importance for Buddhism. A hangyo functions as a doctrine of a particular school of Buddhism for ordering Buddhist doctrines.

KARL BARTH

A passage in Karl Barth's *Church Dogmatics*[4] will serve to add some complexity and depth to this brief account of principles and rules which bear on orderings of doctrines.

The passage occurs in a discussion of dogmatic theology as a function of the teaching church. Barth has been commenting on the lists of doctrines cited by certain orthodox Lutheran and Reformed theologians of the seventeenth century as fundamental to the Christian faith. He speaks of the work of these theologians with considerable appreciation. Then he says,

> This contained so rich a share of biblical truth and reality that it could not greatly harm the freedom of the faith grounded in the freedom of the Word of God. But the principle introduced at this point is one which we cannot wholeheartedly approve. It is, of course, indisputable that for Christian thinking and speaking there have at all times been *articuli fundamentales* and *articuli non fundamentales,* i.e., more and less important elements of dogma. And in its proper use no exception can be taken to the distinction. [p. 864]

Further on he says, of dogmatics,

> Its function is to confront Church proclamation with the Word of God, and in doing this it must not substitute for the Word of God the confession either

---

4. Karl Barth, *Church Dogmatics*, vol. 1, *The Doctrine of the Word of God*, second half-volume (I.2), trans. G. T. Thomson and Harold Knight (New York: Scribner's, 1956), pp. 864–67.

of a Church or of an individual. If it does, it cannot with complete authority call the Church either to hearing or teaching; it will be only the function of a self-centered and self-occupied Church. The establishment of specific, ir-revocable, fundamental articles will block the way to freedom both for itself and for the Church. It will also block the onward course of the Word of God within the Church. Confession cannot and must not be understood as con-stituting an obstacle of this kind. In all seriousness dogmatics must realise that the confession may not be understood in this way but that its function is to point to the Word of God itself. In dogmatics, therefore, traditional notions as to what is fundamental or not, central or peripheral, more or less important, have to be suspended, so that they can become a matter for vital new decision by the Word of God itself. [pp. 864–65]

It is true that dogmatics

makes certain distinctions and choices with regard to the contents of the Word of God. But we have to make it particularly plain in dogmatics that no such discrimination, no choice of special *articuli fundamentales,* must try to anticipate the fresh discrimination and choice which the Word of God itself may make at any time, thus summoning the Church to make a new report and a new confession. . . . In dogmatics we cannot presume to know and declare in ad-vance, as a more than hypothetical certainty, what is and what is not fun-damental. An hypothesis as such is not to be repudiated but exploited. But it cannot be given the rank and function of a principle. A serviceable heuristic canon cannot be treated as if it were a classic text. [p. 865]

So dogmatics "is ready for new insights which no former store of knowl-edge can really confront on equal terms or finally withstand. Essentially dogmatic method consists in this openness to receive new truth, and only in this" (p. 867).

We might say that the passage contains a concession and a warning. The concession is that discriminations between more important doctrines and less important doctrines are necessary. The warning is that no such dis-crimination should be allowed to bar the way to fresh insights which require new orderings of doctrines. From the general tenor of the passage it is clear that Barth's main point is the warning.

If we attend only to the warning we might be reminded of the contrast case with which we began, the case of a community which would regard its body of doctrines as an unweighted list. Its principle would be that none of its doctrines is intrinsically more important than any other. But it may be that there is an important difference. Barth seems to make room for an ordering of doctrines which is not just relative to particular occasions. Otherwise he could not be so respectful and appreciative of seventeenth-century Protestant orthodoxy as he seems to be. Barth implies that the church needs "a serviceable heuristic canon." This is to say, I suppose, that it needs an ordering of its doctrines appropriate for the conduct of the community's ordinary tasks, the proclamation of the gospel and the education of its members in the pattern of life it teaches. The community's certainty of the rightness of this ordering is not "more than hypothetical"; it must be held subject to revision. But, he says also, "an hypothesis as such is not to be repudiated but exploited." Now it seems that a hypothesis cannot be exploited unless it is maintained up to the point where revision becomes necessary, and with this we may suppose that Barth would agree.

So, although it is clear from the passage that Barth's main point is the warning, we should attend to his concession as well. Furthermore, we might ask whether his warning would have a point if there were no such concession. If there are to be revisions there must be something to revise.

Whether what Barth says in this passage is an authentic doctrine of the Christian community is a question which runs beyond the limits of our program. As in other cases we study, the passage is introduced for the sake of giving an example of principles and rules which bear on the ordering of doctrines. But it seems clear that Barth's intention is to propose some principles and rules for ordering Christian doctrines. He is presenting a doctrine which he thinks his community should accept and teach about its doctrines, a doctrine about ordering its doctrines.

Finally, before we close this discussion of orderings of doctrines, something should be said about connections between criteria of authenticity, and principles and rules for ordering doctrines. In the first instance a community needs principles and rules to guide judgments as to whether what is said in this or that sentence, taken one by one, is an authentic doctrine of the community. It needs criteria of authenticity. Then it needs principles and rules about ordering its authentic doctrines in relation to one another. Principles and rules about authenticity bear on the question: What, taken one by one, are the right things for the community to teach? Principles and rules about ordering bear on the question: In what order should the community teach the things it should teach? Are some of them more important than others, and if so, which are more important than which others?

If an ordering of doctrines in importance is relative to some situation, then the community must ask which of its authentic doctrines are the more important ones for it to teach in that situation. What is the right thing to say here and now? It is not as though the community could speak to the situation in any way it might happen to choose. It is bound to teach its authentic doctrines, and only those. Otherwise it would be speaking out of character. Hence we might say that a community's doctrines about ordering doctrines suppose, and are bound by, its criteria of authenticity.

CONSISTENCY

Now we turn to doctrines bearing on consistency. Whether or not a community teaches explicitly that its doctrines are consistent with one another, its teaching practices suppose that they are. Perhaps suspicions or claims that some doctrines are inconsistent with others have simply not arisen. People grow up accepting the doctrines and continue accepting them without raising questions about their consistency. Even so, the practice of the community in its teaching activity supposes that its authentic doctrines are consistent with one another. This holds for the following reason.

In its teaching activities a religious community does not just mention its doctrines; it proposes them for acceptance. In teaching some of its doctrines it is making proposals for belief. Accepting these doctrines involves taking what is said in them as true. In teaching other doctrines the community is proposing courses of inward or outward action. Accepting these doctrines involves taking the courses of action as right. This holds for the doctrines of the community one by one. In teaching some doctrine the community is proposing that it be accepted as true, or, if it is a practical doctrine, that it be accepted as right. But the community does not teach its doctrines just one by one; it conjoins its doctrines. That is why its practice supposes that its doctrines are consistent with one another.

For if what is said in one assertion is not consistent with what is said in some other assertion, these doctrines could not be accepted in conjunction. Perhaps one or the other could be accepted, but not both. Likewise, if some course of action proposed in a practical doctrine is not consistent with a course of action proposed in some other practical doctrine, then perhaps one or the other of these proposals of courses of action could be accepted, but not both.

So if a community conjoins various doctrines which make assertions, this practice supposes that these doctrines are consistent with one another. And if it conjoins various practical doctrines, this practice supposes that they are consistent with one another.

Furthermore, if a community conjoins an assertion and a proposal of a course of action, this practice supposes that those doctrines are consistent with one another. There are two ways in which it could happen that an assertion and a proposal of a course of action would not be jointly acceptable. First, they would not be jointly acceptable if the truth of what is said in the assertion would make the course of action impossible, hence not right. Second, they would not be jointly acceptable if the rightness, and hence the possibility, of the course of action would make what is said in the assertion untrue. So the practice of conjoining doctrines which make assertions and doctrines proposing courses of action supposes that the theoretical doctrines and the practical doctrines are consistent with one another.

Proposals of a different kind also appear among the doctrines of religious communities, namely proposals of valuations. These proposals are aimed at eliciting judgments that something or other is good or bad in one or another particular way, or that something is better or worse than something else in some particular way, or that something is best of all or worst of all, in some category or without restriction. Some philosophers tend to assimilate valuations to beliefs; others tend to assimilate them to courses of action, in this case to inward courses of action. If we should construe valuations in either of these ways, then interpretations of the consistency of valuation doctrines with one another and with doctrines of other kinds would follow as corollaries. My own inclination is to construe valuations as assertions, hence as true or untrue.

I have been arguing that, if a community puts forward and conjoins doctrines, then its teaching practice supposes that the doctrines thus put forward are consistent with one another, that they are not only acceptable one by one but also jointly. As a matter of fact, it is reasonably clear from the teaching practices of the major religious communities that they do put forward their doctrines in this way, as we shall see later on.

Might a religious community unburden itself of the supposition that its doctrines are consistent with one another? Might it teach as a governing doctrine the semantic thesis that none of its primary doctrines makes proposals of any sort? And might it shape its discourse in accord with this thesis? We could explain this hypothetical case as follows.

This would be a community which says that utterances of its primary doctrines may have other kinds of force, but not the force of making proposals for belief, or proposals of valuations, or proposals of courses of action, or claims of other sorts. It renounces for example the claim that some of its doctrines are true. They are helpful myths, it might say. But to say or to imply contextually that the myths are helpful still makes a claim, and the community would have an obligation to explain how they are helpful and to support that claim.

The community might respond by saying that the myths are helpful in the following way. By entertaining or contemplating the myths those who do so are motivated to undertake certain courses of action. But then it would seem that the courses of action motivated by the myths are being proposed and thus are being claimed to be right, and the community would be obligated to explain and support these claims.

Perhaps, to make its doctrine about its doctrines consistent, this community might have to say that utterances of its primary doctrines are meant to have the effect of stimulating the feelings of their hearers. The purpose is to arouse, but not to propose, feelings of apprehension, comfort, or confidence, for example. Or, it might say, the purpose of utterances of its doctrines is to stimulate, though not to propose, certain courses of action. But at least some of the feelings mentioned above are not pure and simple feelings. One is apprehensive of something, however vaguely; one is comforted by something; one is confident in something. Also, if someone undertakes to stimulate someone else to some course of action, he is not shielded from responsibility for the consequences.

Some other objections to the doctrine of this hypothetical community would have to be considered. It seems that to speak of the purpose of an utterance, or of its intended effects, is not to speak of the force of what is said in the utterance. Whether or not what is said in an utterance makes a claim of some sort and thus calls for a judgment on the part of the hearer or reader is not determined by the intention of the speaker; it depends on the logic of the situation in which the utterance occurs.

Another objection is this: would an explicit utterance of the doctrine about doctrines we are considering weaken the effect and thus obstruct the alleged purpose of utterances of its primary doctrines? Normally no one likes to be manipulated. Would therefore the doctrine about doctrines have to be reserved, as an esoteric doctrine? Further, though one might speak of the activities permitted by this doctrine as processes of training, one comes to wonder whether it would be misleading to speak of these activities as teaching or instruction, and hence whether it would be misleading to speak of doctrines at all.

For these reasons it seems that we are dealing with a very shaky hypothesis about the teachings of a religious community. It does not seem likely that a religious community could in this way avoid supposing or claiming that its doctrines are consistent with one another.

Perhaps a somewhat stronger case could be made for the possibility that an individual could engage in religious discourse without making proposals. He might resolve to restrict his utterances to expressions of his religious feelings, let us say. Then he would be bound to disavow, as misinterpretations of what he says, construals of his utterances as proposals for belief, or proposals of valuations, or proposals of courses of action.

It would not be easy for him to live up to his resolution, but if he should succeed there would be no room for speaking of the consistency or inconsistency of what is said in his utterances. The only way in which questions about consistency or inconsistency could arise would be as to whether he succeeds in living up to his resolution or not. For if some of his utterances do in fact make proposals of one sort or another, whether he realizes it or not, then his practice is inconsistent with his resolution, and inconsistent also with his profession, since, to avoid misunderstandings, he should be ready and willing to profess his resolution.

But a religious community is not in the same boat. Even if we could suppose that an individual might embark in such a frail and leaky vessel, a religious community is not at liberty to do so. It must propose a pattern of life to its members and nurture them in it as best it can. To do so it must propose to them the beliefs, valuations, and courses of action which are the constituents of the pattern. If this is so, then it seems that a religious community cannot avoid the supposition that the various proposals made in its discourse are consistent with one another.

To proceed upon a supposition is not to make a claim. But in the major religious communities claims of consistency are commonly made. We have already noticed a principle of consistency in the passage from the Mahāparinibbānasutta considered in chapter 2. The problem discussed in the sutta was how it could be decided whether some sentence ascribed to the Buddha is a genuine Buddha-word or not. And it was laid down, as a necessary condition of accepting such a sentence as a genuine saying of the Buddha, that the sentence must harmonize with what the Buddha is already known to have said. This clearly implies that the genuine teachings of the Buddha are consistent with one another. Another case in point occurs in the *Westminster Confession of Faith,* chapter 1 ("Of the Holy Scriptures"), where it is said that one of the "arguments" whereby the Bible "doth evidence itself to be the word of God" is "the consent of all the parts." Claims to the consistency of authentic doctrines of a community are evident also in the passages to be discussed later on.

STRAINS ON CONSISTENCY

It is common knowledge that in the histories of religious communities principles of consistency undergo severe strains. If this were not so, the doctrinal histories of the major religious communities would be far simpler than they are. A historical reason for these strains is that diversities and disparities in beliefs, valuations, and practices are present from the very beginnings of a community. In the course of time some of these contrasts become sharper and harden into oppositions. Then the community must take heed of them in order to preserve its health and vigor. It is not as though concerns about consistency are introduced into the community only from outside it. To the degree that a community becomes reflective these concerns arise from the necessities of its own existence.

A deeper reason for strains on doctrinal principles of consistency is this: a community has an obligation to do justice to the sources of its doctrines, and these sources are of various kinds. They include narratives, prophetic utterances, moral valuations and directives, directions for ceremonial and liturgical practices, proverbs and other bits of wisdom, patterns for meditation and other forms of inward discipline, assertions about the constitution of the world and the conditions of human existence, records of the past existence of the community, and analyses of emotions and attitudes and their consequences. Also, the sources of a community's doctrines often reflect strains among local cultures which the community as a whole encompasses. Furthermore, in these variegated sources, events and insights appear which are novel and surprising. Nevertheless the community has to live with a pressure to do justice to all these sources of its doctrines.

So there are two pressures operating within a religious community as it undertakes to formulate and shape its body of doctrines. There is the pressure to make its body of doctrines adequate to the sources of its doctrines, to say all the different things which must be said. And there is the pressure to maintain compatible contrasts among all the different things which must be said, to say them consistently. Both of these pressures are internal, and they are reflected in the community's body of doctrines. Comparable pressures, for adequacy and for consistency, operate within communities of other kinds also, and indeed within each of us.

The suppositions of consistency and the claims to consistency which concern us do not imply that all the sentences which happen to be presented within the bounds of some religious community are consistent with one another. It is only sets of authentic doctrines which are supposed or claimed to be consistent with one another. Judging from the literatures of developed religious communities, it is well known in each of them that some sentences uttered within the bounds of the community are not authentic doctrines of the community and hence may well be inconsistent with authentic doctrines or with one another.

Since claims of authenticity and claims of consistency are linked in this way, when a problem about the consistency of its teachings arise within a community, the issue has two faces. It must be asked (1) whether each of the sentences in question are indeed authentic doctrines of the community, and (2) whether the sentences in question are indeed inconsistent with one another.

(1) Members of a community are not bound to accept all sentences which have been claimed to be doctrines of the community, even if some of these have been presented by respected teachers and even if some of these sentences have been generally accepted in the community for considerable periods of time. Decisions as to whether some sentence expresses an authentic doctrine of the community or not have to be guided by the principles and rules constituting the doctrines of the community for identifying its doctrines. So one way of responding to what appears to be an intolerable inconsistency is to ask whether one or more of the sentences in question are indeed authentic doctrines.

(2) Turning to the other face of the issue, some apparent inconsistencies turn out not to be so. This is a general fact about human discourse. Telling whether various utterances of sentences in natural languages are consistent or not is not always a simple matter. Formal syntactical rules are not sufficient in a large number of cases. In many cases the trouble arises because various groups of speakers have developed their own idioms, and along with these, their own rules for consistency. For example, sentences which seem inconsistent to non-physicists are explained as consistent with one another by those who are familiar with the ways the sentences are used in physics. Similarly anthropologists often learn that members of the society they are studying are being consistent in ways they did not previously understand. Prima facie inconsistencies which had puzzled them turn out not to be genuine inconsistencies. Indeed this is just how they work their way into the consistency rules of the unfamiliar society. These are not uncommon experiences, so it should not come as a surprise to anyone that re-

ligious communities and groups of speakers within a religious community develop their own manners of speaking and rules of speech. This is not to say that the consistency rules of physicists or of a relatively isolated and nonliterate society or of a religious community are exempt from criticism, only that their manners of speaking should be understood and taken into account.

The treatise *Against Celsus* by the third-century Christian theologian Origen illustrates the two-faced character of these issues. Celsus had claimed to find many inconsistencies in Christian teachings. In some cases Origen denies that one or another of the sentences which Celsus produces is an authentic Christian doctrine and goes on to explain the authentic doctrines on the points at issue. In other cases Origen undertakes to show that the pairs of sentences which Celsus claims are inconsistent are not inconsistent when they are correctly understood. To take another case from the same period, the early Christian fathers, Irenaeus for example, argued that various gnostic teachings were inconsistent with one another. And it would have been fair for gnostics to reply either that their doctrines had been misunderstood or that the alleged inconsistencies were only apparent and not real.

A SCHEMA OF PRINCIPLES OF INTERNAL CONSISTENCY

So, for some religious community, the schema of a principle of internal consistency would run as follows:

For any pair of sentences *(s1, s2)*, if
(i) *s1* is an authentic doctrine of the community, and
(ii) *s2* is an authentic doctrine of the community, then
s1 and *s2* are consistent.

Hence, if *s1* and *s2* are inconsistent, then
(i) *s1* is not an authentic doctrine of the community, or
(ii) *s2* is not an authentic doctrine of the community, or
(iii) neither *s1* nor *s2* is an authentic doctrine of the community.

Some abbreviations:
'*s* is a doctrine' abbreviates 'what is proposed in *s* is a doctrine' or '*s* expresses a doctrine.'
'*s1* and *s2* are consistent' abbreviates 'what is proposed in *s1* and what is proposed in *s2* are consistent.'

What we have here is a schema of doctrines. A particular community would have its own principle of internal consistency for its doctrines, relying on its own criteria of authenticity. But we may think of the schema as an expression of an abstract principle, a principle abstracted from doctrinal principles of particular communities which fit the pattern of the schema. Notice several points about the principle and the rule which follows from it.

The principle gives no guidance as to whether some sentence or other is or is not an authentic doctrine of some particular community. But if some community embodies the abstract principle in a governing doctrine, a doctrine about its doctrines, this supposes that the community has criteria of authenticity and hence is in a position to judge, at least in some cases (since criteria are not always easy to apply), that some sentences express authentic doctrines of the community and that some other sentences do not. So we might say that adoption of the principle by a community supposes that the community has criteria of authenticity which are applicable and effective.

Notice also that with respect to the diagnosis of an inconsistency, the rule which follows from the principle is impartial. It does not weight the scales in favor of any one of the diagnoses it mentions. It does not suggest that any one of them is more likely than any other. As far as the rule itself goes, when a community confronts an inconsistency it is free to adopt any one of the diagnoses. The only alternative the rule does not admit is that both members of the pair of inconsistent sentences are authentic doctrines of the community.

Notice further that this is not a general principle of consistency. In the schema the only cases where members of a pair of sentences are said to be consistent are cases where both members of the pair are authentic doctrines of the community. The point of principles which fit the schema is to say something about authentic doctrines of a community. That is why we may speak of these principles as principles of internal consistency. Hence it may be supposed that a community which adopts such a principle as a governing doctrine would have reasons of its own for doing so, and that such reasons may be drawn from its own primary doctrines. A community might say, for example, that the sources of its doctrines, if they are rightly understood, can be trusted not to speak inconsistently. We return to this point in chapter 7.

Consider then the following options for dealing with some pair of sentences which pose a problem about consistency.

Option 1. One of the sentences is not an authentic doctrine of the community, or the other is not, or neither is.

If any of these alternatives holds then the problem is resolved. If one sentence is an authentic doctrine of the community and the other is not, the question whether they are consistent would still be pertinent for a spokesman for the community. For knowing that a doctrine of the community is inconsistent with some sentence which is not a doctrine of the community would tell him something about the doctrine. It would help to define the doctrine. So this inconsistency would be of direct interest to a spokesman for the community in a way in which the inconsistency of two sentences which are not doctrines would not be. In chapter 7 we consider cases where a doctrine of a community and some sentence which is not a doctrine of that community are inconsistent. In such cases extended principles of consistency are needed.

If neither of the sentences is a doctrine of the community, then it would not be a matter of special interest to a spokesman for the community. That is to say, it would not concern him as a spokesman for the community any more than it would concern anyone else, though by virtue of various interests he has as a person and various activities in which he is engaged it might concern him as much as anyone else.

Option 2. Both of the sentences are authentic doctrines of the community, and they are not inconsistent with one another.

This would be a different resolution of the problem. If the consistency of the sentences is challenged, the speaker ought to be ready and willing to do what he can to meet the challenge. He may think it can be shown that there is no absurdity in accepting both sentences. He might argue, for example, that though there would be an absurdity in accepting both if some third sentence were supposed, in fact this third sentence is not supposed by these doctrines of the community. Compare a case where a defender of noneuclidean geometry might point out that the parallel postulate is not supposed.

On the other hand the spokesman for the community may find that he is unable to remove the appearance of inconsistency. Still, he may say, there are good reasons for accepting each of the sentences as authentic doctrines of the community. Hence there is reason to believe that they are not inconsistent with one another. Many of us find ourselves in analogous positions, at least for the time being, not only as members of religious communities but also in respect to the perceptual and moral judgments we make in the course of ordinary life, and in scientific inquiries as well. Sometimes we think it is better on the whole to hold on for the time being to both of two apparently inconsistent perceptual judgments, moral judgments, or results of experiments, since there seem to be good reasons for accepting each of them, in hope of finding a consistent resolution which will do justice to both of them.

Sometimes a member of a religious community has strong, indeed compelling, reasons for maintaining that each of some pair of sentences is an authentic doctrine of the community. Each seems well buttressed by authoritative sources, for example by scripture and tradition. Each has been generally accepted in the community over long periods of time. A number of other beliefs and practices of the community have been accommodated to each of these doctrines, so that each has become deeply embedded in the life of the community. Yet it is not clear how they are consistent with one another. Such strains may continue unresolved in spite of the efforts of devout and acute minds to resolve them, though the logical pressure in a community to maintain consistency is still felt. Hence we should expect to find in the body of doctrines of a religious community, along with the principle of internal consistency, other principles and rules which bear on apparent inconsistencies in its doctrines.

To sum up on options 1 and 2: When arguments about apparent inconsistencies grant that the sentences in question are inconsistent but aim to show that one or both of them are not authentic doctrines of the community, taking option 1, then they will rely mainly on such principles and rules for identifying authentic doctrines as those we studied in chapter 2. When, on the other hand, taking option 2, arguments grant or claim that both sentences are authentic doctrines but aim to show that they are not inconsistent, then they will rely mainly on doctrines which implement a principle of internal consistency and apply it to the complexities of a body of doctrines. Consider some of these.

IMPLEMENTING A PRINCIPLE OF INTERNAL CONSISTENCY: THOMAS AQUINAS

Near the beginning of the *Summa Theologica,* Aquinas takes up the question "Whether in Holy Scripture a Word may have Several Senses?"[5] He considers the objection that if in Holy Scripture a word can have several senses this would produce confusion and destroy all force of argument. Against this and other objections he argues that, though the first sense of scripture is the historical or literal sense, scriptural words may have an allegorical sense, a moral sense, and an anagogical sense as well. (These latter senses taken together he refers to also as the spiritual sense.) But, he says,

> no confusion results, for all the [other] senses are founded on one—the literal—from which alone can any argument be drawn, and not from those intended allegorically, as Augustine says. Nevertheless, nothing of Holy Scripture perishes because of this, since nothing necessary to faith is contained under the spiritual sense which is not elsewhere put forward clearly by the Scripture in its literal sense. [Reply Obj. 1]

Aquinas groups history, etiology, and analogy under the literal sense.

> For it is called history, as Augustine expounds, whenever anything is simply related; it is called etiology when its cause is assigned. . . ; it is called analogy whenever the truth of one text of Scripture is shown not to contradict the truth of another. [Reply Obj. 2]

In reply to another objection, he assimilates the use of parables to the analogical sense:

> The parabolical sense is contained in the literal, for by words things are signified properly and figuratively. Nor is the figure itself, but that which is

5. Anton C. Pegis, ed., *Basic Writings of Saint Thomas Aquinas,* (New York: Random House, 1945), Part 1, Question 1, art. 10. Pegis revises the English Dominican translation.

figured, the literal sense. When Scripture speaks of God's arm, the literal sense is not that God has such a member, but only what is signified by this member, namely, operative power. [Reply Obj. 3]

So Aquinas expands the scope of the expression *literal sense* beyond the bounds sometimes set for it.

Notice two principles which Aquinas seems to put forward in this discussion:

1. Arguments for saying that some sentence well and truly expresses a doctrine which is necessary to faith must rely on the literal senses of passages of scripture.

2. The literal senses of passages of scripture include analogical senses, which are needed to show that some scripture passages are consistent with others.

The first of these principles bears directly on the authenticity of doctrines. It has a place among principles and rules for identifying the authentic doctrines of the Christian community. The second principle helps to explain the first, but it bears directly on the relations of authentic doctrines of the community to one another. It is a hermeneutical principle which has a place among principles and rules implementing applications of a principle of internal consistency.

It seems that both principles are being put forward as formulations of Christian teachings. Aquinas is speaking as a Christian theologian, and he is arguing what the Christian community should say on the question he is taking up. Insofar as the church claims to draw its teachings from the Bible, these principles would guide its procedures for settling internal disputes about doctrines.

But it seems that neither of these principles is directly about the world in which human life goes on or about human conduct in the world. They are directly about Christian doctrines. They would function as Christian doctrines about Christian doctrines. Though we should not impute to Aquinas the framework we have been developing for the sake of our own investigation, it seems that in effect, if not in his intention, these principles would have a part, along with various other principles and rules, in governing the process of formulating and shaping the corpus of Christian doctrines. More particularly, they would guide judgments as to the authenticity of formulations of Christian doctrines and as to the consistency of authentic Christian doctrines with one another.

It is the second of these principles which concerns us at this point. Taking the example Aquinas gives, this principle permits the church to say that when Scripture uses the expression "the arm of the Lord," it is not teaching us that God has a certain bodily member. That would be clearly inconsistent with what is said in many other texts of Scripture. God is not a body with such members as arms and eyes, and he does not have such a body. God is present everywhere. (See Question 8, article 2.) Instead, when Scripture uses the expression "the arm of the Lord," it is speaking of his operative power. What the Scripture says in such a text is consistent with what it says elsewhere. Hence the doctrines of the church drawn from such texts and from elsewhere in the scriptures are consistent with one another.

Now consider the following question: Granted that the introduction of analogical senses of Scripture texts would have the effect of resolving some apparent or potential inconsistencies, under what conditions is the introduction of such senses warranted? How is it to be decided whether a particular text calls for interpretation in an analogical sense?

A passage in Aquinas' treatise *On the Power of God*[6] bears on this question. He asks whether, from the words of Genesis 1:2, "The earth was void and empty, and the spirit of God moved over the waters," we can say that formless matter preceded the formation of the earth. He proceeds as follows:

> I answer that as Augustine says (Conf. xii) this question admits of a twofold discussion, one regards the true answer to the question itself [that is, I take it, the question whether formless matter preceded the formation of the earth], the other regards the sense of the text in which Moses inspired by God tells the story of the world's beginning.
>
> As to the first discussion two things are to be avoided: one is the making of false statements especially such as are contrary to revealed truth, the other is the assertion that what we think to be true is an article of faith, for as Augustine says (*Conf.* x), *when a man thinks his false opinions to be the teaching of godliness, and dares obstinately to dogmatise about matters of which he is ignorant, he becomes a stumbling block to others.* The reason why he says that such an one is a stumbling block is because the faith is made ridiculous to the unbeliever when a simple-minded believer asserts as an article of faith that which is demonstrably false, as again Augustine says in his commentary (*Gen. ad lit.* i). As regards the other discussion two things also are to be avoided. One is to give to the words of Scripture an interpretation manifestly false: since falsehood cannot underlie the divine Scriptures which we have received from the Holy Ghost, as neither can there be error in the faith that is taught by the Scriptures. The other is not to force such an interpretation on Scripture as to exclude any other interpretations that are actually or possibly true: since it is part of the dignity of Holy Writ that under the one literal sense many others are contained. It is thus that the sacred text not only adapts itself to man's various intelligence, so that each one marvels to find his thoughts expressed in the words of Holy Writ; but also is all the more easily defended against unbelievers in that when one finds his own interpretation of Scripture to be false he can fall back upon some other. Hence it is not inconceivable that Moses and the other authors of the Holy Books were given to know the various truths that men would discover in the text, and that they expressed

6. Aquinas, *On the Power of God (Quaestiones Disputatae de Potentia Dei)*, trans. English Dominican Fathers (London: Burns Oates & Washbourne, 1933), Second Book, Question 4, art. 1 (pp. 8–9).

them under one literary style, so that each truth is the sense intended by the author. And then even if commentators adapt certain truths to the sacred text that were not understood by the author, without doubt the Holy Ghost understood them, since he is the principal author of Holy Scripture. Consequently every truth that can be adapted to the sacred text without prejudice to the literal sense, is the sense of Holy Scripture.

Notice several points. Some of them bear not only on the present topic but also on relations of doctrines of religious communities to secular claims, which will be studied in later chapters.

1. From what Aquinas says, following Augustine, about the "twofold discussion" it seems that the right answer to the question about formless matter is relatively independent of answers to the question about the sense of a Biblical text, as he goes on to explain later. From the context of the passage it seems this is because he considers the question about formless matter one for natural philosophy, or at least a question on which natural philosophy has an important bearing.

2. What has gone wrong when "a simple-minded believer" "asserts as an article of faith that which is demonstrably false?" What is the trouble? Is it that the simple-minded believer is naive in his judgment that what is said in some sentence is true? Is he just credulous? He has not reflected on the matter? He is not aware of objections to taking what is said in the sentence as true? He does not know that what is said in the sentence is demonstrably false? Or does the trouble lie elsewhere? Is it that he is not aware of the complexities involved in judgments that what is said in the sentence is an article of faith?

That is to say, is the simple-minded believer epistemically naive, or is he theologically naive? Perhaps both, but the distinction is important. Perhaps he is not aware that the conditions for saying that some sentence is true and the conditions for saying that some sentence is an article of faith are not the same.

3. Two errors are to be avoided in interpreting Scripture. The first of these is giving to the words of Scripture an interpretation which is manifestly false. That is to say, I take it, an interpretation where what is said, in a sentence meant to give a meaning of a Scripture text, is itself manifestly false and hence would, if it were a valid interpretation of the text, make what is said in the text false.

The second error is to force an interpretation on the Scripture in such a way as to exclude other interpretations which are actually or possibly true. This holds even if some truth which can be adapted to a text of Scripture was not understood by Moses or some other human author of the Holy Books. From this it seems to follow that it would be wrong to exclude actual or possible truths of natural philosophy (secular truths, we might say) from interpretations of a sacred text if these truths "can be adapted to the sacred text without prejudice to the literal sense" of the text.

We may ask: Would these truths thus come to be not only secular truths but also truths taught in the Scripture? Would they in this way come to qualify as authentic doctrines of the Christian community?

Coming back to our question about conditions for introducing analogical senses of scriptural texts, we can formulate a rule which, it seems, is consistent with what Aquinas says in these passages. Suppose that a scriptural text has no more than one literal sense; it may have a historical sense, in which something is simply related, or it may have an etiological sense, in which a cause of something is given, or it may have an analogical sense. But it has no more than one of these (I do not know whether what Aquinas says supposes this, but let us suppose it), though along with a literal sense a scriptural text may have more than one spiritual sense. Then the rule would be as follows:

1. A claim that some sentence (s) expresses an analogical sense of a scriptural text is warranted if (i) what is said in s is actually or possibly true, and (ii) taking the text in a literal sense of some other kind (i.e., in a historical sense or in an etiological sense) would result in contradictions between what is said in the text and what is clearly said in other scriptural texts.

2. A claim that what is said in some sentence expresses an analogical sense of a scriptural text is not warranted if (i) what is said in s is manifestly or demonstrably false, or (ii) taking the text in a literal sense of some other kind would not result in contradictions between what is said in the text and what is clearly said in other scriptural texts.

AL-GHAZZĀLĪ

A similar question is dealt with by the celebrated Muslim theologian and jurist al-Ghazzālī (1058–1111), though different terms are used. Aquinas speaks of analogical senses of texts and places these, along with certain other senses including historical senses, under the heading of literal senses; al-Ghazzālī speaks of allegorical senses and contrasts these with literal senses. But to deal with what al-Ghazzālī says, all we need is a reformulation of our question: How is it to be decided whether a text should be given an allegorical sense rather than a literal sense?

al-Ghazzālī addresses this question in the course of a judgment on a point in Muslim law.[7] He had been asked to give a legal opinion (a *fatwā*) on the esoteric sects among the Shi'ite Muslims, as to their standing in the Muslim community. As a preliminary to his decision he distinguishes two classes of opinions, which make those who hold them liable to censure in

7. "A *Fatwā* of al-Ghazzālī," pp. 254–79. Jeffery gives Arabic terms in parentheses and his own glosses in brackets.

different ways, "Two categories, one of which makes it necessary to declare that they are in error, are astray, and are guilty of innovation (*bid'a*), and the other of which makes it necessary to declare that they are unbelievers and [the community must] be cleansed of them" (p. 255). Among opinions falling in the second category he places "denying the last Judgment, or disavowing Paradise and Hell and the resurrection" (p. 260). Then al-Ghazzālī poses the following question: "Well, what about a man who believes in the Divine unity and denies all association (*shirk*) [the sin of associating any other with Allah in such a way as to prejudice His absolute uniqueness—from Jeffery's footnote], yet feels himself free to interpret allegorically particular matters concerning Judgment and Paradise and Hell" (p. 260).

This man does not grant that there will be sensuous delights in paradise such as houris and palaces, or that there will be sensuous pains in hell. Instead he interprets the bliss of Paradise as the enjoyment of intellectual and spiritual perfection, and he interprets the distress of Hell as deprivation of that perfection. al-Ghazzālī gives a sympathetic account of the arguments for this position. Indeed he seems to be drawn toward it himself. But his judgment as a jurist is that such a person must be declared an unbeliever, because the description of Paradise and Hell occurs in the Qur'ān not merely once or twice, "and is not given by way of allusion (*kināya*), rhetorical augmentation (*tawassu'*) or literary figure (*tajawwuz*), but in clear terms about which there is nothing doubtful or subject to suspicion. The Master of the religious law meant them to be understood in their literal sense" (p. 262). Then al-Ghazzālī goes on to deal with an ad hominem objection:

> Should someone ask: "But did you yourself not travel this road [when you were dealing] with the images which are presented in connection with [exposition of] the attributes of Allah—exalted be He—, e.g., in connection with the verse of sitting, the Tradition about the coming down, the word 'foot' where it says that the Almighty put His foot in the Fire, the expression 'image' (*sūra*), where he—upon whom be peace—said that Allah created Adam in His own image, and in other such Traditions, perhaps more than a thousand of them, yet you know that the pious early believers were not in the habit of allegorizing these literal expressions, but used to take them in their literal sense. You did not declare anyone who denied the literal acceptation [of these passages], and allegorized them, to be in unbelief, but you professed your belief in the allegorical interpretation and plainly stated this"—our answer is: How can one avoid this [suggesting of] equivalences when the Qur'ān states quite plainly that "He has no similitude" (XLII, 11/9), and the Traditions which indicate the same thing are more than can be numbered? We are aware that in the days of the Companions had anyone stated plainly that Allah—exalted be He—is not confined by space, is not limited by time, is not in contact with matter nor separated therefrom by any distance measurable or immeasurable, that He is not subject to transfer, whether going or coming, appearing or disappearing, that it is impossible that He should be among

things that settle down or are transferred [from place to place], or that are firmly fixed [in a place], and so on with the other expressions which [are used to] deny anthropomorphic attributes, they would have considered such statements the very essence of [true effort at maintaining] the Divine unity and transcendence. Yet were a person [who asserted these things] to deny the [literal acceptance of the] Hūrīs and the palaces, the [celestial] rivers and trees, the Zabāniyya, and the Fire [of Hell], that would have been counted among the various classes of falsity and denial, but there is no equivalence between the two cases.

We have already drawn attention to the difference [between them] in [p. 263] the chapter where we refute [the teachings of] their sect, [where we point out] two aspects thereof. One of them is that the expressions regarding the Judgment, Paradise and Hell are stated so plainly that there is no allegorizing them or avoiding them otherwise than by removing them or treating them as false, whereas the expressions regarding such matters as the sitting, the image, and so forth, are commonly used metaphorical, rhetorical figures (ta-wassu'āt), which may be interpreted allegorically. The other is that there are intellectually satisfying arguments which hinder belief in anthropomorphism and in [notions of] descent, movement, spatial fixation [with reference to Allah], and indicate their impossibility with a clarity that leaves no room for doubt. On the contrary there is no intellectually satisfying proof that what is promised with regard to Paradise and Hell in the after life cannot possibly happen. Nay, indeed, the eternal Power knew all about these [promises] and had them in His control. They are things which in themselves are quite possible, and the eternal Power will not fail to bring about that which in itself is possible. How then can you confuse this with the expressions used of the attributes of Allah—exalted be He? [p. 264]

We can extract from what al-Ghazzālī says the following outlines of arguments:

A. An argument for taking the passages in the Qur'ān about Judgment, Paradise, and Hell literally.

    A1. These passages are so numerous and so plain that they cannot be taken allegorically.

    A2. In the days of the Companions of the Prophet, denials of these passages taken in their literal senses would have been counted as denials of the Muslim faith.

    A3. There are no intellectually satisfying arguments which show that what is said in the passages, taken literally, is impossible. God has the power to bring about what is promised in them.

B. An argument for taking the anthropomorphic expressions about Allah allegorically.

    B1. These expressions are commonly used metaphorical figures which can be interpreted allegorically even though, he seems to grant, "the pious early believers" took them literally.

    B2. The Qur'ān and many traditions say, "He has no similitude."

B3. If a clear and developed statement denying that Allah has anthropomorphic attributes had been advanced in the days of the Companions, it would have been accepted as essential to maintaining the Divine unity and transcendence.

B4. There are intellectually satisfying arguments which clearly show that it is impossible that Allah should have anthropomorphic attributes.

So the two cases are not on the same footing. It is consistent to take the passages about Judgment, Paradise, and Hell literally and to take the anthropomorphic expressions about Allah allegorically. The conclusion of Argument A and the conclusion of Argument B are consistent with one another.

It seems that al-Ghazzālī does not think that the literal meanings of the passages about the Judgment, Paradise, and Hell generate even apparent inconsistencies with other primary Muslim doctrines. At least he does not introduce such questions here, for example whether these passages in their literal meanings are consistent with doctrines about the divine unity and transcendence (though this question might well trouble someone like the man whose position al-Ghazzālī had discussed earlier [on p. 260]). The only problems about the consistency of Muslim doctrines he deals with here are the following:

(1) Whether ascriptions of anthropomorphic attributes to Allah would be consistent with assertions of the divine unity and transcendence.

He thinks the inconsistency is obvious and intolerable. So, since assertions of the divine unity and transcendence are clearly essential to the Muslim faith, ascriptions of anthropomorphic attributes to Allah cannot be authentic doctrines of Islam. Passages mentioning bodily functions as though they were attributes of Allah ought to be interpreted allegorically, as argued above.

(2) Whether a doctrine which requires those passages to be interpreted allegorically is consistent with a doctrine which requires a literal interpretation of the passages about the Judgment, Paradise, and Hell.

He argues that these doctrines are consistent with one another, because the cases are dissimilar. He thinks there could be a consistent hermeneutical rule. Perhaps we could reconstruct this rule as follows:

A passage in the Qur'ān must be taken in a literal sense, especially if it belongs to a set of passages which are numerous and plain, unless what is said in a literal reading of the passage is clearly inconsistent with what is said in some other passage in the Qur'ān. In that case, if (1) the expressions used in the first passage are common metaphors, and if (2a) the other passage belongs to a set of passages which are numerous and plain, and especially if what it says is reinforced by many traditions about the sayings of the Prophet and expresses a consensus of the Companions, or (2b) there are conclusive arguments against what is said in a literal reading of the first passage, then the first passage must be taken nonliterally.

It seems that al-Ghazzālī is arguing that in the case of passages which say that after the creation Allah took his seat on his throne or that he raised his arms, or use similar expressions, the conditions for resort to nonliteral interpretations are satisfied; and that in the case of passages about the Judgment, the bliss of Paradise, and the distress of Hell, those conditions are not satisfied.

We should notice a different hermeneutical doctrine put forward by some earlier Muslim theologians, because it bears on some of the apparent inconsistencies with which al-Ghazzālī was dealing. These theologians, including Ahmad ibn Hanbal (786–855) and al-Ash'arī (873–935), refused to interpret nonliterally the passages in the Qur'ān which say that Allah took his seat on his throne and that he raised his arms, and which speak of his face, his eyes, and his hands. They thought that interpreting such expressions as metaphors was not warranted. The words ought to be interpreted in accord with their ordinary meanings in the Arabic language. For example, they argued that the Arabic word for hand simply does not mean grace.

Yet they held as strongly as al-Ghazzālī did that Allah cannot be assimilated, likened, to any creature. They said that Allah's hands are not like any hands we know. So they felt forced to say that though, since the Qur'ān speaks of Allah's hands, it must be asserted that Allah has hands, this must be asserted *bilā kaifa,* that is to say, "without how," without giving any further qualification or explanation of what is asserted.

They were respected by their followers for their sturdy refusal to tread on shaky ground. If one begins to substitute metaphors for literal meanings, where is one to stop? Also, it might be said, being unable to explain what is meant is not the same as being inconsistent. But al-Ghazzālī seems to have thought that even the appearance of inconsistency had to be removed.

NĀGĀRJUNA

We have been considering some doctrines about doctrines which, with a view to resolving apparent or potential inconsistencies of doctrines, set forth principles and rules for interpreting texts. Now consider a case in which a somewhat different sort of doctrine about doctrines is put forward. Here also a distinction is developed with a view to resolving apparent inconsistencies of doctrines. But this distinction is not between different senses of expressions; it is a distinction between truths of different kinds.

Often distinctions between truths of different kinds have been drawn by philosophers, for example distinctions between logical truths, perceptual truths, truths of physics, and moral truths, and these distinctions have been used for various purposes.[8] Distinctions between truths of different kinds

8. See William A. Christian, "Domains of Truth," *American Philosophical Quarterly* 12 (1975): 61–68.

occur also in the literatures of various religious communities as doctrines about their doctrines. Some such doctrines about doctrines serve to set off doctrines of the community from claims made by philosophers, historians, scientists, and others who do not purport to speak for any religious community. Sometimes, however, such doctrines set off different types of doctrines of the community from one another, and these often bear on apparent inconsistencies between doctrines of the community. We shall study a distinction of this last sort, but let us begin with a distinction more like those we have already considered.

In a Pali text the Buddha says: "There are these two who misrepresent the Tathāgata. Which two? He who represents a Sutta of indirect meaning [neyyattha] as a Sutta of direct meaning [nītattha] and he who represents a Sutta of direct meaning as a Sutta of indirect meaning."[9] Here the teacher makes a distinction which yields a principle for interpreting his own teachings. In some cases the meaning of a passage is obvious; in other cases the meaning of the passage is not obvious but has to be drawn out. It is wrong to confuse passages of one of these types with passages of the other type. K. N. Jayatilleke says that no examples of these two kinds of suttas are given in the Pali canon (p. 362).

This reminds us of the distinction drawn by Aquinas and al-Ghazzālī between literal senses of expressions and nonliteral senses of expressions. Here again a principle for interpreting particular passages in a canonical text is presented. So we might speak of these principles as exegetical principles. They bear directly on instances where what is said in one passage seems inconsistent with what is said in another passage. The point is that if the passages are interpreted in accord with these exegetical principles, they will be seen to be not inconsistent with one another.

Later on, the standard Buddhist commentaries develop from this distinction the notion of two kinds of truth: "The Perfectly Enlightened One, the best of teachers, spoke two truths, viz. conventional and absolute—one does not come across a third; a conventional statement is true because of convention and an absolute statement is true as (disclosing) the true characteristics of things."[10]

It seems that the principle introduced by this distinction is different in character from the exegetical principles. Like them, it does indeed bear on particular passages in texts. But it seems to bear more immediately on functions which doctrines of different kinds have in a body of doctrine. We might say that it has to do with the logic of a body of doctrines as a

---

9. Aṅguttara Nikāya, 1:60, trans. K. N. Jayatilleke, in *Early Buddhist Theory of Knowledge* (London: George Allen & Unwin, 1963), p. 361. A. K. Warder, in *Indian Buddhism* (Delhi: Motilal Banarsidass, 1970), p. 150, translates Sanskrit nītārtha (Pali nītattha) as "having its meaning drawn out" and Sanskrit neyārtha (Pali neyyattha) as "having its meaning requiring to be drawn out."

10. Jayatilleke, p. 364, translating from the standard commentary on the *Kathāvatthu* (34) and the standard commentary on the *Aṅguttara Nikāya* (1:95).

whole. The body of doctrines has a pattern, and doctrines of different kinds have different sorts of places in this pattern. So, if a doctrine of one kind and a doctrine of another kind appear inconsistent, the apparent inconsistency may be resolved by understanding the doctrines in the light of their different places in the pattern. The point of the distinction is in this way logical rather than exegetical.

We shall now study a development of this distinction by Nāgārjuna, the founder of the Mādhyamika school of Mahayana Buddhism in the second century A.D. The text of Nāgārjuna's *Mūlamadhyamakakārikās*, written in highly compressed and enigmatic verses (*kārikās*), is embedded in a commentary by Candrakīrti, a Buddhist monk of the seventh century A.D.[11]

Nāgārjuna's distinction runs as follows: "The teaching of the Buddhas is wholly based on there being two truths: that of a personal everyday world, and a higher truth which surpasses it" (p. 230). The distinction is introduced in the course of a reply by Nāgārjuna to a Buddhist opponent who objects to Nāgārjuna's main thesis.

This thesis is that all things whatsoever are empty (*sūnya*), that is to say, devoid of self-existence (*svabhāva*). Nothing whatever exists independently of other existents. This is not to say that there are no existents. It is only to say that no existents exist of themselves. Our tendency to think of things including ourselves as self-existent is prompted by, and in turn reinforces, attachments to or aversions from particular objects in the world. These attachments and aversions bind us to the world. Realization that nothing whatever is self-existent would cut the roots of these attachments and aversions. Enlightenment is liberation from this bondage. That is the practical point of the doctrine.

The opponent's objection to this thesis is that if it is true then a number of standard Buddhist doctrines would have to be regarded as unintelligible or false, for these standard Buddhist doctrines seem to assert or suppose that there are some self-existent things. He argues that, according to the teaching of the Buddha:

> There are four noble truths (*āryasatya*), namely (i) that suffering (*duhkha*) pervades ordinary existence; (ii) that the cause of suffering is craving (*tanha*); (iii) that cessation of craving is possible; and (iv) that the way to cessation of craving is the noble eightfold path (right view, right thought, right speech, right bodily action, right livelihood, right effort, right mindfulness, right concentration). These truths sum up the *Dharma*, the teaching of the Buddha.

11. *Lucid Exposition of the Middle Way. The Essential Chapters from the Prasannapadā of Candrakīrti*, trans. from the Sanskrit by Mervyn Sprung, in collaboration with T. R. V. Murti and U. S. Vyas (Boulder Colo.: Prajnā Press, 1979). Page numbers refer to this translation. Another translation of Nāgārjuna's kārikās is given in Frederick J. Streng, *Emptiness: A Study in Religious Meaning* (Nashville: Abingdon, 1967). See also Streng's essay in *The Problem of Two Truths in Buddhism and Vedānta*, ed. Mervyn Sprung (Dordrecht and Boston: Reidel, 1973), in which Streng retranslates a number of the kārikās.

There is the Buddhist community of monks, the *Sangha.*

There is the enlightened one, the *Buddha,* at the head of this community.

These are the Three Jewels which are mentioned in the standard formula: I take my refuge in the Buddha. I take my refuge in the Dharma. I take my refuge in the Sangha.

Furthermore, the opponent continues, in Buddhist teachings it is said that some actions are right and some actions are wrong. Also in Buddhist teachings many everyday expressions, such as "cook," "eat," "come," and "go" are used.

All these teachings would have to be abandoned if Nāgārjuna's thesis were accepted. For they suppose that there are a number of real things which can be considered in themselves as subjects of discourse. But Nāgārjuna's thesis is that all things are empty, devoid of self-existence.

For example, the four noble truths speak of causation of suffering and cessation of suffering. But if there are no self-existent beings, then there is nothing to cause something else, and there is nothing which can be said to cease. So the principle of sūnya, that all things are devoid of self-existence, makes the āryasatya and other standard Buddhist teachings unintelligible. It seems to Nāgārjuna's opponent that the foundations of Buddhist doctrines are threatened.

Nāgārjuna defends his thesis by dialectical objections to the notion of self-existence, but also by appealing to the doctrine of *pratityasamutpāda,* which is prominent among the teachings of the Buddha. The Buddha taught that all things are subject to conditions in their origination and in their cessation. This, Nāgārjuna argues, clearly implies that no beings are self-existent, that all things are devoid of self-existence, that all beings depend on other beings for their existence. Indeed, Nāgārjuna seems to speak of *sūnyatā* not just as an implication of pratityasamutpāda but as equivalent to it. For example, "We interpret the dependent arising of all things as the absence of being in them" (p. 238).

So, since it seems clear from the kārikās that Nāgārjuna is not only supporting his thesis by appealing to the teaching of the Buddha, but that he is putting forward the thesis as a Buddhist doctrine, the setting in which his distinction between the two truths is introduced is an apparent inconsistency between different Buddhist doctrines. The immediate point of the distinction between a truth of a personal everyday world (*lokasamvṛtisatya*) and a higher truth which surpasses it (*paramārthasatya*) is to open a way of removing the apparent inconsistency.

Nāgārjuna proceeds as follows to resolve the problem.

1. He does not deny that the doctrines mentioned by his opponent are authentic Buddhist doctrines. That would have been one way to remove the inconsistency, but he does not take that path.

2. He does reject the implication suggested by his opponent, that these

doctrines imply that there are self-existent beings. His reason is that these doctrines are framed in the context of personal everyday experience, and they speak in the ordinary language we use about the everyday world. They are truths of a personal everyday world (lokasamvrtisatya). But the fact that we speak in these ways does not imply that we ourselves or other people or physical objects or anything else is self-existent. It does not imply that the subjects of our discourse exist in complete independence of anything else. It is only when our own attachments and aversions to particular objects bind us to them that we begin to think of them as self-existent. Taking them as they come they are just what they are, nothing less, and especially nothing more.

3. Also, he rejects the further implication suggested by his opponent that if the things mentioned in the standard Buddhist doctrines are not self-existent, then they are nothing. That something is empty (sūnya), devoid of self-existence, does not imply that it is nonexistent. It implies only that what we speak of does not exist in independence of all other things. Hence the higher, surpassing truth (paramārthasatya), that all things are devoid of self-existence, is consistent with the truths of a personal everyday world, and not inconsistent with those Buddhist doctrines which are framed in the context of those truths.

The distinction between the two truths is not a distinction between truths and falsehoods. In everyday discourse there are both truths and falsehoods. The standard Buddhist doctrines are truths, not falsehoods. They prepare the way for a truth of far higher value, the paramārthasatya, the truth of pratityasamutpāda and hence of sūnyatā, in the light of which they must be understood.

4. Here Nāgārjuna turns the table on his opponent. He argues that only in the light of the *paramārtha* truth do the standard Buddhist doctrines make sense. In the first place, only if things are dependent on other things do the four noble truths make sense (*artha*). For if things are self-existent, then nothing could arise or cease, so we could not understand either the arising or the cessation of suffering. The four noble truths make sense only for him for whom dependent arising makes sense (p. 235). And if the four noble truths make sense, and if they truly obtain, then the Buddhist teaching, the Dharma, makes sense. If the Dharma, and with it the Buddhist community which exists to teach it, makes sense, then the idea of an enlightened one at the head of this community, the Buddha, makes sense too. Thus the Three Jewels, the Buddha, the Dharma, the Sangha, make sense. Furthermore, moral and immoral conduct and their consequences make sense. And spiritual wellbeing and spiritual downfall and all everyday practical transactions make sense. Thus, instead of being inconsistent with the standard Buddhist doctrines, the truth that all things are devoid of self-existence is the key to understanding the standard Buddhist doctrines. So Nāgārjuna, as expounded by Candrakīrti, argues.

I have treated Nāgārjuna's distinction between two kinds of truths as a prima facie doctrine of a religious community about the doctrines of that community, and in particular as a doctrine which bears on the consistency of the doctrines of that community. This case in point has been abstracted from a commentary which, like the text it interprets, has occasioned a number of disputes among scholars. There is much more in the commentary than I have taken from it for the purpose of this study of doctrines of religious communities. In defense of the abstraction I offer the following considerations.

The commentary, like its text, develops philosophical distinctions and arguments which are very subtle and complex. Yet it seems clear that Candrakīrti supposes that Nāgārjuna was speaking not just as a philosopher but as a Buddhist teacher. It seems clear also that this is true of Candrakīrti himself as well. He purports to speak to and for the Buddhist community. He is engaged in a process of explaining, developing, and defending the doctrines of the community to which he belongs and for which he intends to speak. This comes out at several points in the commentary.

At the beginning of the commentary Candrakīrti makes his

obeisance to Nāgārjuna,
who was born of the ocean of wisdom of the perfectly enlightened one and
    who rose above the realm of dualities;
who compassionately brought to light the hidden truth of the treasury of
    Buddhism in Buddha's sense. [p. 51]

Further, in the chapter on the four Buddhist truths he takes the objections of the Buddhist opponent quite seriously, as Nāgārjuna did, more seriously indeed than the philosophical merits of the objections would seem to deserve. And, following his text, which says, "The teaching of the Buddhas is wholly based on there being two truths: that of a personal everyday world, and a higher truth which surpasses it," Candrakīrti comments, "That is, the teaching of the illustrious Buddha in this world is effective and valid only as based on the twofoldness of truth" (p. 230). Though this does not seem to go so far as to say explicitly that the Buddha taught the distinction between the two truths, the fact that the teaching of the Buddha depends on it seems to be put forward as a reason for accepting the distinction as a Buddhist doctrine.

Thus it seems that Candrakīrti is not only (1) speaking of the four noble truths and other doctrines framed in the context of truths of a personal everyday world (lokasamvrtisatya), as Buddhist doctrines; and (2) speaking of the paramārthasatya, the higher and surpassing truth of sūnyatā, as a Buddhist doctrine; he is also (3) speaking of Nāgārjuna's distinction itself as a Buddhist doctrine. So it seems clear that we could look on this distinction as a prima facie Buddhist doctrine about Buddhist doctrines.

I have not argued that any of these are authentic Buddhist doctrines.

That would have taken us far beyond the limits of our own investigation. I have argued only that Nāgārjuna and Candrakīrti seem to put them forward as Buddhist doctrines. For our study, prima facie doctrines, doctrines with plausible claims to authenticity, are good enough.

The point of the doctrine of the twofoldness of truth is to put the relevant primary doctrines in their places. In response to the objection by the Buddhist opponent, it shows the place of the standard primary doctrines in the body of Buddhist doctrines; it shows the place of the doctrine of sūnyatā; and it shows how the standard doctrines and the doctrine of sūnyatā are related to one another. The standard doctrines prepare the way for the doctrine of sūnyatā, and they depend on it for their intelligibility. The doctrine of sūnyatā presupposes them and makes them intelligible. And this shows that they are not inconsistent with one another.

Two further questions deserve consideration. The first is this: Is the central Madhyāmaka doctrine of sūnyatā meant to be taken as a purely practical doctrine, not as an assertion with a bearing on practice? Is it to be taken as just a set of directives for the conduct of life, rules for following a path, not as putting forward any propositions, suggestions, or insights which might be true or untrue?

This question arises from Sprung's translation of verse 18 of chapter 24 of the *Mūlamadhyamakakārikās* and Candrakīrti's commentary on this verse. Sprung translates the verse as follows: "We interpret the dependent arising of all things as the absence of being in them. Absence of being is a guiding, not a cognitive, notion, presupposing the everyday. It is itself the middle way." And his translation of Candrakīrti's commentary on the verse includes the following: "Absence of self-existence itself, as it presupposes the everyday, is a guiding, not a cognitive, notion" (p. 238). This seems to say that the real force of the apparent assertion "Nothing exists independently of other things" is not to assert anything but only to recommend a set of noncognitive attitudes and actions.

Several comments are in order. First, recommendations of courses of action bring with them suppositions about existents and conditions of existence. In particular, they suppose that in the relevant situation the recommended course of action is possible. And it seems that if some such supposition is challenged the speaker would be bound to assert what is supposed and to defend the assertion.

Second, even if Sprung is right about the text, this would not stand in the way of studying Nāgārjuna's distinction as a governing doctrine which bears on apparent inconsistencies in a body of doctrines. For practical doctrines may be inconsistent with one another and inconsistent with assertions. So, even if the paramārthasatya were a purely practical doctrine, the formulation of the two truths would still have the force of a principle, put forward as a doctrine, which functions to resolve a potential inconsistency among other doctrines of a community.

Third, it may be that Sprung's translation of verse 18 is misleading on this point. In his essay in *The Problem of Two Truths,* Streng transliterates the text of the verse as follows:

yaḥ pratītyasamutpādaḥ sūnyatāṁ tāṁ pracakṣmahe
sā prajñaptir upādāya pratipat sāiva madhyamā [p. 37, n. 5]

Streng's translation is:

The "originating dependently" we call "emptiness".
This apprehension, *i.e.,* taking into account (all other things), is [the understanding of] the middle way. [p. 28]

This makes one wonder whether there is in the text an equivalent of Sprung's phrase "not a cognitive." I cannot answer this question, though Sanskrit readers whom I have consulted do not find an equivalent in the text.

We should ask also whether the case study I have drawn from Candrakīrti's commentary loses its point in a different way. In the chapter on nirvāna, the principle of sūnyatā, namely that all things are conditioned and that hence there are no self-existent beings, is applied both to the notion of nirvāna (enlightenment) and to the notion of a buddha (an enlightened one). Candrakīrti says: "If there were anything at all called 'Truth' (*dharma*) which in its own nature was absolute (*svabhavarūpatah*), there would be those who were the bearers of this Truth and there would be some ultimate being called the illustrious Buddha, its teacher. This is the way it would be." As, however (here quoting Nāgārjuna's verse), "Ultimate beatitude is the coming to rest of all ways of taking things, the repose of named things, no Truth has been taught by a Buddha for anyone, anywhere." Shortly after this Candrakīrti goes on as follows:

When the illustrious Buddhas are in *nirvāna,* the ultimate beatitude, which is the coming to rest of named things as such, they are like kingly swans in the sky, self-soaring in space or in the nothingness of space on the twin wings of accumulated merit and insight; then, it should be known, that, because they do not perceive objects as signs, no rigid "Truth" whatsoever either concerning bondage or purification has been taught either among or for any gods or men whatsoever. [p. 262]

It seems that it might be argued from this that all the Buddhist doctrines we have been discussing are meant to be subjected to a dialectic, since none is complete in itself, unconnected with other doctrines and thus unconditioned by other doctrines. But it would not follow from this conclusion that the standard Buddhist doctrines do not make sense, or that they are not true (or, if they are practical doctrines, not right). And it would not follow that the paramārthasatya, that is, what is said above about nirvāna, does not make sense, or that it is not true. Nor would it follow that the paramārthasatya supplants the standard doctrines in such a way as to be a substitute for them.

The conclusion to be drawn, it seems, is not that there are really no Buddhist doctrines after all, but that all Buddhist doctrines must be understood in certain contexts. They must not be treated as things in themselves. And the distinction between the two truths seems to imply that if the doctrines are rightly understood in their connections with one another they will be seen to be consistent with one another.

CONSISTENCY UNDER PRESSURE

The cases in the latter part of this chapter show principles and rules for dealing with apparent inconsistencies within a body of doctrines. One lesson we can learn from them is the following: As we noticed earlier, various features of the bodies of doctrines of the major religious communities make them vulnerable to inconsistencies; still, pressures toward consistency are felt and responded to. Consider some such features.

1. The doctrines of these communities are not produced artificially. One way to insulate a set of sentences against inconsistencies is to exclude all ambiguous terms and to construct the sentences in accord with strict and effective formation rules. But this is not the way the doctrines of the major religious communities have been produced. Instead, their doctrines are thought of as responses to concrete events which brought these communities into existence. The doctrines of the Hindu community are thought of as responses to the sayings of the Vedic *rishis*. The doctrines of the Buddhist community are thought of as responses to the life and teachings of the Buddha. The doctrines of the Judaic community are thought of as responses to events in the history of Israel. The doctrines of the Christian community are thought of as responses to the life and teachings of Christ. The doctrines of the Muslim community are thought of as responses to the messages sent down to Muhammad. The significance of events such as these is not free from ambiguities, not by a long shot, and at many points they touch on mysteries, as is often acknowledged in these bodies of doctrines.

2. One might think it would be easier to produce a consistent body of doctrines if all its elements were assertions as to existents and the conditions of existence, eschewing proposals of courses of action and valuations. For, it might be argued, the logic of practical sentences and valuational sentences and their connections with existential sentences is problematical. So if these are included in some body of doctrines, inconsistencies are more difficult to recognize and to track down. But in the bodies of doctrines of the major religious communities, proposals of courses of action and of valuations are not only included but play essential parts in the teaching practices of the communities.

3. It would be easier to insulate a body of doctrines from inconsistencies if it were possible to avoid internal developments of doctrines. But this is scarcely possible without effectively banning reflection by one generation of scholars and teachers on the formulations of previous generations. On the whole the major religious communities have not proposed such bans, and attempts to arrest developments of doctrines have not always been effective. Furthermore, the bodies of doctrines of the major religious communities have undergone strong internal pressures to adapt the patterns of life they reflect to changing circumstances over long periods of time. So their bodies of doctrines reflect layers on layers of reflections by many generations of scholars and teachers, thus increasing liabilities to diachronic tensions.

4. Another feature of these bodies of doctrines which makes them more vulnerable to inconsistencies than they would otherwise be is this: the scriptures and traditions on which they draw include prophetic and poetic passages which are highly imaginative and hence are rife with invitations to inconsistencies. But these communities have thought that their doctrines should be adequate to these prophetic and poetic sayings as well as to other constituents of their sources.

In spite of the liabilities to inconsistency inherent in these features of their bodies of doctrines, it seems clear that internal pressures toward consistency have been felt and responded to in the major religious communities. Otherwise we would not be able to explain how such doctrines as those we have been considering could have come to be taught.

CHAPTER FOUR

Authenticity and Truth or Rightness

In this chapter we study some principles and rules which would connect (1) claims that what is said in some sentence is an authentic doctrine of a certain religious community and (2) claims that what is said in some sentence is true, or, for practical sentences, right. In chapter 2 we studied principles and rules which would yield a community's criteria of authenticity. But some communities seem to claim also that their doctrines are true or right. How could a community connect claims of these different sorts with one another?

In chapter 3 we studied principles and rules which bear on the internal consistency of a body of doctrines. These are also related to claims to truth and to rightness, and hence to our present topic, in the following way. One reason for a community to be concerned about the consistency of its doctrines is this: If the members of some pair of its doctrines are inconsistent with one another, then one or the other of the pair may be true or right, but not both members of the pair. So a concern on the part of a community for the internal consistency of its body of doctrines suggests, though it does not show, that the community claims that its doctrines are true or right.

Our topic also looks toward what we have yet to do. In chapters 7 and 8 we consider positions of religious communities on alien claims, claims which are not authentic doctrines of the community in question. One question is: May what is said in an alien claim be true or right? But we are not yet ready for that question. One reason is that a community's answer to the question depends on its principles and rules for connecting claims to authenticity and claims to truth or rightness. Also, since some alien claims are doctrines of other religious communities, we need a background study, in chapter 6, of connections between doctrines of different religions.

In this chapter we are venturing into less familiar territory than in chapters 2 and 3. The classical literatures of the major religious communities are less forthcoming on the topic of this chapter. Generally, and naturally, religious communities have attended most to their primary doctrines, doctrines about the setting of human life and how human beings should conduct their lives in this setting. When they go further and develop doctrines about their doctrines, they seem to have attended more to doctrines about authenticity and doctrines about consistency than to the doctrines we study in this chapter.

It is as though problems about connections of claims to authenticity and claims to truth or rightness have seemed less urgent to those communities than problems about authenticity and about consistency. That does not make it any easier, to say the least, for us to find our own way into the topic of this chapter.

So the hypothetical character of our discussion must be stressed even more than in the earlier chapters. Consideration of possible doctrines is most needed at points where discussions in the literatures of religious communities are least developed and least clear.

TWO SCHEMAS

We can find a way to get some light on our topic by beginning with the following schemas:

Schema T/R-A
For any sentence (s), if s is true or right, then s is an authentic doctrine of the community. So, if s is not an authentic doctrine of the community, then s is not true or not right.

Schema A-T/R
For any sentence, if s is an authentic doctrine of the community, then s is true or right. So, if s is not true or not right, then s is not an authentic doctrine of the community.

Some notes:
(1) "s is true or right" abbreviates "what is proposed in an utterance of s is true or right," and "s is an authentic doctrine of the community" abbreviates "what is proposed in an utterance of s is an authentic doctrine of the community."

(2) The point of the locution "true or right" is this: if an utterance of s is an assertion, what is asserted is true, and if an utterance of s is a proposal of a course of action, the proposed course of action is right.

(3) Notice that in the schemas the antecedents are sufficient conditions of the consequents, not necessary conditions. The schemas say "if," not "only if". Schema T/R-A does not say that s is an authentic doctrine of the community only if s is true or right. And schema A-T/R does not say that s is true or right only if s is an authentic doctrine of the community.

For our purpose we will take these as schemas of governing doctrines of religious communities. We want to see what the consequences for a community would be if it should judge that the principle of one or the other of these schemas satisfies its criteria of authenticity, and that therefore the community is bound to teach it as a guiding principle for the development of its doctrines. The principle would have the force of a norm for a body of doctrines. Taking them in this way, the schemas will be useful as fulcrums for various levers.

I do not claim to have found the principles expressed in these schemas in the literatures of religious communities. In fact, to my surprise, I have not found discussions of the topic of this chapter plentiful or very helpful either within or outside those literatures.

I do not argue that all religious communities ought to adopt one or the other of the principles, or that any particular community should do so. A community might be constrained by its sources or by other considerations from developing its body of doctrines in the direction of either of the principles. Instead, the schemas are introduced as points of departure for discussions of issues which cluster about the topic of the chapter. There does not seem to be a well-beaten path through these issues; this is one way of making a beginning.

In the next two sections we consider some features and consequences of doctrines which would embody the principles of these schemas, taking the principles one by one. These considerations will suggest (1) that it is problematical whether a religious community could adopt and sustain a doctrine which fits the pattern of schema T/R-A, and (2) that it is plausible that doctrines which fit the pattern of schema A-T/R would be consistent with the doctrines and the teaching practices of the major religious communities.

REMARKS ON THE T/R-A PRINCIPLE

1. If this principle is embodied in a doctrine of a religious community, the doctrine would say that if any sentence is true or right, then that sentence expresses an authentic doctrine of that community. But consider the following sentences:

> Mayor Bonbrake was in Washington last Tuesday.
> The whistle blows at twelve o'clock noon on weekdays.
> There are more small cars in the parking lot of Bob's Surplus than in the parking lot of Kramer's Furs.

It is easy to think of circumstances in which what would be said in utterances of these sentences would be true. Yet it is highly implausible that any of these sentences would count as an authentic doctrine of any religious community.

Consider also the following sentences:

> In an emergency dial 911.
> Take one tablet four times a day.
> Put in the stopper before shaking the bottle.

Here again it is easy to think of circumstances in which the courses of action proposed in these sentences would be right, prudentially or otherwise. Yet, if we were told that any of these practical sentences is an authentic doctrine of some religious community we would be incredulous.

We could extend these lists indefinitely by adding to the first list various assertions drawn from perceptual experience, historical study, natural and social sciences, and otherwise, and by adding to the second list various recommendations drawn from practices in the fine arts and arts of coarser sorts, from legal rules, moral codes, instructions for technical operations, and otherwise. And it seems clear that a selection of sentences could be made in such a way that (1) it would be highly plausible that the sentences are either true or, in the case of the practical sentences, right, and (2) it would be highly implausible that the sentences are authentic doctrines of any of the major religious communities.

Even if we remind ourselves that there are a number of nonstandard religious communities, applications of the principle of T/R-A to sentences on the lists would remain implausible. It might indeed be possible to connect up what is said in some of the sentences with doctrines of various religious communities. But to reach a conclusion that the sentences themselves are doctrines of religious communities, one might have to argue that any sentence directly or indirectly connected with an authentic doctrine of a religious community, in any way save by way of opposition, is itself an authentic doctrine of that community. That seems a far-fetched and shaky thesis. It seems highly unlikely that any religious community would want to include that thesis among its principles and rules for identifying its doctrines. It is plausible that a community may teach its members to tell the truth and to do what is right. But it would not seem to follow from these precepts that the whereabouts of the mayor last Tuesday or the right number to dial in an emergency are authentic doctrines of the community.

We cannot conclude from this that there never has been and never will be a religious community which adopts the principle of schema T/R-A. One reason is that we have not drawn a firm line between religious communities and other communities. Another reason is that we have not assured ourselves that authenticity cannot be construed in a way which would lend significance to saying that the sentences on our lists are authentic doctrines of religious communities. But these cases do seem to make it initially implausible that a religious community could adopt the principle as a doctrine.

2. A part of the trouble is that it seems essential for a religious community to have specific criteria for deciding whether some sentence expresses one of its doctrines or not. Without specific criteria of authenticity at hand, would not a claim of authenticity for some sentence lose its force? What sense could we make of the principle of T/R-A in that case?

Would the effect of adopting the principle of T/R-A as a governing doctrine be this; that the community is substituting this principle for such principles and rules as those we studied in chapter 2? The community means to eliminate distinctive criteria for what it should teach? When the community asks itself whether it ought to teach what is said in some sentence, it needs only to satisfy itself that what is said in the sentence is or is not true or that it is or is not right?

If this would be the point of adopting the principle of schema T/R-A as a doctrine, then what would be the force of utterances of sentences of the form *s is an authentic doctrine of R*? How could such claims be construed? In that case what is being said of a sentence when it is said to be authentic?

In the absence of specific criteria of authenticity, perhaps such utterances would have to be construed as simple approvals. A community is putting its stamp of approval on what is said in *s*. It is not attributing any quality or character to what is said in *s*. So it would be a mistake even to construe *s is an authentic doctrine of R* as asserting that *s* has been, as a matter of fact, authorized by *R*. If it is a simple approval it is not an assertion at all, thus not an assertion of some matter of historical fact. But if *s* is known to be true or right, what is the point of approvals?

Furthermore, if the object of adopting the principle of schema T/R-A is to eliminate specific criteria of authenticity, how could the negative counterpart of the principle be construed? For this says that if *s* is not an authentic doctrine of *R,* then *s* is not true or not right.

This seems to lead to the following question: Can we give an adequate explanation of the doctrines of a religious community without introducing into our account the community's norms for them and its rules for applying these norms? Consider a comparable question. Can we give an adequate explanation of the legal system of a society without introducing into the explanation that society's norms for its laws and its rules for applying those norms? The question is not whether someone who studies the legal system must adopt or approve its norms. The question is whether he can explain the legal system without taking into account the society's own principles and rules for determining whether or not some custom, statute, or administrative ruling is binding or not.

Similarly, the question for us is whether we can give a good account of the doctrines of a religious community without introducing into our account its own normative principles for shaping and developing its doctrines and rules for applying these principles. For it seems hardly possible for a religious community to maintain its existence without doctrines of its own. Otherwise how could we explain the unity of the community? And what would it have to say to the world around it which the world does not already know? And if it has doctrines of its own, it seems that there must be doctrines to guide the development of its doctrines and to relate them to what the world already knows.

3. Another related consideration tends to make adoption of a T/R-A doctrine problematical. Put briefly and abstractly it runs as follows.

The multiplicity of truths, taken together with the multiplicity of courses of action which would be right in some circumstances or other, is so vast and so multifarious that it does not bring with it, on its face (so to speak), any principle of organization powerful enough to lend unity to the teachings of a religious community, or for that matter any other human community.

So we must ask ourselves again whether there could be in this world a concrete historical religious community without distinctive doctrines of its own and without specific criteria of their authenticity.

4. If a religious community should adopt the principle of schema T/R-A, would the notion of secular claims lose its force for that community?

The question arises because, according to that principle, a community would be bound to teach, as its doctrines, all sentences which are true or right. Now a secular claim is a claim arising in an inquiry in which success is not measured by the distinctive standards of any religious community. So when we ask whether the principle of schema T/R-A permits the notion of secular claims, we seem to have a dilemma on our hands.

On one hand if, along with all sentences which are true or right, a community should take over, as governing doctrines of that community, all the standards by which these sentences are judged to be true or right, then there would be no standards of success in any inquiry which are not also doctrines of that community. In this way it seems there could be no secular claims, no claims independent of the standards of that community.

On the other hand, if a community which adopts the principle of schema T/R-A does not take over as doctrines the standards of success which govern the various secular inquiries, then it seems that the community would have no standards for judging whether the claims it accepts are true or right. Is the community then accepting and teaching sentences which it has no good reasons of its own to accept? For, having and giving good reasons for accepting some proposal for belief or some valuation as true, or for accepting some directive as right, requires principles by which such claims can be judged. Yet in this case it seems that the community would have no principles whatever to guide its judgments.

So we are brought to wonder again what motive there could be for a religious community to adopt the principle of schema T/R-A as a doctrine. Again we might imagine an intention to abolish distinctions between authentic doctrines and secular claims. One thinks of mass baptisms, and of their consequences! But in the present case, what would be the equivalent of baptism? And this brings us back to our earlier questions about the significance, in this case, of saying that some sentence is an authentic doctrine of the community. What would be happening if a religious community should undertake to adopt all true assertions and all right directives for conduct as its doctrines?

By way of contrast, all the major religious communities have had to confront and to deal with, in various ways and to varying extents, claims arising from inquiries in which success is not measured by their own standards or those of any other religious community. Proponents of the doctrines of these communities have taken account of claims arising from, among other sources, the study of grammar, elementary mathematics, perceptual experience, magical practices, astrology, historical study, speculations about bodies and souls and about the general constitution of the world, the legal and moral codes of various societies and, in recent times, modern sciences and technology.

The question we have been raising about the status of secular claims under the principle of schema T/R-A leads on to a question with a wider compass, namely this: Could a religious community which adopts the principle of schema T/R-A grant, consistently with that principle, that there may be truths and right actions which the community is not bound to teach? Here not only secular claims but also doctrines of other religious communities would have to be considered.

We shall return to this question, but it seems clear enough that if a religious community adopts the principle of T/R-A, then it could not, consistently, grant that there are truths or right actions that it is not bound to teach.

So there are a number of conceptual problems about governing doctrines for a hypothetical religious community patterned by schema T/R-A. Furthermore, we might be hard put to find cases where religious communities have purported to teach such doctrines. Still, however implausible such doctrines may seem to be, we can be instructed by considering them and by studying contrasts between their features and consequences and those of governing doctrines patterned by schema A-T/R.

REMARKS ON THE A-T/R PRINCIPLE

1. Some of the teaching practices of the Hindu, Buddhist, Judaic, Christian, and Muslim communities seem to suppose this principle, whether or not it is taught explicitly. From the manners in which they conduct their teaching activities it seems that (1) they aim to present teachings which are faithful to their sources, and that (2) they claim that these teachings are true or right. They seem bent on bringing it about that hearers and readers will accept the doctrines as true or right, and that they will adopt and live out the pattern of life of which the doctrines are constituents.

Though lively figures of speech, parables and other imaginative narratives, and poetic forms are abundant in their presentations of their doctrines, and though communication in words is enhanced by music, painting, sculpture, and architecture, it seems clear that the general intent is not only that what is said should be entertained or enjoyed by hearers and readers, and not only that what is said should be seriously considered by hearers and readers. It seems clear that there is a further intent along with these, an intent that the teachings should be accepted as true or right. This feature of the teaching practices of these communities seems to suppose the principle that, if some sentence is an authentic doctrine of the community, then if that sentence occurs in an assertion, what is asserted is true, and, if the sentence occurs in a proposal of a course of action, that course of action is right.

The following passage conveys the quality of intent of the teachings of the major religious communities. In a Buddhist scripture it is said that when the Buddha was staying at a certain monastery he engaged the monks in conversation. He asked them what sort of a monk is an unworthy teacher of the Doctrine, and what sort of a monk is a worthy teacher of the Doctrine. They asked him for instruction on these points. Part of his response runs as follows.

> Any monk, O monks, who in teaching the Doctrine to others thinks as follows: "O that they may hear from me the Doctrine! and be won over by what they hear, and manifest delight towards me," such a monk, O monks, is an unworthy teacher of the Doctrine.
>
> Any monk, O monks, who in teaching the Doctrine to others thinks as follows: "The Doctrine has been well taught by The Blessed One, avails even in the present life, is immediate in its results, is inviting and conducive to salvation, and may be mastered by any intelligent man for himself. O that they may hear from me the Doctrine, and be enlightened by what they hear, and as a result of their enlightenment begin to act accordingly!" and thus teaches the Doctrine to others because of that Doctrine's intrinsic goodness, and because of compassion, mercy, and kindness, such a monk, O monks, is a worthy teacher of the Doctrine.[1]

A worthy teacher is not one for whom his teaching is instrumental to his desire that those whom he teaches will think well of him. His teaching is governed by his awareness of the intrinsic values of the Doctrine and his compassion for those whom he teaches. What matters to him is the truth and the rightness of the Doctrine and its consequences in the lives of those who accept it.

If this feature of the teaching activities of these communities should be overlooked, it would be harder to explain why internal disputes about the authenticity of doctrines have been so serious and so potentially divisive as they have been in the histories of these religions. Also, it would be harder to explain why, when the truth or the rightness of some doctrine is challenged by external critics, and these challenges are brought home to the community, they are thought to require serious attention. Furthermore, if the principle of schema A-T/R were not supposed by the teaching practices of these communities, it would be harder to explain the fact that these communities propose their doctrines not only to their members but to others, as they often do.

2. Representative proponents of the doctrines of some of the major re-

---

1. Henry Clarke Warren, ed. and trans., *Buddhism in Translations* (New York: Atheneum, 1974), p. 419. I have substituted "monk" for "priest."

ligious communities have claimed more or less explicitly that authentic doctrines of their communities are true, or right. Consider some examples.

The first Question of the *Summa Theologica* of Thomas Aquinas deals with "The Nature and Domain of Sacred Doctrine."[2] In the second article of that Question he argues that sacred doctrine is a science. In the fourth article he considers whether sacred doctrine is a practical science. He says: "Every practical science is concerned with the things man can do; as moral science is concerned with human acts, and architecture with buildings. But sacred doctrine is chiefly concerned with God, Who is rather the Maker of man. Therefore it is not a practical but a speculative science." But then he goes on to qualify that as follows: "It is more speculative than practical, because it is more concerned with divine things than with human acts; though even of these acts it treats inasmuch as man is ordained by them to the perfect knowledge of God, in which consists eternal beatitude." (And well he might so qualify his first response, since the massive second part of the *Summa* deals in great detail with human acts!)

It becomes even clearer that sacred doctrine, as Aquinas understands it, makes serious claims to truth and rightness, when, in the eighth article of the Question, he contends that sacred doctrine is argumentative. It "does not argue in proof of its principles, which are the articles of faith, but from them it goes on to prove something else." In this respect it is like the "philosophical sciences," for even the highest of these, metaphysics,

> can dispute with one who denies its principles, if only the opponent will make some concession; but if he concedes nothing, it can have no dispute with him, though it can answer his arguments. Hence Sacred Scripture, since it has no science above itself, disputes argumentatively with one who denies its principles only if the opponent admits some at least of the truths obtained through divine revelation.

Not necessarily, may we suppose, admitting that the truths are revealed? But objections to the articles of faith can be answered, and the proponent of sacred doctrine can argue "from articles of faith to other truths."

For another example from a different setting and with a somewhat different angle of incidence on our topic, consider the following passage by Rāmānuja (1077–1157?), the chief exponent of the Viśistādvaita Vedānta school of Hinduism. He has been discussing connections among various Vedānta texts and arguing against certain interpretations of them.

> The assertion again that a statement referring to some accomplished thing gratifies men merely by imparting a knowledge of the thing, without being a means of knowledge with regard to its real existence—so that it would be comparable to the tales we tell to children or sick people—, can in no way be upheld. When it is ascertained that a thing has no real existence, the mere

2. Pegis, ed., *Basic Writings of Aquinas*, 1:5–17.

knowledge or idea of the thing does not gratify. The pleasure which stories give to children and sick people is due to the fact that they erroneously believe them to be true; if they were to find out that the matter present to their thought is untrue their pleasure would come to an end that very moment. And thus in the case of the texts of the Upanishads also. If we thought that these texts do not mean to intimate the real existence of Brahman, the mere idea of Brahman to which they give rise would not satisfy us in any way.

The conclusion therefore is that texts such as "That from whence these beings are born" &c. do convey valid instruction as to the existence of Brahman, i.e., that being which is the sole cause of the world, is free from all shadow of imperfection, comprises within itself all auspicious qualities, such as omniscience and so on, and is of the nature of supreme bliss.[3]

Perhaps it would be fair to construct from this passage, taken in its context, the following argument. The authentic teachings of Hinduism are given in the texts of the Upanishads (the Vedānta). Now the texts of the Upanishads, such as those mentioned in the passage, do not have the same force as stories told for the sake of the entertainment they give, whether or not they are true. Instead, the texts claim to give instruction as to the real existence of Brahman and the attributes of Brahman. Furthermore, the claims made in the texts are valid; what they say is true. So if what is asserted in some sentence is an authentic doctrines of Hinduism, then what is said in the sentence is true.

A supporting case can be drawn from al-Ghazzālī's fatwā on the esoteric sects, introduced in chapter 3. It seems that al-Ghazzālī would have endorsed the following argument:

1. Statements ascribing certain anthropomorphic characteristics to God, for example, that God has hands or that he is located in some place, are false. They are false because (i) they are inconsistent with clear teachings of the Qur'ān, and (ii) there are sound and conclusive philosophical arguments against them.
2. Since these statements are false they are not authentic Muslim doctrines.

Now this is just what we would expect if we should suppose that al-Ghazzālī was proceeding on a doctrine patterned by schema A-T/R, a doctrine saying that if some sentence is an authentic doctrine of the Muslim community then what is said in that sentence is true or right. For that doctrine would bring with it the consequence that, if what is said in the sentence is not true or not right, then the sentence is not an authentic doctrine of the Muslim community.

We may suppose that the philosophical considerations al-Ghazzālī refers to would count as examples of secular claims. It seems clear that he had a deep and genuine respect for these considerations. Furthermore, he seems

3. *The Vedānta-Sūtras with the Commentary of Ramanuga,* trans. George Thibaut (Oxford: Clarendon, 1904), pp. 199–200.

to have thought that the conclusions of these arguments, i.e., that God is one and that God is transcendent, coincided with some of the clear teachings of the Qur'ān. Hence, we might say, although the arguments for these conclusions do not rely on the distinctive norms of the Muslim community, the claims made in these conclusions are not alien claims. They are secular claims, but they are not alien claims.

A further point should be noticed. The argument set out above, concluding that the anthropomorphic statements are false, hence not authentic doctrines of Islam, does not depend on the philosophical arguments al-Ghazzālī refers to. It seems that the inconsistency of the anthropomorphic statements with the clear teachings of the Qur'ān would be a sufficient reason for saying that the anthropomorphic statements are false. Perhaps he would have said that the philosophical arguments are another reason (another sufficient reason?) for saying they are false.

3. To understand how governing doctrines patterned by schema A-T/R would function in the bodies of doctrines of religious communities, we need to develop further a distinction which was introduced earlier.

An A-T/R doctrine would say that if a sentence is an authentic doctrine of the community, then it is true or right. But how does one tell whether some sentence is an authentic doctrine of the community? All that can be learned from an A-T/R doctrine on this point is that if the sentence is not true or not right, then it is not an authentic doctrine of the community. So the truth or rightness of the sentence is a condition of its authenticity. But, as far as the A-T/R doctrine goes, there might be many sentences which are true or right but not authentic. The truth, or rightness, of a sentence is a condition, but not a sufficient condition, of its authenticity.

Hence we might say that an A-T/R doctrine calls for, but does not give, conditions of authenticity other than the truth or rightness of the sentence in question. We have spoken of these other conditions of authenticity as specific criteria of authenticity or, more simply, as criteria of authenticity. So we need to distinguish between (1) the condition of authenticity which is given in the A-T/R doctrine, this condition being the truth or rightness of the sentence in question, and (2) specific criteria of authenticity, which are not given in the A-T/R doctrine.

It is a fair assumption that any religious community which holds and teaches a doctrine patterned by schema A-T/R will also hold and teach doctrines which yield specific criteria of authenticity. We studied some examples of such doctrines in chapter 2. The reason for the assumption is this: if the body of doctrines of a community is reflectively developed far enough to include an A-T/R doctrine, then it will be evident to the community that specific criteria of authenticity are needed.

Perhaps the converse of the assumption would not have to hold. Perhaps a community could have specific criteria of authenticity without an A-T/R doctrine. It might have principles and rules for identifying its doctrines without claiming that its doctrines are true or right. It might think that if it makes this latter claim it is venturing beyond the limits set for it by its sources, that this claim would commit it to general principles of truth and rightness which its sources do not require it to adopt. We consider this possibility later on.

However that may be, the immediate point is that A–T/R doctrines, on one hand, and, on the other hand, doctrines giving specific criteria of authenticity, have different kinds of functions in the bodies of doctrines of religious communities. Doctrines of the latter sort give principles and rules for determining whether some sentence is an authentic doctrine of the community or not. Doctrines patterned by schema A–T/R (and, for that matter, doctrines patterned by schema T/R–A, though we are not immediately concerned with those) relate authenticity to truth and rightness.

This distinction corresponds roughly to a distinction made by J. M. Bochenski. One of the structural features of a body of doctrines, he says, is "a heuristic rule indicating which sentences are to be considered as elements of objective faith."[4] These heuristic rules are comparable with the principles and rules for identifying authentic doctrines studied in chapter 2.

From the heuristic rule of a body of doctrines Bochenski distinguishes another structural feature of a body of doctrines,

> the basic assumption, . . . a meta-logical rule, according to which every element of objective faith—that is, every sentence designated by the heuristic rule—has to be accepted as true. Thus a Mohammedan would admit that whatever has been revealed by Mohammed has to be considered as true; and a Catholic catechism says that whatever God revealed and the Church proposes to be believed is true, and so on. [p. 61]

(A Muslim would want to say it is God who does the revealing.) These basic assumptions of religious communities are comparable with the principles for relating claims to authenticity and claims to truth or rightness we have been considering.

There are differences between Bochenski's distinction and the distinction developed here. We have been introducing principles as well as rules. Also, we have been considering practical doctrines as well as assertions; hence the locution "true or right" has been needed. Still, Bochenski's distinction between heuristic rules and basic assumptions as structural features of bodies of doctrines, and our distinction between doctrines which yield criteria of authenticity and doctrines which relate claims to authenticity and claims to truth or rightness, make similar points. Religious communities need to be able to identify their doctrines. And they may, and often do, it seems, wish to say that their doctrines are true or right. Reflections arising from these different interests would lead toward different though interconnected sorts of doctrines about their doctrines.

4. Bochenski, *Logic of Religion*, p. 60.

SOME CONTRASTS

Consider some contrasts between some features and consequences of a T/R-A doctrine and some features and consequences of an A-T/R doctrine.

1. The first contrast has to do with doctrines about alien claims, so we should begin with some remarks about such doctrines.

Recall that the primary doctrines of a community, unlike its doctrines about its doctrines, are directly about the world. They say something as to what existents and what conditions of existence go to make up the world. Or they propose valuations of various existents and conditions of existence. Or they propose courses of outward or inward action to be undertaken.

Recall also that an alien claim, alien with respect to some community, is a claim that some proposition is true, or that some proposed course of action is right, which is not an authentic doctrine of the community. Since it is not an authentic doctrine of the community, it is a feature of the environment of the community of which the community may, or may not, take account. An alien claim is a claim made by some other religious community, or a claim which does not depend on the distinctive doctrines of any religious community, in which case it is a secular alien claim. But a community may have doctrines of its own about alien claims. These doctrines, which are about certain features of the environment of the community, would be primary doctrines of the community.

A community may teach, for example, that there may be alien claims which are true or right. Or it may teach positive or negative valuations of knowing what is proposed for belief in some alien claim, provided that what is said in the claim is indeed true, or of knowing how to carry out some course of action proposed in an alien claim, provided that the course of action is indeed right. Or a community may teach that no alien claims are true or right.

Now if a community should hold and teach a T/R-A doctrine about its doctrines, it could not consistently hold and teach the primary doctrine that there may be alien claims which are true or right. For a T/R-A doctrine would say that if what is proposed in some sentence is true or right, then what is proposed in the sentence is an authentic doctrine of that community. So the community could not, consistently, grant that there may be alien claims, claims which are not authentic doctrines of the community, which are true or right. A condensed version of the argument would run as follows. If true or right, then authentic. Hence if not authentic, then not true or not right. So if *s* is an alien claim, then *s* is not true or not right. Conversely, if a community should hold and teach the primary doctrine that there may be alien claims which are true or right, it could not consistently hold and teach a T/R-A doctrine about its doctrines.

In contrast, if a community should hold and teach an A-T/R doctrine about its doctrines, it would be consistent for the community to hold and teach the primary doctrine that there may be alien claims which are true or right. An A-T/R doctrine would not say or imply that all sentences which are true or right express authentic doctrines of the community, as a T/R-A doctrine would do.

2. Consider another contrast. A doctrine about doctrines which fits the pattern of schema T/R-A would permit a community to say that some of its authentic doctrines are not true or not right. It would not say or imply that all the authentic doctrines of the community are true or right. It does not block off the possibility of saying that some authentic doctrines are not true or not right. In contrast, an A-T/R doctrine would not permit this. It would say that the authentic doctrines of the community are true or (if they are practical doctrines) right. Furthermore, it would imply that if what is said in a sentence is not true or not right, that sentence would not express an authentic doctrine of the community.

This contrast gives rise to a special problem. It seems highly problematical, to say the least, whether a community could say that an authentic doctrine of the community is not true or not right. It is clear enough that a community could teach that various sentences which have been claimed to be authentic doctrines of the community are not true or not right. But it would be quite a different matter for a community to say of some sentence that (1) it expresses an authentic doctrine of the community and that (2) what is said in that sentence is not true or not right. Could a community say this without absurdity?

Recall what was said in chapter 2 about the normative force of assertions of the form s is an authentic doctrine of R. To say that what is proposed in some sentence is an authentic doctrine of some community is to say, among other things, that the community ought to teach what is proposed in the sentence. Or it is to say that insofar as the community is true to itself the community does teach it. Either way a norm is introduced which may contrast with what has been taught in the past or what happens to be going on within the bounds of the community at present. It may be that at some point in its teaching activities the community was not, or is not, being true to itself.

So there would be no absurdity in a community's saying that what is proposed in some sentence is not true or not right, even if the sentence has been claimed to express an authentic doctrine and even if it has been accepted as such by some (perhaps many) members of the community. But it seems there would be an absurdity in a community's saying (1) that what is proposed in a sentence satisfies the community's criteria of authenticity and hence is an authentic doctrine of the community, hence a doctrine the community ought to teach, and (2) that what is said in the sentence is not true or not right.

Imagine a decision of a court of law which would say of some statute that it satisfied the society's criteria of a valid law (it is constitutional; it is not contrary to precedents; it is in accord with the society's moral standards; and so on), but that the statute is unacceptable. It may be said that sometimes courts act on previously unrecognized principles. Perhaps *Brown v. Board of Education* would be a case in point. But, confining ourselves now to religious communities, is there any general principle—a principle which would be independent of any community's doctrines about its doctrines, which would validly rule out changes in a community's list of criteria of authenticity, by way of additions, subtractions, or modifications of items in the list, or by way of alterations of the community's priorities among items in the list?

It is true that a T/R-A doctrine would not require a community to say that some of its authentic doctrines are not true or not right, though it permits this. Similarly, an A-T/R doctrine would not require a community to say that alien claims may be true or right, though it permits this. In this respect the consequences of the two principles would be symmetrical. Would the apparent absurdity of the doctrine which the T/R-A principle permits (that an authentic doctrine may be not true or not right) mar this symmetry?

In defense of the symmetry it could be argued that the doctrine permitted by the A-T/R principle is also problematical. It is problematical whether a community could teach that some alien claims are true or right. I believe that this issue is far less serious, less fraught with the threat of absurdity, than the issue whether a community could teach that some authentic doctrine is not true or not right. If so, an asymmetry between the consequences of the principles would remain. Discussion of the schemas J2 and K2 in what now follows will bear on this point.

The contrasts we have noticed may be epitomized with the aid of some simpler schemas:

J1 All true sentences are C-authentic (from schema T/R-A).
K1 All C-authentic sentences are true (from schema A-T/R).

J2 Some C-authentic sentences are not true.
K2 Some true sentences are not C-authentic.

(Let "C-authentic sentences" stand for authentic doctrines of the Buddhist community, or the Muslim community, or some other community. Sentences which are not C-authentic would be, relative to the community in question, alien claims.)

Now J2 is consistent with J1 but inconsistent with K1. And K2 is consistent with K1 but inconsistent with J1. So J1 leaves open a possibility which K1 excludes. And K1 leaves open a possibility which J1 excludes. It is as though a traveler could take either of two roads. But if he takes one road there is something he could do which he could not do if he should take the other road.

Something more must be said about K2. The position on alien claims mentioned in the first contrast was not that some alien claims are true or right, but that there may be alien claims which are true or right. The point is this: to grant there may be alien claims which are true or right, a community does not have to produce such a claim. It is enough to say of some alien claim that it may be true or right, provided that it is consistent with authentic doctrines of the community.

This makes a difference for the problem about K2 alluded to earlier. That problem is how a community could be competent to judge the truth or rightness of an alien claim. No doubt members of a community would be competent to judge various alien claims. But the question is whether a community itself, by virtue of its sources or otherwise, would be competent to judge various alien claims. What does the community itself really know?

A community might be competent to judge whether various alien claims are consistent or inconsistent with its authentic doctrines, though it may not be able to do even this in some cases. (It may not be able to trace out the implications of some alien claim.) And if some alien claim is inconsistent with its doctrines, the community would be bound to say that the claim is not true or not right—assuming that the community has an extended principle of consistency.

But suppose a community judges that some alien claim is not inconsistent with its authentic doctrines. The community would not thereby be in a position to judge whether the claim is true or right. That is the problem about K2. Still, the community might be in a position to say that since the claim is not inconsistent with its doctrines the claim may be true or right.

Put this way, the doctrine which the A-T/R principle permits seems unproblematical, certainly less problematical than the doctrine which the T/R-A principle permits (that some authentic doctrines may be untrue or not right).

ARE THE PRINCIPLES DISPENSABLE?

Could a community maintain a refusal to adopt either a T/R-A doctrine or an A-T/R doctrine? Could it dispense with both of the principles these doctrines would embody? In its teaching activities could it take that course without involving itself in inconsistencies or other unhappy consequences?

It is not hard to think of states of affairs in which the body of doctrines of some community would fail to exhibit the features of either of the principles. Suppose a body of doctrines is not reflectively developed. Stories and precepts have been transmitted from one generation to another with a minimum of reflection on their connections or on reasons for teaching them. There are only rudiments of doctrines about its doctrines.

Or suppose that, though there has been reflection on other topics, connections between claims to authenticity and claims to truth or rightness, have not been reflected on. This might be true of a community even if its primary doctrines have been elaborated and even if it has developed doctrines about its doctrines on other topics. This is not just a theoretical possibility; the literatures of various communities seem to have less discussion of this topic than one might expect.

More interesting cases would be those in which a community decides after reflection that it ought to do without either of the principles. What reasons could it give for taking this position?

Suppose a community holds that in its teaching activities its first responsibility is to be faithful to the sources of its doctrines. What is to be found in them is a wisdom which speaks to all the situations, old and new, in which human beings find themselves, and to all the kinds of activity by which human beings respond to their situations. So there is more in these sources than meets the inattentive eye. More light for thought and for practice may be shed by them. For this very reason the wandering eye, seeking elsewhere to find what the community ought to teach, would show an unfaithful heart.

Maybe the community has in the past allowed its teachings to be shaped by alien customs, valuations, and beliefs which prevailed in its social environment, perhaps without clear awareness of the consequences. The result has been a loss to the community and to the world. The vitality of the community has been impaired. The salt has lost its savor. What the community has to offer the world beyond what the world already has (why say that over again?) has been diminished.

So, the community thinks, it ought to guard well its teachings from being shaped by sources which are not its own. It should not allow its voice to be confused with other voices. Hence the only principles and rules for its doctrines it can accept are those which are derivable from its sources. We may speak of this as the guarding principle. It is plausible that a community might embody this principle in a doctrine about its doctrines.

Here an incidental remark about some philosophical treatments of doctrines of religious communities may be inserted. It is not argued in this inquiry that religious communities generally adopt the guarding principle as set forth here, or that any religious community should do so, though some of the notes just sounded are familiar in the literatures of the major religious communities. There are however occasional tendencies in philosophical treatments of religious communities to deal with their bodies of doctrines as though they are detachable from their sources, as though a community's body of doctrines amounts to a philosophy of life. But a philosophy of life is for individuals. There are indeed different schools of thought in religious philosophy, but doctrines of religious communities have to be understood in another way.

The sources of a community's doctrines would be indicated in its criteria of authenticity. Sayings and practices of revered or respected teachers of the community, especially of a founder; canonical scriptures; a consensus of some group or class of teachers, or of the community as a whole, on some doctrine; decisions of valid councils or other magisterial, judicial, or legislative bodies of the community; and perhaps sources of other types such as common sense or an inward light or natural reason would be pointed to as authentic sources of doctrines of the community. In any case, whatever the authentic sources of a community may happen to be, in adopting a guarding principle as a doctrine about its doctrines a community says that its doctrines, including its principles and rules for deriving its doctrines, must be derivable from these sources.

We ought to distinguish two versions of the guarding principle. One version would require that principles and rules for doctrines, as well as primary doctrines, must be derivable from the community's sources, but it would go further. It would rule out principles and rules which, though they are derivable from its sources, are also derivable otherwise, from sources of other religious communities or from secular sources. It would require that its principles and rules should be derivable only from its own sources. We can speak of this as a stringent version of the guarding principle.

An objection to this version of the guarding principle would be that, to ensure the faithfulness of the community to its sources, it would not be necessary to go so far. It would be enough to require that its principles and rules for its doctrines should be derivable from its own sources.

Another objection might be advanced. How could this version of the guarding principle be effective? How could a community know that some principle or rule cannot be derived otherwise than from its sources? To know this, would the community have to know more about possible premises and possible forms of argument, and more about possible alien sources, than could be reasonably expected?

A nonstringent version of the guarding principle would be less problematical. This would say that, if principles and rules for doctrines of the community are derivable from its authentic sources, they are acceptable even if they are also otherwise derivable. If they are derivable from the community's sources, the community would not have to rely on other derivations of them.

Suppose now that a community finds that its sources warrant a nonstringent version of the guarding principle and that it adopts this principle. Suppose also that the community examines its sources further, with a view to the consequences of the T/R-A principle and the consequences of the A-T/R principle. Notice the following possible outcomes of this examination.

1. The community finds that its sources warrant adoption of a T/R-A doctrine about its doctrines.
2. The community finds that its sources warrant adoption of an A-T/R doctrine about its doctrines.
3. The community finds that its sources warrant adoption of both a T/R-A doctrine and an A-T/R doctrine about its doctrines.

Assuming that the community has a principle of internal consistency, this third outcome would be possible only if the T/R-A principle and the A-T/R principle are compatible with one another, so that the principle of internal consistency could be satisfied.

4. The community finds that its sources do not warrant adoption of a T/R-A doctrine about its doctrines and that its sources do not warrant adoption of an A-T/R doctrine about its doctrines.

Then it seems that this absence of warrants in its sources would be reason enough for a refusal by the community to embody either of these principles in a doctrine about its doctrines. The community could dispense with both of them and undertake to carry out its teaching activities without them.

CHAPTER FIVE

Deriving Doctrines and Arguing for Them

When members of a community reflect on deriving its doctrines from its sources, questions of the following sorts would be directly relevant.

1. What are the authentic sources of the community's doctrines?
2. Are some of the sources more important than others for this purpose?
3. How is it to be decided whether the sources warrant a decision that what is said in some sentence is an authentic doctrine of the community?

Questions of the first sort would call for principles and rules for identifying authentic sources of a community's doctrines. If the answer to a question of the second sort is affirmative, ordering principles and rules would be called for. Questions of the third sort would call for hermeneutical and logical principles and rules.

IDENTIFYING AUTHENTIC SOURCES

In the passage from the *Mahāparinibbānasutta* considered in chapter 2, it seems clear that the collections of the Buddha's teachings in the Suttas and in the Vinaya are taken to be authentic sources of Buddhist doctrines. The passage mentions also "the summaries of the doctrines and the law." It seems that the passage supposes the following principle: if some body of sentences is a faithful collection of teachings of the Buddha or a faithful summary of the teachings of the Buddha, then it is an authentic source of doctrines of the Buddhist community. It is not hard to imagine how this doctrine about doctrines could be supported by primary doctrines of the Buddhist community, including doctrines about the Buddha's enlightenment and its consequences for his trustworthiness as a teacher.

THE WESTMINSTER CONFESSION

For another example, *The Westminster Confession of Faith* gives in its first chapter a list of the thirty-nine books of the Old Testament and the twenty-seven books of the New Testament "under the name of Holy Scripture, or the word of God written." All the books on these lists, the *Confession* says, "are given by inspiration of God, to be the rule of faith and life." It then proceeds as follows: "The books commonly called Apocrypha, not being of divine inspiration, are no part of the canon of the Scripture; and therefore are of no authority in the Church of God, nor to be any otherwise approved, or made use of, than other human writings."

We may notice in passing what the Anglican *Articles of Religion* say of the books of the Apocrypha. Article VI says these books "the Church doth read for example of life and instruction of manners; but yet doth it not apply them to establish any doctrine."

In the passages from the *Confession* we seem to have a principle for identifying authentic sources of the Reformed community. The principle says in effect that all the books of the Old and New Testaments on the lists are authentic sources of doctrines of the community and that none of the books of the Apocrypha are. This would be a doctrine of the community about its doctrines, a governing doctrine.

In the passages from the *Confession* we seem to have also a primary doctrine of the Reformed community, a claim that the books of the Old and New Testaments "are given by inspiration of God" and that the books of the Apocrypha are not given by inspiration of God. As in the Buddhist case it is easy to see how this primary doctrine of the community could be advanced in support of the governing doctrine.

This helps to show the distinction between primary doctrines of a community and its governing doctrines. It also helps to show one kind of connection between primary doctrines and governing doctrines. Sometimes it seems that in the teaching practices of a community the emphasis on such primary doctrines as those about revelation and inspiration is so strong that the difference in type between them and governing doctrines is not noticed. It is not unnatural that such emphases should occur. But the difference should be noticed. In the present case the primary doctrine asserts an event or a process in the world (we might say). The governing doctrine is a norm for a community's formation and development of its body of doctrines. The primary doctrine could be advanced in support of the governing doctrine.

A little later the *Confession* goes on to say:

The whole counsel of God, concerning all things necessary for his own glory, man's salvation, faith and life, is either expressly set down in Scripture, or by good and necessary consequence may be deduced from Scripture: unto which nothing at any time is to be added, whether by new revelations of the Spirit, or traditions of men. Nevertheless we acknowledge the inward illumination of the Spirit of God to be necessary for the saving understanding of such things as are revealed in the word; and that there are some circumstances concerning the worship of God, and government of the church,

common to human actions and societies, which are to be ordered by the light
of nature and Christian prudence, according to the general rules of the word,
which are always to be observed. [pp. 13–14]

We remarked on the first part of this paragraph in the discussion of criteria of authenticity in chapter 2. Now notice the latter part, for it suggests
some interesting questions:

Would it be fair to take what is said in the long last clause as a principle
for identifying authentic sources of doctrines of the community? If so, could
we conclude that, with respect to certain practical doctrines concerning the
worship of God and the government of the church, the light of nature and
Christian prudence would count as authentic sources of doctrines of the
community? This question bears on a topic mentioned briefly in chapter
2—authentication of principles and rules which do not depend on distinctive
doctrines of a community. We come back to that topic later in the present
chapter.

Would this principle and its consequences be consistent with the other
principles in the passage? Notice that the practical doctrines which are to
be ordered by the light of nature and Christian prudence must be in accord
with "the general rules of the word ["the word of God written," we may
suppose], which are always to be observed."

DŌGEN

Written texts are not the only sources from which religious communities
draw their doctrines. Zen Buddhists speak of

A special transmission outside the scriptures;
No dependence upon words and letters;
Direct pointing at the soul of man;
Seeing into one's nature and the attainment of Buddhahood.[1]

Consider some passages from a short treatise, *Bendōwa*, written in 1231
by Dōgen,[2] a Zen master who is revered especially in the Sōtō Zen school.
The main thesis of *Bendōwa* is that *zazen* is the "right entrance" to the
Buddha Dharma, the teaching of the Buddha. Zazen is the practice of sitting
upright with legs crossed, in meditation. So Dōgen is proposing and explaining a practice which, he thinks, is the right entrance to the Buddha
Dharma.

From what source did Dōgen derive this doctrine about zazen? He tells
us how he traveled through Japan calling upon various teachers. Then he
visited Zen masters in China. "Ultimately, I went to T'ai-pai peak and

1. William Barrett, ed., *Zen Buddhism: Selected Writings of D. T. Suzuki* (Garden City:
Doubleday, 1956), p. 61.
2. "Dōgen's *Bendōwa*," trans. Norman Waddell and Abe Masao, with an introduction, in
The Eastern Buddhist, n.s., 4/1 (May 1971): 124–57.

engaged in religious practice under the Zen master Ju-ching, until I had resolved the one great matter of Zen practice for my entire life" (p. 130). So the direct source from which Dōgen derived the doctrine was his master Ju-ching. But not from Ju-ching as an isolated individual.

Dōgen goes on later to explain:

> Patriarchs and buddhas, who have maintained the Buddha Dharma, all have held that practice based upon proper sitting in zazen in *jijuyū* samādhi was the right path through which their enlightenment opened. In India and China, those who have gained enlightenment have all followed in this way of practice. It is based upon the right transmission of the wonderful means in private encounter from master to disciple, and their receiving and maintaining of its authentic essence.
>
> According to the authentic tradition of Buddhism, this Buddha Dharma, transmitted rightly and directly from one to another, is the supreme of the supreme. From the first time you meet your master and receive his teaching, you have no need for either incense-offerings, homage-paying, nembutsu, penance disciplines, or silent sutra-readings; only cast off body and mind in zazen. [p. 133]

Some explanations are needed: *jijuyū* samādhi is a state in which the joy of awakening is sustained; *nembutsu* is the practice of repeating the name of the Buddha; sutra-readings are scripture readings.

Then, after a discussion of the benefits of zazen (another primary doctrine brought forward in support of a doctrine about doctrines, we may say), Dōgen embarks on a series of questions and answers. Notice the first two.

> *Question* 1: Now I have heard and understand the sublime merits of zazen. [However] an unthinking person might have doubts and say, "There are many entrances to the Buddha Dharma. What is the reason for your advocacy of zazen alone?"
>
> *Answer* 1: Because it is the right entrance to the Buddha Dharma.
>
> *Question* 2: Why is it alone the right entrance?
>
> *Answer* 2: The great teacher Śākyamuni Buddha, beyond doubt, rightly transmitted [zazen as] the wonderful means for attaining the Way. Also, the tathāgatas of the three periods all attain the Way through zazen. That is the reason they have transmitted it from one to another as the right entrance. That is not all. Patriarchs from the western skies of India to the eastern earth of China all have gained the Way through zazen. Therefore I now point it out to men and devas as the right entrance. [pp. 137–38; glosses are the translators'.]

Sōtō Zen Buddhists will say: Only sitting.

So it seems that, to authenticate the source of his doctrine, Dōgen claims that the doctrine has been transmitted in a long line of private encounters from master to disciple, "from buddha to buddha," apart from scriptures, going back to the historical Buddha, Śākyamuni. Further, he claims that all the patriarchs and buddhas have taught the doctrine. So he is appealing also to a consensus.

ORDERINGS OF SOURCES

Now we come to the second of the sorts of questions posed at the beginning of the chapter. In the early part of chapter 3 we considered an ordering of the sources in the Jodo Shinshu school of Buddhism. This ordering gives a priority to a certain canonical Mahayana text over certain other canonical Mahayana texts. It seems that the arguments for this priority would be that Shinran, the founder of the Jodo Shinshu community, gave more weight to this text than to the others, and that this text expresses a certain doctrine which is central to Mahayana Buddhism more clearly and fully than the other texts do.

Similarly, many Hindu teachers seem to give a priority in importance to the Vedas (including the Upanishads) over all other sources of Hindu doctrines. Many Judaic scholars rank the first five books of the Hebrew Bible over other parts of the Bible, especially for legal doctrines. Also, many Judaic scholars seem to give more weight to Rabbi Judah's Mishna in the Talmud than to other extrabiblical legal texts. Christian communities take the New Testament as more important for deriving Christian doctrines than the Old Testament, though they recognize the Old Testament as an authentic source of Christian doctrines. Muslim teachers give more weight to the Qur'ān as a source of doctrines than to the reports of what Muhammad said and did which are handed down in traditions (hadīth).

Various reasons could be advanced for such priorities. A certain ordering is justified because it reflects a clear consensus of the community. Or, a source is given more weight if it is more clearly of divine origin or otherwise more trustworthy than some other source. Or, with respect to a certain topic, one source gives clearer and more extensive guidance on that topic than other sources do.

HERMENEUTICAL PRINCIPLES

Now we move from questions about identifying and ordering sources to questions about how doctrines are to be derived from these sources. We can distinguish two different but interconnected sorts of questions.

It may be asked just what is said (asserted or recommended or commanded or otherwise expressed) in some source or in some part of a source or in the sources of a community as a whole. How are the sources to be interpreted?

And it may be asked how the community is to move from understanding what the sources say to formulating its doctrines. Given an understanding of what is said in the sources, how is it to be decided just what the community ought to teach? We can approach the question from a different direction. Suppose that what is said in some sentence, short or as long as may be, seems worth considering as a candidate for being taught as an authentic doctrine of the community. From this point of view it does not matter how the sentence comes to be considered. It may occur in the sources of the community; it may occur elsewhere; or it may be constructed hypothetically. Then the question would be: Do the sources of the community warrant a decision that what is said in the sentence is an authentic doctrine of the community? Is it a doctrine which the community ought to teach on the basis of warrants in the sources?

We may say that questions of the former sort call for hermeneutical principles and rules and that questions of the latter sort call for logical principles and rules. Since we are studying doctrines of religious communities, this gives us a focus for our interest in principles and rules of these sorts. We are concerned with hermeneutical and logical principles and rules of religious communities, considered as doctrines about their doctrines.

At several places we have touched on hermeneutical principles and rules of religious communities. In the latter part of chapter 3, we considered some ways in which communities implement their principles of internal consistency in the face of apparent inconsistencies in their teachings. We noticed some distinctions between literal and nonliteral readings of texts, made by Thomas Aquinas and by al-Ghazzālī, and some of their norms for interpreting texts. Also, by way of Candrakīrti's commentary, we studied Nāgārjuna's distinction between truths of different kinds and his norm for placing those Buddhist doctrines which are expressed in the speech of everyday life in the right relation to the doctrine that all things are devoid of self-existence. Thus he put the whole body of Buddhist doctrines in a perspective. His argument advances logical principles as well as hermeneutical principles.

At various other points later on, hermeneutical issues will come before us. But we do not go far into that territory, not by a long way as far as philosophers would find it interesting and fruitful to go. Here I make only a comment on the topic and then give a case in point.

Hermeneutical principles and rules serve various purposes, depending on the underlying interest of an inquirer. Texts of many different sorts are studied and interpreted by readers of many different sorts: by historians, by literary theorists, by individuals who look for light and help on their personal problems, and by readers who have interests and purposes of other sorts.

But the readers with whom we are concerned are members of religious communities, and especially teachers of religious communities, who want to know what their own communities ought to teach. That is the purpose for which the hermeneutical principles and rules with which we are concerned are needed. Questions of other sorts about interpreting texts, if any should arise, would be worth considering only if that would contribute to learning what the community ought to teach.[3]

THE ROMAN CATHOLIC CHURCH AND THE BIBLE

In Pope Pius XII's encyclical *Divino Afflante spiritu*[4] (1943) the part of the encyclical headed "Interpretation of Sacred Books" begins as follows:

> 23. Being thoroughly prepared by the knowledge of the ancient languages and by the aids afforded by the art of criticism, let the Catholic exegete undertake the task, of all those imposed on him the greatest, that namely of discovering and expounding the genuine meaning of the Sacred Books. In the performance of this task let the interpreters bear in mind that their foremost and greatest endeavor should be to discern and define clearly that sense of the biblical words which is called literal. Aided by the context and by comparison with similar passages, let them therefore by means of their knowledge of languages search out with all diligence the literal meaning of the words; all these helps indeed are wont to be pressed into service in the explanation also of profane writers, so that the mind of the author may be made abundantly clear.
>
> 24. The commentators of the Sacred Letters, mindful of the fact that here there is question of a divinely inspired text, the care and interpretation of which have been confided to the Church by God Himself, should no less diligently take into account the explanations and declarations of the teaching authority of the Church, as likewise the interpretation given by the Holy Fathers, and even "the analogy of faith" as Leo XIII most wisely observed in the Encyclical Letter *Providentissimus Deus*. With special zeal should they apply themselves, not only to expounding exclusively these matters which belong to the historical, archeological, philological and other auxiliary sciences—as, to Our regret, is done in certain commentaries,—but, having duly referred to these, in so far as they may aid the exegesis, they should set forth in particular the theological doctrine in faith and morals of the individual books or texts so that their exposition may not only aid the professors of theology in their explanations and proofs of the dogmas of faith, but may also be of assistance to priests in their presentation of Christian doctrine to the people, and in fine may help all the faithful to lead a life that is holy and worthy of a Christian.

Some comments may be ventured. We may suppose that the instructions given here to Catholic Biblical scholars would apply also to those who

3. Hans W. Frei considers some general hermeneutical theories and some hermeneutical doctrines of religious communities in "The 'Literal Reading' of Biblical Narrative in the Christian Tradition," in Frank McConnell, ed., *The Bible and the Narrative Tradition* (Oxford: Oxford University Press, 1986).

4. Pope Pius XII, *Divino Afflante Spiritu*. Enclyclical Letter on Promotion of Biblical Studies. English translation provided by the Vatican (Washington, National Catholic Welfare Conference, n.d.).

exercise the teaching authority of the church, with due regard for the specific functions of each of these classes. So we may suppose that the explanations and declarations of those who exercise teaching authority would themselves be informed by the hermeneutical principles and rules which are set forth here.

Notice the strong emphasis the Pope gives to theological exposition of the Scriptures for the sake of the doctrinal studies and the teaching practices of the church. Though historical studies, philological studies, and literary studies may be helpful to this end, the proper aim of Catholic Biblical scholars is to contribute to learning what the church ought to teach. The Catholic community has an aim of its own in interpreting the Scriptures.

This aim is connected with the emphasis of the encyclical on the literal senses of texts. We may recall here what Aquinas said about the literal sense of a text: it is from the literal sense of a text alone that any argument can be drawn. Further, nothing necessary to faith is contained in other senses of texts which is not elsewhere put forward clearly by the Scripture in its literal sense.

After discussion of the literal sense, the encyclical goes on to say that, as well as expounding the literal senses of texts, exegetes should also expound the spiritual sense of the Scriptures "provided it is clearly intended by God" (par. 26). But "let them scrupulously refrain from proposing as the genuine meaning of Sacred Scripture other figurative senses." A broader use of Scripture in the figurative sense, especially in preaching, is approved "provided this be done with moderation and restraint" (par. 27).

Some later paragraphs bear on determination of the literal senses of texts. Two considerations are brought forward. One is that, on the principle that an inspired writer "is the living and reasonable instrument of the Holy Spirit," Catholic theologians in our age rightly observe that from the book an author composed his special character may be inferred. "Let the interpreter then, with all care and without neglecting any light derived from recent research, endeavor to determine the peculiar character and circumstances of the sacred writer, the age in which he lived, the sources written or oral to which he had recourse and the forms of expression he employed" (par. 33).

The other consideration is as follows.

> 35. What is the literal sense of a passage is not always as obvious in the speeches and writings of the ancient authors of the East, as it is in the works of the writers of our own time. For what they wished to express is not to be determined by the rules of grammar and philology alone, nor solely by the context; the interpreter must, as it were, go back wholly in spirit to those remote centuries of the East and with the aid of history, archeology, ethnology and other sciences, accurately determine what modes of writing, so to speak, the authors of that ancient period would be likely to use, and in fact did use.

In his later encyclical *Humani Generis*[5] (1950), Pius XII developed this last consideration further. He refers to a letter sent by the Pontifical Commission on Biblical Studies to the Archbishop of Paris in 1948, saying,

> This Letter, in fact, clearly points out that the first eleven chapters of Genesis, although properly speaking not conforming to the historical method used by the best Greek and Latin writers or by competent authors of our time, do nevertheless pertain to history in a true sense, which however must be further studied and determined by exegetes; the same chapters (the Letter points out), in simple and metaphorical language adapted to the mentality of a people but little cultured, both state the principal truths which are fundamental for our salvation, and also give a popular description of the origin of the human race and the chosen people. If, however, the ancient sacred writers have taken anything from popular narrations (and this may be conceded), it must never be forgotten that they did so with the help of divine inspiration, through which they were rendered immune from any error in selecting and evaluating those documents. [par. 38]

We may suppose that the "simple and metaphorical language" of the first eleven chapters of Genesis would have to be taken into account in formulating and teaching doctrines on the topics of those chapters. So the next question would be: How would it be taken into account?

At this point we turn away from further developments in Roman Catholic interpretation of the Bible, thereby leaving much undone, to sketch briefly a contrast case. A proponent of this contrasting position might explain it somewhat as follows.

The Bible tells a story. So when we find in the Bible "simple and metaphorical language," this should not occasion surprise or wonder. Nor should it require learned historical explanations or hermeneutical dissertations. Instead, a community which lives by the Bible should teach its members to listen to the story the Bible tells, to learn its rhythms, to follow the twists and turns of the deep-laid plot, to tremble at the warnings it has in store, and to celebrate the victories it relates. In short, the community should induct its members into the Bible in such a way that they will themselves live the story.

So the point of reading the Bible is not to look for evidence that God created the world, that Eve succumbed to the tempter's wiles, that a tower of Babel was built, that a great flood covered the earth, that a man named Abraham did what God told him to do. These are parts of the story the Bible tells.

The so-called simple and metaphorical language of the Bible is not a concession to "the mentality of a people but little cultured," an expression of something which could have been said better otherwise. Instead, it is

5. Pius XII, *Humani Generis*. Encyclical Letter Concerning Some False Opinions Which Threaten to Undermine the Foundations of Catholic Doctrine. (Washington, National Catholic Welfare Conference, n.d.).

an integral feature of the story the Bible tells, and the community should teach its members to take the story as it comes.

Certainly there is much which might occupy the curiosity of historians and other scholars. But the community's concern should be to nurture its members to live in the story the Bible tells and to live by it. So from the point of view of this position it might be said that Pius XII conceded too much to secular studies of the Bible.

SOME LOGICAL ISSUES

Some questions about deriving doctrines from sources call for principles and rules which would be logical rather than hermeneutical. They would deal with conditions for drawing conclusions.

1. For example, it may be asked whether some topic is treated in some source, or in the sources of a community taken together, sufficiently and sufficiently clearly to give a basis for a doctrine on that topic. Is enough said on the topic to warrant formulating and teaching a doctrine of the community? No doubt knowing the vocabularies and grammars of the languages of texts or other sources, and consideration of alternative interpretations, would be essential. But this would not be enough to settle the question, for the question raises a logical issue. Would the community be warranted in drawing a doctrinal conclusion on the topic from the source or sources?

Suppose a certain topic in geography or history, for example, comes up for consideration by a community. Suppose the community turns to some source which seems to promise light on that topic. Suppose that after studying the source the community is brought to the conclusion that it does not really deal with the topic at all, or that it does so so scantily or so obscurely that it gives the community no warrant for speaking on that topic. Then the community might turn to other sources for light on the topic, but with the same result. Suppose that taking its sources together, eking out what one source says with what others say, the community gets no further.

Suppose now that the community holds and teaches a version of the guarding principle, which would require that its doctrines should be derivable from its sources. Then it seems that the community would have to be silent on that topic, at least for the time being, except for giving the reason for its silence.

This outcome would point to a limitation on the scope of its doctrines, a limitation the community would have to accept if it is to be true to its principles. One consequence would be that the community would acknowledge that there may be truths, or (if the topic is a practical one), right courses of action, which the community is not bound to teach. We explore this and other sorts of limitations on the scope of the doctrines of a community in chapter 8.

2. A very simple logical rule for deriving doctrines from sources would be the following: If some sentence occurs in the community's sources, it may be concluded that what is said in the sentence (i.e., what is asserted or recommended) is an authentic doctrine of the community. But this rule might turn out to be too simple.

Suppose for example that in an authentic source of the community some sentence is attributed to some opponent of a revered teacher of the community. Could the community adhere to the rule in such cases? In the literatures of religious communities objections are often cited for the sake of criticism or refutation.

So contexts would have to be taken into account. It may be clear that a certain doctrine is taught in a passage, or in a source taken as a whole, even though what is said in some sentence which occurs in the passage, or in some other passage of the source, is inconsistent with the doctrine. In this case there are hermeneutical considerations which would count against the rule. This suggests that, though logical principles and rules can be distinguished from hermeneutical principles and rules, hermeneutical considerations cannot be dispensed with.

3. A community's principle of internal consistency, which would be a logical principle, would bear on its derivations of doctrines from its sources. For suppose that a study of one of its sources suggests that what is said in some sentence (s) ought to be taught by the community as an authentic doctrine. But suppose also that what is said in s appears to be inconsistent with what is said in some other sentence s' which is well entrenched in the current teaching practices of the community. Suppose further that after reflection the community is brought to acknowledge that s and s' are indeed, not just apparently, inconsistent. Then by its principle of internal consistency the community would have to acknowledge that:

s is not an authentic doctrine of the community, or
s' is not an authentic doctrine of the community, or
neither s nor s' is an authentic doctrine of the community.

So it seems that the community would have to reconsider (1) the authenticity of the source which suggested s, (2) whether s is indeed derivable from that or other sources, and (3) its warrants for teaching s' as an authentic doctrine of the community.

4. How close and strong a connection must there be between what is said on some topic in the sources of a community and what the community ought to teach on that topic? How clear and sure must a community be that some doctrine is taught in its sources before the community adopts that doctrine as one of its authentic doctrines? With respect to this con-

nection, how good must the community's warrant for teaching the doctrine be?

Insofar as communities reflect on such questions, we should be prepared to find them responding in different ways. The *Westminster Confession* says that some doctrines are "expressly set down in Scripture," and that some doctrines "by good and necessary consequence may be deduced from Scripture." (We may suppose that a doctrine might be found to be expressly set down in one part of Scripture and deduced from another part.)

But recalling Dōgen's *Bendōwa,* we should keep in mind that the sources of religious communities are of different kinds. Also, we should keep in mind that some passages in a source may be less didactic, more suggestive and incitive, than other passages in the same source, as the Westminster divines would no doubt have agreed.

So we should not be surprised if we should find some community requiring, for derivations of its doctrines from its sources, connections which are not as tight and firm as those some other community requires. Furthermore, we should recall that a community's criteria of authenticity may be of different kinds. So its practical certainty of the authenticity of a doctrine may not depend entirely on the strength of a logical connection between the doctrine and the source from which it is derivable.

ARGUING FOR DOCTRINES

A refrain which can be heard throughout this essay is that religious communities have, or may have, principles and rules of their own to govern the formation and development of their bodies of doctrines. Here we study some rules to govern the arguments a community advances for the doctrines it proposes. A community may think that if it advances arguments of a certain sort for its doctrines it will not be true to itself. Arguments of that sort would commit the community to assumptions it cannot really call its own. Or, arguments of that sort would rest on premises which the community is not in a position to sustain. If the community ventures beyond the limits of its competence in the arguments it advances it will find itself in a false position. So it thinks it must consider what sorts of arguments are consistent with its principles, and it must build doctrines about doctrines on this point into its body of doctrines.

We begin with some background considerations. It seems clear that a community could give reasons, drawn from its primary doctrines or otherwise, in support of a claim that some sentence expresses an authentic doctrine of the community. It seems clear also that a community could give reasons in support of a claim that what is said in some doctrine is true or right, if its principles permit this. Consider some cases.

Suppose that what is said in some sentence, for example: (1) The cause of suffering is craving—is claimed to be an authentic doctrine of the

Buddhist community. Then a reason for accepting this claim to authenticity would be: (2) What is said in the sentence was clearly taught by the Buddha. Suppose it is claimed, further, that what is asserted in sentence (1) is true. Then a reason for accepting this further claim would be: (3) Whatever the Buddha asserted is true. Let us call this a schematic reason. Another reason for accepting this claim to truth would be: (4) The Buddha knew the cause of suffering and how to overcome it (in the suttas he is spoken of as the *jina,* conqueror), because he himself attained nirvāna. Let us call this a substantive reason.

Again, suppose that what is said in some practical sentence, for example: (1) Remember the Sabbath to keep it holy—is claimed to be an authentic doctrine of the Judaic community. Then a reason for accepting this claim would be: (2) What is said in this sentence is clearly taught in Exodus as a command of God. Suppose it is claimed, further, that it is right to keep the Sabbath holy. Then a schematic reason for accepting this further claim would be: (3) It is right to obey God's commands. In turn this could be supported by substantive reasons, for example: (4) Obedience to this command brings many blessings.

In these cases reasons are given for judging that some sentence expresses an authentic doctrine of the community in question, and reasons are given for judging that what is asserted in some sentence is true, or for judging that the course of action proposed in some practical sentence is right. It is possible to discriminate between reasons for judgments of one sort and reasons for judgments of the other sort, though in these cases reasons of the two sorts are connected.

Now whether or not something would count as a reason for accepting a claim to authenticity would depend on that community's criteria of authenticity. But what would count as a reason for accepting a claim that some doctrine is true or right is another matter. Criteria of authenticity are not as such criteria of truth or rightness. More must be said about this, for it seems that claims to truth or to rightness would lose their force if criteria of truth and criteria of rightness were not at least somewhere in the offing.

Of course if a community embodies the A-T/R principle in a doctrine about its doctrines, then applications of this principle would extend the force of arguments for the authenticity of a doctrine. An argument for the authenticity of a doctrine would then support, indirectly, a claim that the doctrine is true or right. So a reason for saying that a sentence is authentic would also be, indirectly, a reason for saying that it is true or right. But, we should ask, if a community adopts an A-T/R doctrine, is it thereby bound to advance, or at least to permit, other reasons in support of claims that its doctrines are true or right? We may speak of such other reasons as direct reasons for judging that doctrines are true or right. And we may speak of arguments which depend on direct reasons as direct arguments for the truth or rightness of a doctrine. Arguments for the authenticity of a doctrine could support a claim that it is true or right, only indirectly, relying on an A-T/R doctrine to bridge the gap.

SOME RULES FOR ARGUMENTS

With these distinctions in hand, consider the following types of rules for arguments as doctrines of a community about its doctrines. I believe that rules of all these types, taken one by one, would be consistent with the guarding principle, though they are not all consistent with one another. And I believe that rules of types II and III, though not rules of type I, would be consistent with A-T/R doctrines.

  I. Doctrines of the community are supportable only by arguments for their authenticity.
 II. Doctrines of the community are supportable by direct arguments for their truth or rightness, as well as by arguments for their authenticity.
III. Substantive reasons advanced in direct arguments for the truth or rightness of doctrines of the community must themselves be authentic doctrines of the community.

First some explanations of doctrines of these types. Then we can consider some questions about the consistency and the connections of doctrines of these different types with the guarding principle, with the A-T/R principle, and with one another. We may suppose that a rule for arguments would apply to the discourse of members of the community generally, and especially to teachers and other recognized spokesmen of the community.

A rule that doctrines of a community are supportable by arguments of a certain sort would say that introduction of an argument of that sort is consistent with the principles of the community. And it would suppose that arguments of that sort are available, that they can be found or constructed.

Doctrines of type I would allow arguments of the following sorts in support of doctrines of the community:

(1) arguments to show that what is said in some sentence is derivable, in accord with the community's hermeneutical and logical principles and rules, from its sources;
(2) arguments to show that what is said in some sentence is consistent with the community's authentic doctrines; and
(3) arguments to show that what is said in some sentence is derivable from authentic doctrines and hence is itself authentic, provided that the criteria of authenticity of the community permit this.

But doctrines of type I would not allow direct arguments in support of claims that what is asserted in some doctrine is true, or that a course of action proposed in some practical doctrine is right.

Doctrines of type II allow direct arguments in support of claims that doctrines are true or right, as well as arguments for their authenticity. Also, they do not restrict the range of the substantive reasons advanced in direct arguments, as doctrines of type III do.

Doctrines of type III admit direct arguments for the truth or rightness of doctrines of the community, as doctrines of type II do. But they restrict the range of the substantive reasons advanced in direct arguments. They say that the substantive reasons advanced in direct arguments must themselves be authentic doctrines of the community. The thought behind the rule would be that if the community keeps to its own authentic doctrines it will walk on firm ground. What else can it be sure of? The distinction between schematic reasons and substantive reasons is developed in what follows.

To put these distinctions to use let us develop further the Buddhist and Judaic cases introduced earlier. In the Buddhist case the sentence we began with was:

(1) The cause of suffering is craving.

A reason for accepting the sentence as an authentic doctrine of the Buddhist community was:

(2) The Buddha taught that the cause of suffering is craving.

We may suppose that this is ruled in, as a reason for saying that the sentence expresses an authentic doctrine, by Buddhist criteria of authenticity. Notice that so far nothing has been said about the truth of the doctrine.

Then a reason for accepting the initial sentence as true would be:

(3) Whatever the Buddha taught is true or right.

This does not refer specifically to what is asserted in the initial sentence. So we will speak of this as a schematic reason.

But a reason of a different sort could also be given for accepting the initial sentence as true:

(4) The Buddha knew the cause of suffering, and how to overcome it, because he himself attained nirvāna.

This does refer specifically to what is asserted in the initial sentence. So we will speak of this as a substantive reason. It may be that (4) is itself an authentic doctrine of the Buddhist community. If that is so, then this would go toward satisfying the restriction on arguments which is made in doctrines of type III.

Similarly, in the Judaic case we began with:

(1) Remember the Sabbath to keep it holy.

A reason for accepting this practical sentence as an authentic doctrine of the Judaic community was:

(2) This precept is taught in Exodus as a command of God.

We may suppose that this is ruled in, as a reason for accepting the precept as an authentic doctrine of the Judaic community, by Judaic criteria of authenticity. So far nothing has been said about whether it is right to do what is proposed in the precept.

Then a reason for accepting, as right, the course of action proposed in the initial sentence would be:

(3) Whatever is taught in the scriptures as a word of God is true or right.

As with the comparable sentence in the Buddhist case, we will speak of this as a schematic reason. It does not refer specifically to the course of action proposed in the initial sentence.

But a reason of a different sort could also be given for accepting that course of action as right:

(4) Obedience to this and other commands of God brings many blessings.

As with the comparable sentence in the Buddhist case, we will speak of this as a substantive reason. Another substantive reason would be: the Sabbath itself is a blessing, and we ought to show our gratitude to God for it by keeping it holy. It may be that both of these substantive reasons for accepting the doctrine as right are themselves doctrines of the Judaic community. If so, this would go toward satisfying the condition for arguments given in doctrines of type III.

In these cases we have not developed complete arguments for the authenticity of a doctrine, or for the truth or rightness of a doctrine. We have been considering only various sorts of reasons which might be advanced in the courses of arguments for the authenticity of a doctrine and in arguments for the truth or rightness of what is said in a doctrine.

Notice that the schematic reasons for the truth or rightness of what is said in the initial sentences—the reasons given in the sentences numbered (3), seem to rely on the A-T/R principle. In contrast, the substantive reasons, in the sentences numbered (4), for the truth or rightness of what is proposed in the initial sentences do not seem to rely on that principle. They are not incompatible with it, and they might be said to implement it. They are reasons other than the authenticity of the initial sentences in support of claims to their truth or rightness. They are direct reasons for the truth or rightness of what is said in the initial sentences.

An instructive case can be developed from the Dogmatic Constitution on the Catholic Faith *(Dei Filius)* promulgated by Pope Pius IX, *sacro approbante concilio,* at the first Vatican Council (1869–70). Chapter 2 of this constitution, "Of Revelation," begins as follows:

> The same Holy Mother Church holds and teaches that God, the beginning and end of all things, may be certainly known by the natural light of human reason, by means of created things, "for the invisible things of Him from the creation of the world are clearly seen, being understood by the things that are made" (Rom. i. 20); but that it pleased His wisdom and bounty to reveal Himself and the eternal decrees of His will, to mankind by another and a supernatural way: as the Apostle says, "God, having spoken on divers occasions, and many ways, in times past, to the fathers by the prophets; last of all, in these days, hath spoken to us by His Son" (Heb. i. 1, 2).

> It is to be ascribed to this divine revelation, that such truths among things divine as of themselves are not beyond human reason, can, even in the present condition of mankind, be known by every one with facility, with firm assurance, and with no admixture of error. This, however, is not the reason why revelation is to be called absolutely necessary; but because God of His infinite goodness has ordained man to a supernatural end, viz. to be a sharer of divine blessings which utterly exceed the intelligence of the human mind: for "eye hath not seen, nor ear heard, neither hath it entered into the heart of man, what things God hath prepared for them that love Him" (I Cor. ii. 9).[6]

Keeping the Buddhist and Judaic cases in mind, notice the first parts of these paragraphs. Let us develop from them a case which would roughly parallel those cases. Condensing the main thesis of these parts of the passage, let us begin with:

(1) God can be known by the natural light of human reason.

A reason for accepting what is said in this sentence as an authentic doctrine of the Roman Catholic Church would be:

(2) It is taught in St. Paul's Epistle to the Romans that God can be known by the natural light of human reason.

We may suppose that this would be ruled in, as a reason for holding that the initial sentence is authentic, by the church's criteria of authenticity. We may suppose also that the church's criteria of authenticity would rule in, as another reason for holding that the initial sentence is an authentic doctrine, the following: "It is asserted in a dogmatic constitution of a church council that God can be known by the natural light of human reason."

Then a reason for accepting the further claim that what is said in the initial sentence is true would be:

(3) Whatever is taught in St. Paul's Epistle to the Romans is true or right.

6. Dom Cuthbert Butler, *The Vatican Council* (London: Longmans, Green, 1930), Vol. 2, Appendix, pp. 254–57.

This is a schematic reason for holding that what is said in the initial sentence is true. It does not refer specifically to what is said in the initial sentence. Another schematic reason would be: "Whatever is taught by the church in a valid exercise of its teaching authority is true or right." Both of these reasons, it seems, could rely on the principle that if some sentence expresses an authentic doctrine of the community, then what is said in that sentence is true or right.

So far our construction of a case parallel to the Buddhist and Judaic cases has had clear sailing. But now we have to ask what substantive reasons could be given for holding that what is said in the initial sentence is true. Here we might encounter cross winds and choppy seas.

Suppose that, with a view to offering a substantive reason for accepting the initial sentence as true, an argument for some proposition about God should be constructed, for example an argument to show that God is wise. Let us call this argument G. It would include, as a subordinate argument, an argument for the existence of God. The argument would not include among its premises any claims based on supernatural revelation. It would rely only on natural reason. Now suppose that the following is put forward as a direct reason for holding that God can be known by the natural light of human reason:

(4) Argument G is a sound argument.

This says that all the premises of the argument are true and that the reasoning in the argument is valid. Since the first paragraph of the passage says "certainly known," (4) might be strengthened to read: "Argument G is a sound and conclusive argument." But for our purpose we can leave that possibility to one side.

The point of introducing (4) would be that if argument G is sound, then we would have an actual case of knowing God by the natural light of human reason. The initial sentence says that such knowledge is possible. Here we would have a case of it. The reasoning would run as follows: if there is an actual instance of natural knowledge of God, then natural knowledge of God is possible. So it would seem that (4) would count as a substantive reason for holding that what is said in the initial sentence is true. No doubt other substantive reasons might be found.

Now it seemed plausible in the Buddhist and Judaic cases that the substantive reasons given in the sentences numbered (4) are authentic doctrines of those communities. Could that be said of (4) in the present case? Is it plausible that there is an authentic doctrine of the Roman Catholic church which asserts of some argument, which satisfies the conditions for argument G, that the argument is sound? More particularly, is the authenticity of (4) in this case as plausible as the authenticity of the sentences numbered (4) in the Buddhist and Judaic cases?

Whether or not there is some version of (4) which is an authentic doc-

trine of the Roman Catholic church is, at least in the first instance, a theological question, and giving answers to such questions is not a part of our
program. But consider one reason why the authenticity of such a doctrine
might seem implausible. It might seem that the question whether the reasoning in some argument is valid, in argument G for example, is a secular
question, a question to be settled without reference to the distinctive standards of any religious community. But this objection is not conclusive. It
will be argued in chapter 6 that it is possible that some sentence which can
be used to express a doctrine of some religious community can also be used
to express a doctrine of some other religious community. In such a case
it could be said that both communities teach the same thing, that is, each
of them teaches what would be said in that sentence. A similar point holds
for doctrines of a religious community and secular claims. It is possible
that a sentence which expresses a conclusion of a secular inquiry might also
satisfy a religious community's principles and rules for the authenticity of
its doctrines.

So we ought to speak only hypothetically. If the claim made in sentence
(4) is only a secular claim, and not also an authentic Roman Catholic doctrine, then the argument in which it occurs would be in accord with a doctrine of type II. But it would not be in accord with a doctrine of type III,
which would allow, as substantive reasons for the truth of a doctrine, only
those reasons which are themselves authentic doctrines of the community.
But if sentence (4) is not just a secular claim, if it is also an authentic doctrine of the church, then the argument would be in accord with a doctrine
of type III.

This Roman Catholic case has a bearing on discussions of natural theology by theologians and discussions of comparable topics by teachers in
nontheistic religious communities. In these discussions the validity of various arguments is one sort of issue. But other issues arise. Do the distinctive
principles of the community permit the use of certain arguments for its
doctrines? Is the use of these arguments in harmony with the sources of
its doctrines? Is the use of such arguments consistent with the pattern of
life set forth in its doctrines? Can the community advance such arguments
and still be true to itself?

When such questions are raised within a religious community it would
need doctrines about its doctrines to guide its responses to them. The discussions in this chapter bear on these questions, though they are not aimed
at settling them for any particular community.

SOME CONSISTENCIES AND CONNECTIONS

Now consider some points about the consistency and the connections of
these rules for arguments with the A–T/R principle (that authentic doctrines
of a community are true or right), with the guarding principle (that doc-

trines of a community must be derivable from its own sources), and with one another. This will tell us something about how doctrines about doctrines of different types are related.

The A-T/R principle and the guarding principle

First notice that if we take these principles abstractly, without respect to some particular community, they are independent of one another. They would have different sorts of functions in the body of doctrines of a community. The A-T/R principle would speak to the question: What force does the community intend its proposals of its doctrines to have? The guarding principle would speak to the question: From what sources should doctrines of the community be derivable?

Notice further that whether or not a community ought to embody the A-T/R principle in a doctrine about its doctrines would depend on that community's criteria of authenticity. Likewise, whether or not a community ought to embody the guarding principle in a doctrine about its doctrines would depend on that community's criteria of authenticity.

So a community might hold and teach an A-T/R doctrine about its doctrines without holding and teaching the guarding principle. Suppose a community exists in a social environment in which there are no temptations, so to speak, to substitute other sources of doctrines for its own or to add other sources to its own. Suppose the community is isolated socially, perhaps also geographically, from other likely sources of doctrines. Then it seems the guarding principle would not be needed.

Also, the guarding principle does not depend on the A-T/R principle. Suppose a community is content to carry out its teaching activities without claiming that its doctrines are true or right in any senses of those terms which would extend beyond claims to the authenticity of its doctrines. Perhaps indeed a community could say that it is prevented by its sources from claiming that its doctrines are true, or right, in ordinary, or general, senses of those terms. It has no warrant to go further than to claim that its doctrines are faithful to its sources.

Though the principles are independent of one another, no inconsistency is apparent in a community's (1) claiming that its doctrines are true, or right, in senses which go beyond saying they are authentic, and (2) requiring that its doctrines should be derivable from its own sources. It is not apparent how an argument for the inconsistency of (1) and (2) would run.

Something more can be said. The principles are indirectly connected in the following way. The guarding principle supposes that the community has sources of its own. Now if, to the contrary, a community should have no sources of its own, then it would have no distinctive claims to truth or rightness. How then could it have any unity, unless it should define itself only by reference to some set of natural facts such as a geographical location, a political identity, or a biological ancestry? But the major religious communities do not seem to define themselves only in such ways.

Doctrines of type I and the A-T/R principle

An A-T/R doctrine would institute claims that authentic doctrines of the community are true or right. But would such claims be empty if no direct arguments for their truth or rightness are permitted? We have been supposing a distinction between (1) authenticity and (2) truth or rightness. Would this distinction vanish if both a doctrine of type I and an A-T/R doctrine are taught?

Sometimes we find uses of "true" and "right" in the literatures of religious communities which cause us to wonder whether the distinction does indeed vanish. One wonders whether saying that something is true or right amounts only to saying that it satisfies the criteria of authenticity of the community in question.

But if the distinction between authenticity on one hand and truth or rightness on the other hand is retained, then it seems that the consistency of an A-T/R doctrine and a rule for arguments of type I is problematical. What makes it problematical is this: if a claim to truth or rightness would add something to a claim to authenticity, then it seems that arguments for truth or rightness, as well as arguments for authenticity, should be at least permitted, if not required. But a rule for arguments of type I would not permit this.

It is understandable that a community which claims that its doctrines are true or right might in certain situations fail to advance direct arguments for them. Suppose the community is relatively unreflective. Or suppose objections to the truth or rightness of its doctrines have not happened to occur within the bounds of the community. If there are objections from nonmembers in its social environment, perhaps these have not struck home to the teachers or other members of the community.

But the situation we are considering is of a different sort. In this case it does not just happen, for one reason or another, that direct reasons for the truth or rightness of the community's doctrines are not offered. There is a rule of the community against offering such reasons and arguments.

Furthermore, it is not just arguments claimed to be conclusive or demonstrative which are ruled out. Arguments which do not go that far, arguments which are claimed only to be supportive of the truth or rightness of what is said in doctrines, are ruled out too.

A doctrine of type I would not rule out liturgical or meditative uses of sentences which express doctrines of the community if these uses do not pose direct reasons for the truth or rightness of the doctrines, and if these uses are not meant to stimulate such reasons in the reflections of the par-

ticipants. We should not suppose that the only arguments we should consider are those which occur in public debates. Many arguments occur in
the reflections of individuals.

So it seems that a doctrine of type I would say that no reasons should
be given by teachers or other members of the community to others or to
themselves for the truth or rightness of doctrines of the community except
reasons for their authenticity.

It would not be inconsistent for a community (1) to claim for its doctrines only that they satisfy its criteria of authenticity, and (2) to rule out
direct arguments for their truth or rightness. But it seems that a community
which (1) claims that its doctrines are not only authentic but also true or
right and (2) rules out direct arguments for their truth or rightness would
be acting inconsistently.

A community might say that its doctrines point to mysteries. So, though
the doctrines are true or right, no direct arguments for them can be given,
because what they point to cannot be understood. Would this mean that
what the doctrines point to cannot be understood at all? Some hedging on
this point is likely. But further, and more to the issue at hand, saying that
a doctrine points to a mystery is not the same as saying that the doctrine
itself is mysterious and hence that its truth cannot be argued for. Another
question is this: is it possible for a community to say that all its doctrines
are mysterious?

A community might say that the truth or rightness of its doctrines is
guaranteed in some way. For example, it might claim that the doctrines
are revealed by God. But, in saying and explaining this, would not the
community be giving direct arguments for the doctrines, contrary to the
rule for arguments in a doctrine of type I?

It seems that a dilemma would be posed for a community which considers the consequences of an A-T/R doctrine on one hand and the consequences of a doctrine of type I on the other hand: either (1) allow direct
arguments for doctrines, or (2) do not claim that doctrines are true or right.
I do not see a way through this dilemma. So I have to conclude that, unless
some resolution not now on my horizon can be found, an A-T/R doctrine
and a doctrine of type I are inconsistent.

In the preceding chapter we saw how a refusal to adopt the A-T/R
principle, and therewith a refusal to go beyond claiming that doctrines of
the community are authentic, would be defensible. With that position, a
rule for arguments of type I would be consistent.

Doctrines of type I and the guarding principle

It does not seem inconsistent for a community (1) to allow its doctrines
to be supported only by arguments for their authenticity, and (2) to require
that its doctrines should be derivable from its own sources. The community
might wish to guard against dilutions and distortions of its doctrines, which

might result from giving direct arguments for them. It might find that its sources require this position. And it might argue that knowing that the doctrines are faithful to their sources would be enough to live by. Indeed, a rule against direct arguments for doctrines would have the effect of reinforcing the guarding principle. It would be a further countering of tendencies to secularization and eclecticism.

Doctrines of types I and II

Rules for arguments of these types are clearly inconsistent with one another. The former do not allow direct arguments for the truth or rightness of doctrines of the community; the latter allow them.

Doctrines of types I and III

One might expect that a community with concerns which incline it toward ruling out direct reasons for its doctrines would look more favorably on rules of type III than on rules of type II, for type III rules do not admit direct arguments without restriction. They require that substantive reasons advanced in direct arguments should themselves be authentic doctrines of the community. Recall that a substantive reason, in contrast with a schematic reason, refers specifically to what is claimed in the doctrine it is meant to support.

Still, direct arguments would be allowed. Without them the restriction would have no application. So type III rules would still be inconsistent with type I rules.

Doctrines of type II and the A-T/R principle

It seems that rules which allow direct arguments for doctrines are not only consistent with claiming that doctrines are true or right; it seems that claiming doctrines are true or right calls for direct arguments. This has been argued above. It seems that if a community teaches that its doctrines are true or right, it ought to allow support of its doctrines by direct arguments.

Doctrines of type II and the guarding principle

It does not seem inconsistent for a community (1) to allow direct arguments in support of its doctrines and (2) to require that its doctrines be derivable from its own sources. It is not the guarding principle which excludes direct arguments for doctrines; it is a rule for arguments of type I which does that. The guarding principle is consistent with rules excluding direct arguments, but it is also consistent with rules allowing them.

Suppose a community requires that its doctrines should be derivable from its sources. Consistently with this, as we have seen, it may claim that its doctrines are true or right. Suppose the community is confident that its doctrines are indeed true or right, so it fears no harm from advancing direct arguments for them.

Suppose now further that this community holds and teaches an extended principle of consistency. As we will see in chapter 7, an extended principle of consistency would rely on a general principle of consistency. That principle would say that, for any pair of claims, if each member of the pair is true or right, then the members of the pair are consistent with one another. Suppose also that both the community's extended principle of consistency and the general principle of consistency are derivable from its sources, in accord with the guarding principle.

Then this would strengthen the case for (1) allowing direct arguments for doctrines and (2) maintaining the guarding principle. For the community would then be in a position to say, of the considerations to which it would expose itself by offering direct arguments for its doctrines, that if any of these considerations is true or right, then it would be consistent with its authentic doctrines.

Doctrines of types II and III

A rule of type II and a rule of type III would be clearly inconsistent with one another. A type II rule tacitly allows the use in direct arguments of substantive reasons which are not authentic doctrines of the community. That is to say, it allows the use of alien claims as substantive reasons for its doctrines. A type III rule would not permit this.

Doctrines of type III and the A-T/R principle

It seems evident that a rule which restricts substantive reasons in direct arguments to authentic doctrines of the community would be consistent with claiming that authentic doctrines of the community are true or right. But the A-T/R principle does not require this rule; a rule which permits direct arguments without this restriction would also be consistent with the A-T/R principle. A community which claims that its doctrines are true or right may or may not require the restriction made in rules of type III.

Doctrines of type III and the guarding principle

No inconsistency is apparent between (1) requiring that the substantive reasons in direct arguments should be authentic doctrines of the community and (2) requiring that the community's doctrines be derivable from its sources. Indeed, as we have noticed, a rule of type III would reinforce the guarding principle. The guarding principle would exclude alien sources of doctrines of the community; a rule of type III would exclude alien claims as substantive reasons for doctrines of the community.

We have been studying, as possible doctrines of religious communities about their doctrines, some rules for arguments and some principles which would bear on them. It seems that the only combinations of these rules and principles which would be inconsistent would be the following.

(x) Holding and teaching that authentic doctrines of the community are true or right, as in an A-T/R principle, and (y) ruling out direct arguments for doctrines of the community as in a rule for arguments of type I.

(x) Ruling out direct arguments as in a rule for arguments of type I, and (y) permitting direct arguments as in a rule for arguments of type II.

(x) Permitting alien claims to be advanced as substantive reasons in direct arguments for doctrines of the community, as in a rule for arguments of type II, and (y) requiring that these substantive reasons should be authentic doctrines of the community, as in a rule for arguments of type III.

Along the way we noticed other connections among the principles and rules we have been considering.

MAY ALIEN CLAIMS BE GIVEN AS REASONS FOR DOCTRINES?

Let us attend to the last of the issues listed above, as it would be posed for some community. In direct arguments for the truth or rightness of doctrines of the community, must substantive reasons be authentic doctrines of the community? Or may substantive reasons which do not happen to be doctrines of the community be advanced in such arguments? May, for example, conclusions from archeology or philology or physics be advanced even if these conclusions are not doctrines of the community?

Consider the patriarchal narratives in Genesis. Suppose these narratives, or some of them, express authentic doctrines of the Judaic community, or of the Christian community, or of the Muslim community (since Muslims also regard Abraham as the ancestor of their community).

Suppose now that some recently discovered ancient inscription seems to bear on what is said in the patriarchal narratives, and hence on doctrines based on them. Suppose this inscription is studied in its linguistic, geographical, and historical contexts, and in relation to the patriarchal narratives. Suppose this inquiry is conducted without essential reference to the distinctive norms of any religious community, as for example in Speiser's commentary on Genesis. Then we could speak of this inquiry as a secular inquiry.

Suppose that in the course of this inquiry a conclusion of the following form is reached: Such and such a practice, ascribed to Abraham in Genesis, is representative of social practices in that region at that time. Then we may speak of this conclusion as a secular claim.

Suppose this conclusion does not satisfy the criteria of authenticity of the community in question. It is not an authentic doctrine of that community. Then we may speak of the conclusion not only as a secular claim but also as an alien claim. The conclusion may be consistent with doctrines of the community. Or it may be inconsistent with them. (The community might be bound to teach that the practice was a novel one.)

There are various ways the community might take account of this conclusion. (1) If the conclusion is inconsistent with its doctrines, then it seems the community is bound to regard it as untrue, and to argue against it if circumstances so require. Even so, (2) it could be introduced, without asserting it, into dialectical arguments against objections to doctrines of the community, arguments to show that some objection is self-inconsistent. (3) If the conclusion is consistent with doctrines of the community, the community may be in a position to grant that the conclusion, though an alien claim, may be true. This position, which does not commit the community to undertaking to judge whether or not it is true, will be studied in chapter 7.

Then one issue for the community is whether or not it should (4) allow this alien claim to be advanced as a substantive reason in arguments for the truth or rightness of its own doctrines.

Consider a consequence of advancing alien claims as substantive reasons for the truth or rightness of doctrines of a community. An alien claim could be introduced into dialectical arguments without supposing it is true or right. But if spokesmen for the community advance a claim as a substantive reason for the truth or rightness of its doctrines, then it is contextually implied that they accept it as true or right.

Now in the case of the conclusion about Abraham's practice there are specific criteria for judging whether it is true. Knowledge of the language in which the inscription is written, of cognate languages, and more generally of the history and literatures of the ancient Near East are required for responsible judgments. So, in advancing this alien claim as a substantive reason for accepting a doctrine as true, spokesmen for the community would be making themselves responsible for knowledge of Semitic philology and related secular disciplines. In doing so they would have to take account of the secular criteria of truth which are built into these disciplines. If some of these criteria are alien criteria, not authentic doctrines of the community, they would have to take account of alien criteria of truth.

Notice that, though these spokesmen may in fact be competent scholars in these disciplines, they are not speaking now just as scholars in these disciplines; they are speaking now for the community to which they belong. Hence they ought to be guided by the principles and rules embodied in the community's norms for its doctrines. So the question for the community is whether it should have a rule which would permit its spokesmen to be guided, in their arguments for its doctrines, by alien criteria of truth and of rightness. That issue is involved in a choice by a community between a rule for arguments of type II and a rule for arguments of type III. With a type II doctrine, it seems, though the community's criteria of the authenticity of its doctrines would be its own, the criteria of truth and of rightness which it would recognize in arguments for its doctrines would not be just its own.

In defense of a type II rule for arguments, it could be said by faithful members of a community that, since the community teaches that its authentic doctrines are true or right, it ought to be confident that any truths and right courses of action which can be learned from the study of doctrines of other religious communities or from secular disciplines will turn out to be consistent with its authentic doctrines. Also, it ought to be confident that its authentic doctrines can stand up to any relevant objections and satisfy any criteria of truth or rightness which may be relevant.

On the other hand, equally faithful members of the community might object that, if it advances alien claims as substantive reasons in support of its doctrines, it risks unfaithfulness to its authentic teachings; hence it risks its own health and vigor. Drawn by the attractions of learning to understand and appreciate doctrines of other religious communities and of acquiring skills in secular arts and sciences, its teachers will become less faithful to their own vocations. Their fascinations with what they find in these adventures will affect their teaching. Those whom they teach will become more and more aware of what goes on beyond the bounds of the community and less and less aware of the resources for life the community itself has to offer. In this way the community will tend to look away from its own homeland, so to speak, and to look toward other lands. In learning the languages of other religious communities, of current secular philosophies of life, of secular arts and sciences, and of the popular tastes and values of the times, the community is likely to forget the accents of its own language and to lose its own voice. (In the histories of all the major religious communities there are chapters which could be pointed to in support of such warnings.) Hence, the objection would conclude, the community should not adopt a rule of type II, which would permit alien claims to be advanced as substantive reasons in support of its doctrines. Instead, a rule of type III would guard against extending the claims made in doctrines of the community into domains in which the community is not authorized to speak or in which it is not competent to speak.

Could these contrasting considerations be reconciled and harmonized? Some relevant points will be developed in later chapters. But this is an issue for each community to settle for itself. It seems that, for a community which comes to reflect on the issue, the first consideration of all would be: What is indeed its homeland, and what are the features of its landscape? What is its native language, and what is the grammar of that language? How do its land and its language stand in relation to other lands and other languages? And how, in the midst of a world which the community itself has not created, can the community maintain its sense of its own homeland, still speak its own language, and continue to live from its own resources? In this way, a community would have to reflect on its doctrines and develop its norms for its doctrines. Its answers to such questions, taken together, would be what the community has to say to itself about its doctrines.

Finally, notice a point about the primary doctrines of a religious community. These are its doctrines about the setting of human life and how human beings should conduct their lives in this setting. These doctrines are what the community has to say to the world. It puts them forward not just one by one but also as a whole, as a pattern of life.

A community nurtures its members in this pattern of life and, in various circumstances, proposes it to nonmembers of the community. In those circumstances it puts forward the pattern of life in the public domain. What sort of claim for the pattern of life the community teaches is then being made? And what can be said about criteria for judging such claims?

If a community holds and teaches as a norm of its doctrines that its authentic doctrines are true or right, it would not be enough to say that a pattern of life is being claimed to be better than some other, that is to say more comprehensive, or more coherent, or yielding more satisfaction in a whole of life for those who accept it, though all this could be said. It seems that something more than such comparative judgments would be called for. For the courses of action proposed in the pattern are being claimed to be right, and the valuations and beliefs proposed in the pattern are being claimed to be true. So criteria of the rightness of courses of action and criteria of the truth of assertions, as well as criteria of comprehensiveness, of coherence, and of fruitfulness for wholes of life, would have to be included among the criteria in view of which such a pattern of life would have to be judged.

CHAPTER SIX

Doctrines of Different
Religious Communities

Here we study some types of connections between doctrines of different religious communities. This will give us some background for dealing with positions of religious communities on alien claims in chapters 7 and 8, since some alien claims are doctrines of other religious communities. Also, some of the distinctions made in the early part of the chapter will apply to secular alien claims as well as to alien claims which are doctrines of other religious communities.

Historians of religion study, among other topics, causal connections between the activities of different religious communities, including their teaching activities. For instance, they ask whether Buddhist teachings were influenced by Hindu traditions, and if so, how. Or they ask whether early Christian teachings were shaped in part by influence from the Hellenistic mystery cults. These interests focus on historical processes and particularly on causal connections between different sets of historical facts. Is the fact that some religious community taught certain doctrines in a certain span of time due in part to the fact that some other religious community taught certain doctrines in some earlier span of time?

Philosophers ought to learn from what historians discover. But philosophers who study doctrines of different religions ought to give special attention to connections of a different kind. Asking whether Ananda's saying something is connected with Benedict's saying something is different from asking whether what Ananda said is connected with what Benedict said. Connections of the latter sort might be called logical connections. The interest here is in the force, the grounds, and the consequences of what is said rather than in how it came to be said or the effects of the saying of it. With doctrines, the interest is in what is taught rather than in how the teaching of it came about. We do not have to divorce logical connections from historical connections, but we do need to distinguish them.

Suppose that as we study some prima facie doctrine of some religious community it puts us in mind of a prima facie doctrine of some other religious community. Some similarity or contrast in tone, form, or subject matter leads us to consider them together. Suppose that as we do so it occurs to us that there is a stronger relation between them than similarity or contrast. We think they may be connected. Then we work away at understanding them better, studying each of them in its context and constructing various paraphrases which might help us get at what is being said in each case.

Thus our initial intuition will be tested. It may become clear that there is indeed a connection, not just a similarity or a contrast. Or it may happen that our intuition of a connection evaporates. The suggestion does not lead to what it seemed to promise.

If in some such case there is indeed no connection, but at most a similarity or a contrast, what would the consequences be? Suppose that each of the prima facie doctrines has the force of an assertion. Then we would not be in a position to tell, from the truth of one of them, whether the other is true or not. And if one should turn out to be untrue, we would not be in a position to tell from that whether the other is true or not. Or suppose that in each case the force of what is said is to recommend some course of action. Then, if one course of action should turn out to be right, we could not tell from that whether the other is right or not. And if one should prove to be not right, we would not be in a position to tell from that whether the other is right or not.

LOGICAL CONNECTIONS

Let us count, as logical connections between a doctrine of one religious community and a doctrine of some other religious community, cases of the following sorts:

I. Cases where some sentence, which can be used to express a doctrine of some religious community, can also be used to express a doctrine of some other religious community.

Whether some sentence can be used responsibly and correctly to express a doctrine of a religious community depends on the principles and rules of that community for identifying its doctrines. Even if a community prefers some one natural language, for example Hebrew, Sanskrit, Pali, Greek, Latin, or Arabic, its principles and rules may permit translation into some other natural language.

II. Cases where if some sentence, which can be used to express a doctrine of some religious community, is true or right, then some other sentence, which can also be used to express a doctrine of some other religious community, is true or right.

Some explanations are needed before going further.

(1) Saying a sentence is true is a short way of saying that what is asserted in an utterance of the sentence is true. Saying a sentence is right is a short way of saying that the course of action proposed in an utterance of the sentence is right.

(2) Sometimes, taking assertions and proposals of courses of action together, I shall speak of sentences as acceptable or unacceptable. That will be a short way of saying that what is proposed in an utterance of a sentence is acceptable as true, if the utterance has the force of an assertion, or acceptable as right, if the utterance has the force of a proposal of a course of action. So accepting what is proposed in an utterance of a sentence goes further than just entertaining it.

(3) I shall not speak of acceptability relative to persons ("acceptable to *m*"). I shall suppose that what is said in a sentence may be true or right, and thus acceptable, even if someone does not think so.

With these explanations, we can characterize the cases mentioned in II by saying that in these cases, if some sentence is acceptable, then some other sentence is acceptable.

III. Cases where the acceptability of some sentence, which can be used to express a doctrine of some religious community, depends on the acceptability of some other sentence, which can also be used to express a doctrine of some other religious community. If the latter sentence is not acceptable, the former is not acceptable.

IV. Cases where some sentence, which can be used to express a doctrine of some religious community, is opposed to some other sentence, which can be used to express a doctrine of some other religious community. If one of the sentences is acceptable, then the other is not acceptable. The two sentences are not jointly acceptable, though both may be unacceptable.

Now with I–IV in hand, and with some important qualifications to be brought out as we go along, we can say that the body of doctrines of some religious community is logically connected with the body of doctrines of some other religious community if any of the following conditions holds.

I*.   Some doctrine of one religious community is the same as some doctrine of the other religious community.
II*. Some doctrine of one religious community follows from some doctrine of the other religious community.
III*. Some doctrine of one religious community depends on some doctrine of the other religious community.
IV*. Some doctrine of one religious community and some doctrine of the other religious community are opposed.

If none of these conditions holds, then we can say that the body of doctrines of one religious community and the body of doctrines of the other religious community are logically isolated from one another.

The following considerations will help to distinguish and to connect the first set of formulations, I–IV, and the second set of formulations, I*–IV*.

The teaching activity of a religious community includes presentations of spoken or written sentences. (We can call presentations of both sorts utterances by stretching the range of that term a little.) It includes also various practical arrangements which organize the settings of the utterances and help to nurture and shape the attitudes of those who hear or read them. The warrants for these arrangements are given in various doctrines of the community, for example in principles and rules for liturgies.

In these utterances of sentences, various proposals are being made to the hearers and readers of the sentences. In some cases it is being proposed to them that they should undertake and carry out certain courses of action in their inward lives or in their outward behavior. To accept such a proposal is to judge that the proposed course of action is right and to undertake to carry it out. Other teachings are proposals for belief or proposals of valuations. In these cases propositions are being asserted. To accept a proposal for belief or a proposal of a valuation is to judge that what is asserted is true and to make a place for it in one's stock of beliefs and valuations. (By extending the range of "proposition" the term could be used to cover what is proposed in a practical proposal also. Though this has a warrant in common usage, for example "What is your proposition?" uttered in the course of a business deal, it is better to resist this temptation.)

It is such proposals as these, made in utterances of various sentences, which constitute the teachings of a religious community; its doctrines are what is proposed in such proposals. So it is a simplification to say that a religious community teaches sentences or that a sentence is a doctrine of a religious community. But if we have in hand the formulations in I–IV such shorthand expressions need not be misleading. We shall need the distinction between sentences and doctrines at several points as we consider further the different sorts of connections between doctrines of different religions.

IDENTITIES

From the Psalms, the Prayer Book, and other sources, it is plausible that the following sentence could be used to express a doctrine of the Judaic community:

God is merciful.

From Islamic literature and practice, it is equally plausible that this sentence could be used to express a doctrine of the Muslim community. In English translations of the Qur'ān, at the head of each *sura* except one there stands the following: In the name of Allah, the Compassionate, the Merciful.

Now if we could conclude that it is a doctrine of the Judaic community

that God is merciful and that it is also a doctrine of the Muslim community
that God is merciful, could we say that in this case the two communities
teach the same doctrine? There are some pitfalls we would need to avoid.

Saying this would seem to suggest that the Judaic community teaches
a doctrine of the Muslim community, a Muslim doctrine, and that the
Muslim community teaches a doctrine of the Judaic community, a Judaic
doctrine. There are several ways this might lead us astray.

(1) Each of these communities would very likely object strongly to saying that it teaches some doctrine because it is a doctrine of the other. For
on one hand, the Judaic community taught the doctrine centuries before
the time of Muhammad. And on the other hand, the Muslim community
stands on the revelation sent down to Muhammad. Though it teaches that
the Torah is also a book sent down by God, it teaches also that the Judaic
community has at some points distorted what is said in that book. More
generally, a community's warrants for teaching some doctrine are given
in its own principles and rules for identifying its doctrines.

(2) We may suppose that a member of the Judaic community would
recoil from the suggestion that when he says that God is merciful he is
speaking for the Muslim community or for any other community to which
he does not belong. He might say that proposing the doctrines of his own
community is enough for him to do and that it would be presumptuous
for him to claim to speak for any other. He might indeed welcome the
fact that some other community teaches a doctrine taught by his own
community, but he would wish to point out that he himself accepts and
teaches it as a member of his own community, not of any other. It is for
other communities to decide what they will teach. We might expect analogous reactions from a Muslim. So it would be misleading to say that the
two communities teach the same doctrine, insofar as that should suggest
that either is teaching the doctrine as a doctrine of the other. We could say
of some pair of communities (R1, R2):

R1 teaches s as a doctrine of R1, and
R2 teaches s as a doctrine of R2.

But we could rule out saying:

R1 teaches s as a doctrine of R2, or
R2 teaches s as a doctrine of R1.

This would help to show some of the limitations on agreements in doctrines.

Further it should be noticed (3) that if there should be some identity of
doctrines of different religious communities we would not be warranted
in inferring therefrom that the doctrine is taught by these communities in
concert. Saying there is an identity of doctrines of different religions does
not even imply that those who speak for the different communities know

that the identity exists. That goes for the other sorts of connections as well. Whether some connection holds in some case does not depend on its being known to hold by members of the communities in question.

So all that is needed for a case of identity of doctrines of different religious communities is that it happens that some community makes direct use of some sentence to propose a doctrine and that it happens, perhaps quite independently, that some other community makes direct use of that sentence to propose a doctrine.

Other troubles cluster about the notion of identities of doctrines. Continuing with the example we have taken, suppose that the reasons given in the Judaic community for believing that God is merciful are not exactly the same as those given in the Muslim community, though not entirely different. Or suppose that the kinds of situations in which Muslim teachers utter the sentence "God is merciful" are not exactly like the kinds of situations in which Judaic teachers introduce the sentence, though not altogether different, either. Or suppose the sentence has a somewhat different kind of place in the body of Judaic doctrines than the place it has in the body of Muslim doctrines. Or suppose that Muslims are taught to accept the doctrine with a somewhat different set of attitudes than those with which members of the Judaic community are taught to accept it.

Then it could be objected that the sentence, when it is put forward as a teaching of the Judaic community, could not have the same sense as when it is put forward as a teaching of the Muslim community. Therefore we cannot say that at this point the two communities teach the same doctrine.

Certainly such differences have to be taken into account. And in some cases it may turn out that the differences are so stark that we could not say we have found an identity of doctrines. We have been misled into thinking so by mistranslations or otherwise. There are plenty of cases of mistaken identity. But it seems wrong to assume as a general principle that no part of one complex whole can be a part of another complex whole. It seems there might be cases where we would be justified in saying of two religious communities that there is a doctrine which each of them accepts and teaches, and that this doctrine, for example that God is merciful, has a different set of connections and associations in the body of teachings of one of the communities than in the body of teachings of the other. We could say that there is a set of implications and associations which each of the communities would accept as implications and associations of the doctrine, though each of the communities also accepts, along with these, some implications and associations of the doctrine which the other community does not accept.

In our hypothetical case, what is said in the sentence "God is merciful" has the force of an assertion, and this assertion would function as a primary doctrine of a community. Something is being said about the world. The subject matter of what is said in the sentence is a certain feature of the setting of human life; its subject matter is not the doctrines of a community which teaches what is said in the sentence.

Speaking of God or of some other feature of the setting of human life is different from speaking of doctrines of a community. God can be said to be powerful or merciful or just, or to have done something or other in the course of history. A doctrine of a community can be said to satisfy criteria of authenticity, or to be consistent or inconsistent with some other claim, or to be true, or right. This is a grammatical remark in aid of explaining primary doctrines.

So if we could say that it is an authentic doctrine of the Judaic community that God is merciful, and that it is an authentic doctrine of the Muslim community that God is merciful, then we could say that the primary doctrines of the Judaic community and the primary doctrines of the Muslim community overlap at this point.

As we have seen, a religious community needs, along with its primary doctrines, doctrines about its doctrines. It needs principles and rules to guide and regulate the formation and development of its body of doctrines. These are its norms for its doctrines. We have spoken of these as its governing doctrines.

Now it seems that though identities of primary doctrines of different communities may be possible, the possibility of identities of governing doctrines of different communities is problematical. It seems that no sentence could be used responsibly and correctly to express both a governing doctrine of one community and a governing doctrine of some other community. The reason for this is that a fully explicit statement of a governing doctrine of a community mentions that community essentially, and that the doctrine is meant to apply to that community only; it is not meant to apply to other communities. It is the formation and development of the doctrines of that community that the principle or rule is meant to govern. So a governing doctrine of the Judaic community is meant to govern the formation and development of Judaic doctrines, and a governing doctrine of the Muslim community is meant to govern the formation and development of Muslim doctrines.

It seems clear that the members of the following pair of sentences are not identical:

To qualify as an authentic doctrine of the Muslim community s must be consistent with what is taught in the Qur'ān.

To qualify as an authentic doctrine of the Buddhist community s must be consistent with the teachings of the Buddha.

The following are not identical either:

To qualify as a Muslim doctrine s must be self-consistent.

To qualify as a Buddhist doctrine s must be self-consistent.

Nor are the following identical:

If *s1* is an authentic doctrine of the Hindu community and *s2* is an authentic doctrine of the Hindu community, then *s1* and *s2* are consistent.

If *s1* is an authentic doctrine of the Judaic community and *s2* is an authentic doctrine of the Judaic community, then *s1* and *s2* are consistent.

We could speak of these as pairs of parallel doctrines. But a parallel is not an identity. So it seems that there cannot be identities of governing doctrines of different communities.

It seems natural to interpret cases of agreements in doctrines between proponents of different communities as cases where identities of doctrines can be found. Of course, members of different communities often agree with one another on various matters as individuals when they speak, for example, as historians or as scientists or just as human beings engaged in the search for practical wisdom. But this is not precisely relevant to our study of doctrines of religious communities.

CONSEQUENCES

Dialectical arguments between proponents of different bodies of doctrines lean heavily on connections or supposed connections of this sort. Those arguments begin with premises which are taken to belong to one body of doctrines and end with conclusions which are taken to belong to the other body of doctrines. The speaker is arguing that if some sentence, which he takes to be a doctrine of the community of which his respondent is a member, is acceptable, then some other sentence, which is a doctrine of the community of which the speaker is a member, is acceptable. He argues that some doctrine of his own community follows from some doctrine of the other community.

For example consider the following passage from the Qur'ān: "And *remember* when Jesus the son of Mary said, 'O children of Israel! of a truth I am God's apostle to you to confirm the law which was given before me, and to announce an apostle that shall come after me whose name shall be Ahmad!' But when he (Ahmad) presented himself with clear proofs of his mission they said, 'This is manifest sorcery!' "[1] This suggests that a Muslim might argue that if the teachings of Jesus are acceptable, then the apostleship of Muhammad [Ahmad] is acceptable. Since Christians accept the teachings of Jesus, then, supposing that Jesus said what the passage claims he said, Christians ought to accept the apostleship of Muhammad.

Christians would no doubt respond that the church does not teach what Jesus is here alleged to have said, and that thus the dialectical argument

1. *The Koran,* trans. J. M. Rodwell (London: J. M. Dent; New York: E. P. Dutton, 1909), Sura LXI (in Rodwell's numbering, XCVIII), pp. 405–06.

fails. Also it would no doubt be said that Jesus did not in fact say what he is alleged to have said, or at least that there is no good reason to believe that he said it, and hence that the argument is not only dialectically but categorically unsound. One can imagine that a member of the Judaic community might respond in similar ways if a Christian should put forward an argument from prophecies about the Messiah in the Hebrew Bible to the Messiahship of Jesus.

The weakness of these arguments, which seem to aim at deducing a doctrine of one religious community from what is presumed to be a doctrine of another community, makes us wonder about them. Are there clear cases where a doctrine of one religious community follows directly from a doctrine of another religious community, except some trivial cases? At any rate it seems that dependences are easier to find than consequences.

DEPENDENCES

In connections of this sort, the acceptability of what is said in some sentence depends on the acceptability of what is said in some other sentence. If the latter is not acceptable, then the former is not acceptable. We need some distinctions to see how this would work in the case of doctrines of different religions. These distinctions may be brought out by use of the following schemas.

A $s1$ depends on $s2$.
B. $s1$ is an authentic doctrine of $R1$.
$s2$ is an authentic doctrine of $R2$.
C. ($s1$ is an authentic doctrine of $R1$) depends on
($s2$ is an authentic doctrine of $R2$).

The first point to notice is that statements of form A are independent of statements of form B. If what is said in some sentence depends on what is said in some other sentence, it does so whether or not either sentence is an authentic doctrine of some religious community. For example, let $s1$ be:

Jesus is the Messiah God promised to send.

And let $s2$ be:

God promised to send a Messiah.

Then the truth of the first of these sentences depends on the truth of the second. If God did not promise to send a Messiah then Jesus is not the promised Messiah. But the second does not depend on the first. Dependence is asymmetrical.

So far nothing has been said about religious communities. It is indeed plausible that the first expresses an authentic Christian doctrine and that the second expresses an authentic Judaic doctrine. (It is plausible that the second is an authentic Christian doctrine also. In that case we would have in *s2* an identity of primary doctrines of different religions.) But whether or not those statements of form B are true, it could still be true that the truth of *s1* depends on the truth of *s2*. We can be right in statements of form A and at the same time wrong in statements of form B.

Analogous points would apply to the other sorts of connections we have been considering. Whether or not identities or consequences or oppositions hold does not depend on correct identifications of sentences as doctrines of communities. The issues and problems about connections of sentences are not the same as the issues and problems about identifying sentences as doctrines of particular religious communities.

The second point to notice about dependences is that the acceptability of statements in which forms A and B are combined does not depend on the acceptability of statements of form C. Statements of form C say that some sentence is an authentic doctrine of some particular community only if some other sentence is an authentic doctrine of some other community.

Statements of form C seem problematical in themselves. Would any religious community wish to commit itself to a doctrine of this sort? Would the Christian community wish to say that "Jesus is the Messiah" is an authentic Christian doctrine only if "God promised to send a Messiah" is an authentic doctrine of the Judaic community? Instead, would the Christian community say that its doctrine depends on what is taught in the Bible, not on what the Judaic community defines as its authentic doctrines? (Suppose, implausibly, it turns out that the Judaic community does not regard "God promised to send a Messiah" as an authentic doctrine of the community, or that in the course of time it should cease to do so.) Or would the Judaic community wish to tie its doctrines to Christian doctrines in some such way?

The incongruity would be even more striking if we were considering some pair of religions with weaker historical connections than Judaism and Christianity, for example Buddhism and Islam. But the problem would be the same. A religious community has principles of its own for determining its doctrines. This is necessary for its integrity and hence for its unity and durability.

It seems that the only plausible contexts for statements of form C would be cases where one community is a subcommunity of another, perhaps a cult association or a religious order whose constitution is approved tacitly or explicitly by the parent community. Or perhaps one community is a radical reform movement within the other; it claims that its doctrines are the authentic doctrines of the larger community. In either case a claim of an underlying doctrinal unity of the two communities is being made, a unity which consists not just in agreement on some primary doctrines but in the two communities' constitutions. And such claims would seem initially implausible, at the least, if they should be applied to some pair of the major religious communities.

Returning now from this excursion on statements of form C considered in themselves, the main point is this: a claim that a doctrine of some religion depends for its acceptability on the acceptability of a doctrine of some other religion does not require statements of form C, though it requires statements of form A and, independently, statements of form B. Arguments for such cases of dependence must try to show (1) that the acceptability of some sentence depends on the acceptability of some other sentence, and they must try to show, independently of (1), (2) that the two sentences are authentic doctrines of different religions. An argument would thus have to proceed on two different fronts.

If someone does not wish to argue for statements of form B, because he does not think that in the circumstances he is called upon to speak for his own community, if he has one, and he thinks he is not in a position to speak for some other community, or for other reasons, then he must content himself with making a hypothetical though perhaps plausible case. He would modify the claim so that it would take the following form:

$s1$ depends on $s2$. So, if $s1$ is an authentic doctrine of R1, and if $s2$ is an authentic doctrine of R2, then this doctrine of R1 depends on that doctrine of R2.

OPPOSITIONS

Oppositions are in some ways the most interesting connections between doctrines of different communities. Certainly they are more interesting than consistencies. They are more informative, we might say. If we know that two sentences are consistent, and we know that one of them is acceptable, we are not yet in a position to know whether the other is acceptable or not. But if we know that two sentences are opposed and that one is acceptable, then we know that the other is not acceptable. That is why, if we know only that two doctrines of different religions are consistent with one another, we have not yet found a connection between them. Consistency is a logical relation, but not in our sense a logical connection. Also, an opposition is evidence that in their bodies of doctrines these communities are not saying the same thing.

To say that two sentences are consistent is just to say that it may turn out that they are jointly acceptable. If they are used in assertions both could be true, though it may turn out that one or both are untrue. If they are used in directive utterances, for example in commands or recommendations, both could be right, though it may turn out that one or both are wrong. Saying that it may turn out that both sentences are acceptable does not give a good reason for accepting either one of them, and it does not put us in a position to infer, from the acceptability of one of them, the acceptability or the unacceptability of the other.

The epistemic weakness of the consistency relation can be brought out by considering a further point. Two sentences may be consistent even if what is said in one has nothing to do with what is said in the other. "Jesus died on a cross" is consistent with "Barabbas died on a cross." It is also consistent with "Oil production in Indonesia declined by 5 percent last year." One might say that, if two sentences are irrelevant to one another, that guarantees their consistency. Indeed, questions about the consistency of a pair of sentences do not ordinarily come up unless some relevance is apparent or is suspected. So we would be strongly inclined to say that the following are consistent with one another:

Only a Buddha can recognize a Buddha.
Abu Bakr was the rightful successor to Muhammad in the Caliphate.

And the reason for this is that we see no connection between what is said in one of them and what is said in the other.

On the other hand, to say that two sentences are opposed is to say they are not jointly acceptable; they are inconsistent. It may turn out that one of them is acceptable and the other is not, or it may turn out that neither is acceptable. But it cannot turn out that both are acceptable.

Thus it seems that the consequences of an opposition are more weighty than the consequences of a consistency, and that is why oppositions, if we can find them, are more important in the study of doctrines of different religions than consistencies are.

Finding them would be simpler if doctrines of religious communities explicitly negated doctrines of other religions more often than they seem to do. One reason why finding oppositions is often complicated is this: the main intent of a religious community in developing its doctrines is to nurture its own members in the pattern of life it teaches. It must bend its main efforts to that end. The concepts it uses must be drawn from or harmonized with its own starting point and kept steadily in tune with this intent, which is certainly not to make life simpler and easier for philosophers who study doctrines of different religious communities.

A CASE STUDY IN FINDING OPPOSITIONS

We can learn something about the possibilities and difficulties of finding oppositions of doctrines of different religious communities by considering together a passage from a Buddhist scripture and a passage from a Christian scripture.[2]

2. See also William A. Christian, *Oppositions of Religious Doctrines: A Study in the Logic of Dialogue among Religions* (London: Macmillan; New York: Seabury, 1972).

The *Sāmannaphalasutta* [The Fruits of the Life of a Recluse] relates a dialogue between the Buddha and the king of Magadha. The king asks whether there are any immediate fruits, in this world, of the life of a monk *(bhikshu)*. The Buddha engages to show that there are some such fruits; among them are mindfulness and self-possession. He proceeds as follows:

> And how, O king, is the Bhikshu mindful and self-possessed?
> In this matter, O king, the Bhikshu in going forth or in coming back keeps clearly before his mind's eye (all that is wrapt up therein—the immediate object of the act itself, its ethical significance, whether or not it is conducive to the high aim set before him, and the real facts underlying the mere phenomenon of the outward act). And so also in looking forward, or in looking round; in stretching forth his arm, or in drawing in it again; in eating or drinking, in masticating or swallowing, in obeying the calls of nature, in going or standing or sitting, in sleeping or waking, in speaking or in being still, he keeps himself aware of all it really means. Thus it is, O king, that the Bhikshu becomes mindful and self-possessed.[3]

The translator explains that he added the parenthesis in the second sentence to explain "the principal points of what is implied, according to the Pitakas [the canonical scriptures], in this famous passage." We can take his phrase "the high aim . . ." to mean the aim at attainment of *nibbāna* (Sanskrit *nirvāna*), and we can take "the real facts . . ." to mean the process of conditioned origination, thus eliminating the notion of a permanent soul, as the translator says, along with the notion of unconditioned objects.

It seems clear that this is a practical doctrine. The point of the dialogue is to give the teaching of the Buddha on the conduct of the life of a monk. Though the doctrine is not put explicitly as a command or a recommendation of a course of action, it seems clear that the Buddha is not giving a description; he is presenting a paradigm. The way the bhikshu carries on natural bodily activities is the way any monk would insofar as he is on the right path. So what is being said in the passage has the force of a practical doctrine.

Since it appears to be a saying of the Buddha, it is plausible that this passage expresses an authentic doctrine of the Buddhist community. But, since I shall not undertake to show that this is so, we can speak of it as a prima facie Buddhist doctrine.

Now consider the other passage. In the tenth chapter of his first letter to the Corinthians, the apostle Paul draws some practical lessons from the experiences of the Israelites in the wilderness of Sinai, especially their temptations to idolatry. Then he moves on to discuss pagan sacrifices and current problems about buying and eating food which may have passed through the hands of pagan priests. He explains the liberty of Christians

3. *Dialogues of the Buddha*, Part I, trans. T. W. Rhys Davids, from the Pali *Dīgha Nikāya* (London: Pali Text Society, 1899), pp. 80–82.

in this respect, "for the earth is the Lord's, and the fulness thereof" (Psalm 24:1), adding that the consciences of others have also to be taken into account. Then in verse 31 he gives a general principle as a guide for conduct in such matters: "Whether therefore you eat, or drink, or whatsoever you do, do all to the glory of God."

Clearly this passage presents a practical doctrine. It has the form as well as the force of a recommendation of a general course of action.

It seems plausible that this is an authentic doctrine of the Christian community, but since this will not be argued, we can speak of it as a prima facie Christian doctrine. But often I shall use the briefer phrases "the Buddhist doctrine" and "the Christian doctrine" to refer to the doctrines expressed in the passages given above and in other passages introduced later on. That is all we need for the sake of the argument.

We have here in these two passages directive utterances, utterances in which courses of action are proposed. And it is plausible that they express doctrines of different religious communities. So we ask whether there are connections between what is said in one passage and what is said in the other. More particularly, are these directives opposed to one another?

It is not obvious that they are connected. What is said in one is not the same as what is said in the other; neither seems to follow from the other; neither seems to depend on the other; and no oppositions lie on the surface of the passages. Why then should anyone undertake such an apparently unpromising inquiry? One striking point, which the translator of the Buddhist passage mentions in a footnote, is that there are a common subject matter and some parallels in their phrasings. Each of the passages gives a very general recommendation for conducting simple bodily activities. Also, if a reader has some acquaintance with the literatures of the communities this may lead him to suspect connections which are not immediately apparent.

It seems natural to begin with a distinction between the bodily activities such as eating and drinking which are mentioned in the passages and the intentions and suppositions with which, the doctrines say, these activities should be carried on. It seems that in each case the passage does not recommend that these bodily activities should be carried on. Instead it seems to be taken for granted that they will be carried on in some way or other. What is being recommended in each case is that the bodily activities should be carried on in certain ways, with certain intentions and suppositions.

In this respect these practical doctrines differ from some other types of practical doctrines. For example, some Buddhist doctrines recommend to the serious striver after enlightenment that he should leave behind the life of a householder and take up the life of a monk, and there are recommendations that laymen should give alms to monks. Similarly, there are Christian practical doctrines which recommend meeting with other Christians for common prayers and the celebration of the Lord's supper. These are activities which cannot be taken for granted, as eating and drinking can ordinarily be taken for granted.

The Buddhist doctrine recommends that the bodily activities it mentions should be carried on mindfully and with clear consciousness. In the *Satipatthanasutta*[4] [Discourse on the Applications of Mindfulness] the discipline of mindfulness is discussed systematically and in detail. There are four applications of mindfulness.

A monk "fares along" arousing mindfulness, training himself to be mindful and clearly conscious of what is going on. In this way he contemplates (1) his body in all its movements, or some other body. He reflects also on "precisely this body itself, encased in skin and full of various impurities, from the soles of the feet up and from the crown of the head down, that: 'There is connected with this body hair of the head, hair of the body, nails, teeth, skin, flesh, sinews, bones, marrow, kidneys, heart, liver, membranes, spleen, lungs, . . . saliva, mucus, synovic fluid, urine' " (pp. 73–74). Similarly, he contemplates (2) the feelings in the feelings, pleasant and unpleasant; he contemplates (3) mind in the mind; and he contemplates (4) mental objects in mental objects. In each case "his mindfulness is established precisely to the extent necessary just for knowledge, just for remembrance, and he fares along independently of and not grasping [not clinging to] anything in the world" (p. 79). It seems that the object of the exercise is to cut the roots of attachment to, aversion from, and confusion about what is going on in the world. Mindfulness is "just for knowledge, just for remembrance." It seems that the discipline is aimed at a certain devaluation of all worldly objects. This would free the monk from dependence on them.

At the beginning of the sutta, and again at the end, the Buddha is reported to have said: "There is this one way, monks, for the purification of beings, for the overcoming of sorrows and griefs, for the going down of sufferings and miseries, for winning the right path, for realising nibbāna, that is to say, the four applications of mindfulness" (p. 82). So the cutting off of positive and negative valuations of worldly objects, bodily and mental, is linked to a strong positive valuation of realizing nibbāna.

The recommendations of these intentions in carrying on bodily and other activities carries with it at least two important suppositions. First, it supposes that all the constituents of experience are conditioned in their arising and in their passing away *(paticcasamuppāda)*. Hence there is no independent, unchanging self underlying the bodily and mental activities which are contemplated in the application of mindfulness. These are "the real facts," as

4. *The Collection of the Middle Length Sayings* (Majjhima-Nikāya), vol. 1, trans. I. B. Horner (London: Pali Text Society, 1954): 70–82. Horner translates *sampajanna,* which Rhys Davids translates "self-possession," as "clarity of consciousness." See also Nyanatiloka, *Buddhist Dictionary,* 3d ed., ed. Nyanaponika (Colombo: Frewin, 1972), s.v. "sampajañña" and "satipatthāna."

Rhys Davids puts it, "underlying the mere phenomenon of the outward act." "Distracting forces have the power to act as enemies to our calm when the ego identifies itself with what takes place on the surface of the mind, participating heartily in it. The illusion then arises that these activities are 'my doings,' 'my' concerns, and the sphere in which 'I' live and have 'my' being. Mindfulness begins to dispel these illusions."[5] Second, the recommendation supposes the real possibility of attaining nibbāna.

The Christian doctrine recommends that eating and drinking and other activities be carried on to the glory of God. John Calvin amplifies the doctrine when he calls attention to Paul's exhortation, that believers "be not conformed to the fashion of this world, but be transformed by the renewal of their minds, so that they may prove what is the will of God" (Rom. 12:2). Then he proceeds as follows: "Now the great thing is this: we are consecrated and dedicated to God in order that we may thereafter think, speak, meditate, and do, nothing except to his glory. . . . If we, then, are not our own [cf. 1 Cor. 6:19] but the Lord's, it is clear what error we must flee, and whither we must direct all the acts of our life. . . . We are God's: let his wisdom and will therefore rule all our actions."[6]

The general course of action recommended here is different from that recommended in the Buddhist doctrine, different in its intentions and suppositions. The main intention recommended here is to carry on activities with a view to manifesting the wisdom, power, and goodness of God. So the primary valuation is a strong positive valuation of God, to whom life is conceived as a response.

From this certain valuations of the ordinary activities of life and their objects and conditions follow. In a chapter he devotes to meditations on the future life, holding the present world in contempt, Calvin says:

> But let believers accustom themselves to a contempt of the present life that engenders no hatred of it or ingratitude against God. Indeed, this life, however crammed with infinite miseries it may be, is still rightly to be counted among those blessings of God which are not to be spurned. Therefore, if we recognize in it no divine benefit, we are already guilty of grave ingratitude toward God himself. For believers especially, this ought to be a testimony of divine benevolence, wholly destined, as it is, to promote their salvation. For before he shows us openly the inheritance of eternal glory, God wills by lesser proofs to show himself to be our Father. These are the benefits that are daily conferred on us by him. Since, therefore, this life serves us in understanding God's goodness, should we despise it as if it had no grain of good in itself? We must, then, become so disposed and minded that we count it among those gifts of divine generosity which are not at all to be rejected. For if testimonies of Scripture were lacking, and they are very many

5. Edward Conze, *Buddhist Meditation* (London: George Allen & Unwin, 1956), p. 29.
6. John Calvin, *Institutes of the Christian Religion,* ed. John T. McNeil, trans. Ford Lewis Battles, 2 vols. (Philadelphia: Westminster, 1960), 1:689–90.

and very clear, nature itself also exhorts us to give thanks to the Lord because he has brought us into its light, granted us the use of it, and provided all the necessary means to preserve it.

And this is a much greater reason if in it we reflect that we are in preparation, so to speak, for the glory of the Heavenly Kingdom. For the Lord has ordained that those who are one day to be crowned in heaven should first undergo struggles on earth in order that they may not triumph until they have overcome the difficulties of war, and attained victory.

Then there is another reason: we begin in the present life, through various benefits, to taste the sweetness of the divine generosity in order to whet our hope and desire to seek after the full revelation of this. When we are certain that the earthly life we live is a gift of God's kindness, as we are beholden to him for it we ought to remember it and be thankful. Then we shall come in good time to consider its most unhappy condition in order that we may, indeed, be freed from too much desire of it, to which, as has been said, we are of ourselves inclined by nature. [pp. 714–15]

With this may be placed the General Thanksgiving from the *Book of Common Prayer:*

Almighty God, Father of all mercies, we, thine unworthy servants, do give thee most humble and hearty thanks for all thy goodness and loving-kindness to us, and to all men. We bless thee for our creation, preservation, and all the blessings of this life; but above all, for thine inestimable love in the redemption of the world by our Lord Jesus Christ; for the means of grace, and for the hope of glory. And, we beseech thee, give us that due sense of all thy mercies, that our hearts may be unfeignedly thankful; and that we show forth thy praise, not only with our lips, but in our lives, by giving up our selves to thy service, and by walking before thee in holiness and righteousness all our days; through Jesus Christ our Lord, to whom, with thee and the Holy Ghost, be all honour and glory, world without end. Amen.

The blessings of life are to be enjoyed and remembered with gratitude. Further, all the occasions of life, whether attended by misery or joy, are opportunities for so conducting our activities as to bring to light and to celebrate the wisdom, power, and goodness of God.

All this supposes the reality of God. The world is his creation; the course of nature and human history is governed by his providence; and he promises and brings about the renewing of our minds and our eternal salvation.

Now let us consider the Buddhist doctrine and the Christian doctrine together. To develop suspected connections between doctrines of different religions, especially when oppositions are suspected, it is necessary to consider symmetries and asymmetries. The Buddhist passage with which we began, putting aside for the moment the translator's gloss, says in effect: Act mindfully. The initial Christian passage says in effect: Act to the glory of God. It seems that these formulations are asymmetrical; their constituents do not match. For it seems that "act mindfully" prescribes a manner of acting, and that "act to the glory of God" prescribes an end in view. It is possible that a certain manner of acting might turn out to be consistent, or inconsistent, with a certain end in view. But for the time being let us pursue the thought about symmetry a little further.

We took a step toward symmetry of formulations when from Rhys Davids' gloss and the *Satipatthānasutta* the Buddhist doctrine was amplified into: "Act mindfully, for realizing nibbāna." Acting mindfully is not only intrinsically good, an "immediate fruit"; it is good also as a step on the path which leads to the extinction of all cravings, the attainment of nibbāna. Now we have an end in view to match "to the glory of God." This puts us in position to ask whether some connection holds between practical doctrines which recommend courses of action with these different ends in view.

Meanwhile, might another step toward symmetry be taken? Would the Christian passages we have considered, or others which might be adduced, warrant introducing some manner of acting to match the manner of acting recommended in the Buddhist passages? Indeed, we might ask whether the following would have some initial plausibility as a Christian doctrine: "Act mindfully to the glory of God," in an extended sense of "mindfully." Certainly the passages we have considered do not seem to preclude this.

Since I have not yet discovered in the literature a clearly developed set of rules for Christian mindfulness in bodily activities to match those in the *Satipatthānasutta,* let us proceed hypothetically. Let us suppose that Christian mindfulness in bodily activities could be construed as requiring the following:

(1) attending to what one is doing, acting with presence of mind, not absentmindedly; and
(2) reflecting on the antecedents of the bodily activities, on their consequences, and on their connections with one another; and
(3) not ascribing magical power to them and thus becoming obsessed by them.

So far it seems that these rules are at least consistent with acting to the glory of God. Perhaps we could go further. Perhaps (1) and (2) could be derived from the precept that one should love God with all one's mind, and perhaps (3) could be derived from prohibitions of idolatry. However that may be, it seems that these rules, considered apart from their possible warrants, are consistent also with the applications of mindfulness in the *Satipatthānasutta.* They do not seem to yield oppositions between the practical doctrines with which we began. It seems that it might even turn out that some rules of Christian mindfulness are identical with some Buddhist rules of mindfulness.

But suppose that to these Christian rules another should be added, namely:

(4) valuing positively the powers exercised in the bodily activities and the natural objects of those activities, not just the use of these powers and objects, and accordingly treating them with respect.

This additional rule seems consistent with acting to the glory of God. Indeed, a warrant for it might be derived from the passages in Christian literature we have noticed, as also from Psalm 24:1, which is quoted by the apostle Paul at 1 Cor. 10:26 in his discussion of food which may have passed through the hands of pagan priests:

The earth is the Lord's, and the fulness thereof.

On this verse Calvin comments as follows:

> If *the fulness of the earth is the Lord's,* there is nothing in the world that is not sacred and pure. We must always keep in view, what the question is of which the Apostle treats. It might be doubted, whether the creatures of God were polluted by the sacrifices of the wicked. Paul says they are not, inasmuch as the rule and possession of the whole earth remain always in the hands of God. Now, what things the Lord has in his hands, he preserves by his power, and consequently sanctifies them. The sons of God, therefore, have the pure use of everything, because they receive them no otherwise than from the hand of God.[7]

A somewhat similar note is struck in an incident related in the *Journal* of George Fox:

> After the meeting was over I went to John Audland's, and there came John Story to me and lighted his pipe of tobacco. And said he, "Will you take a pipe of tobacco?" saying, "Come; all is ours." And I looked upon him to be a forward bold lad; and tobacco I did not take, but it came into my mind that the lad might think I had not unity with the creation. For I saw he had a flashy, empty notion of religion. So I took his pipe and put it to my mouth, and gave it to him again to stop him lest his rude tongue should say I had not unity with the creation.[8]

By speaking here of warrants for rules, I have gone beyond the immediate point and anticipated discussion of the suppositions of the practical doctrines we are considering. The immediate point is concerned with the rules of mindfulness themselves, abstracted from the ends in view and the suppositions with which they would be embedded in bodies of doctrines. Would these rules yield oppositions with Buddhist rules of mindfulness?

That depends on how Buddhist rules of mindfulness are construed and developed. It was suggested above that the applications of mindfulness in the *Satipatthānasutta* seem to aim at a certain devaluation of worldly objects;

7. John Calvin, *Commentary on the Epistles of Paul the Apostle to the Corinthians,* trans. John Pringle (Grand Rapids: Eerdmans, 1948), p. 344.

8. George Fox, *The Journal of George Fox,* revised by Norman Penney (London: J.M. Dent; New York: E.P. Dutton, n.d.), p. 63.

the discipline seems to involve withholding from them both positive and negative valuations. The suggestion is not that the mindful person will have no feelings about worldly objects. It is clear that the second application of mindfulness supposes to the contrary that such feelings, pleasant or unpleasant, will occur. It recommends that these feelings themselves, as well as the worldly objects, be contemplated mindfully, "just for knowledge, just for remembrance."

In rule (4) I am supposing that valuations are judgments, not feelings, though no doubt feelings occur too. So rule (4) does not propose having pleasant feelings about worldly objects; it proposes that worldly objects be judged to be good in some certain way or other. Various specifications of how bodily powers and worldly objects are good are spelled out in the Christian passages given above. They are divine blessings which ought to be enjoyed, used, and remembered with gratitude and praise. Hence they are sacred and pure, and they are to be used so as to manifest the wisdom, power, and goodness of their divine giver. Seventeenth-century Puritans stressed that Christians should love the world with "weaned affections," the affections of a child who no longer depends on its mother for sustenance. But weaned affections are still affections. Furthermore, it may be that judgments are even clearer when affections are weaned.

Now rule (4) does not include these or any other specifications, for it is worth asking whether there is a Buddhist doctrine opposed to this rule just as it stands. That would be the case if in the teachings of the Buddhist community there is some recommendation, derivable from the *Satipatthānasutta* or otherwise, against judging that the powers exercised in bodily activities and the worldly objects of those activities are good in some certain way or other, and hence against treating them with respect.

If that were so we would have the following pair of recommendations:

Carry on bodily activities without valuing bodily powers and worldly objects as good in some way and hence without treating them with respect.

In carrying on bodily activities value bodily powers and worldly objects as good in some way and accordingly treat them with respect.

I am supposing that treating something with respect is not the same as treating it with caution.

In this case we would have an opposition of recommendations. Different courses of action are being recommended, and each course of action embodies an intention which runs counter to an intention embodied in the other. So no one could carry out both courses of action. So no one who understands the recommendations could undertake to carry them out jointly without absurdity. Hence they are not jointly acceptable. They are opposed.

Of course, before we could be in a position to say that we have here an opposition between an authentic Buddhist doctrine and an authentic

Christian doctrine, both Buddhist teachings and Christian teachings would have to be explored much further. But it seems that we have here at least a lively possibility of an opposition of doctrines of different religions.

We have been considering rules of mindfulness. Now consider the ends in view which are built into the prima facie Buddhist practical doctrine and the prima facie Christian practical doctrine with which we began. In the Buddhist doctrine mindfulness in bodily and other activities is recommended as "the one way . . . for winning the right path, for realising nibbāna." The Christian doctrine recommends that bodily activities be carried on "to the glory of God."

Notice first that a very strong positive valuation of the end in view is built into each of the recommendations. In his *Buddhist Dictionary,* the venerable Nyanatiloka says:

> Nibbāna constitutes the highest and ultimate goal of all Buddhist aspirations, i.e. absolute extinction of that life-affirming will manifested as Greed, Hate and Delusion, and convulsively clinging to existence; and therewith also the ultimate and absolute deliverance from all future rebirth, old age, disease and death, from all suffering and misery.[9]

It is not said here that attainment of nibbāna is the only end in view a Buddhist should have. But it is clearly not just one of many ends in view. It is the highest and ultimate goal of all the aspirations countenanced by Buddhist teachings.

Also, a strong positive valuation of the end in view is built into the prima facie Christian doctrine. It seems arguable that, according to Christian teachings, God is not the only object of positive valuation, the only good, some of the language of mystics and pietists to the contrary notwithstanding. But it seems clear from the passages given above that God is regarded as the fount of every blessing. From this would follow a strong valuation of glorifying God, that is to say of bringing to light and making clear all the facets of his wisdom, goodness, and power.

If we compare these valuations of ends in view, we can find not only differences but asymmetries. The Buddhist doctrine proposes as the end in view attainment of a state in which all cravings, aversions, and confusions have been extinguished. This is not a pre-existing state, like a heaven, though many have already attained it. And because the buddhas have attained it, especially because the historical buddha, Sakyamuni, has attained it, it is not an unattainable state and in that sense an ideal, like a utopia or like a mathematical point which can only be approximated. A Buddhist life is aimed at this attainment. In contrast, the Christian doctrine puts forward as the end in view a certain response to an existing and present reality, the creator and sustainer of the universe. The end in view is to witness

9. Nyanatiloka, *Buddhist Dictionary,* s.v. "nibbāna," p. 105.

steadily and in all sorts of circumstances to the wisdom, power, and goodness of this present reality.

These are not only different ends in view; they are ends in view of different kinds. On one hand there is an aim at a final but attainable state; on the other hand there is an aim at steadily carrying out a certain pattern of activity in response to an existing present reality. No doubt it would be possible to bypass this asymmetry by developing a plausibly Christian doctrine of a state of perfection and eternal blessedness as an end in view. Then this could be compared with the aim at nibbāna, and from this comparison perhaps an opposition would emerge. But it seems that the bypass would sooner or later lead us back to the route we have been traveling, for Christian doctrines of perfection seem to include the notion of a response to a present existing reality. So let us see whether the asymmetry can be dealt with more directly.

One way of instituting a symmetry in the hope of finding an opposition would begin as follows. The Buddhist aim does not ignore present existing realities. Indeed, it is generated and in part governed by reaction to an existing reality, namely the web of conditioned arisings and passings away which constitutes the world of phenomena. The aim at attaining nibbāna arises from a negative reaction to the conditioned world as a whole. For though in the world one's lot may be a happy one now and then, on the whole the world is a source of misery. It is an endless cycle of rebirths, some better, some worse. It yields no prospect of "ultimate and absolute deliverance from all future rebirth, old age, disease and death, from all suffering and misery." A wise man will look for a way out of its tangles, and a way has been found in the teachings and example of the Buddha.

Thus we have two different reactions to conceived realities, and these reactions shape aims at different ends in view. One is a negative reaction; the other is a positive response. So perhaps an opposition might be formulated as follows:

In this life on the whole the right aim is an aim at freedom from the tangles of conditioned existence.
In this life on the whole the right aim is an aim at responding positively to the reality which creates the world of conditioned existence and acts in the midst of it.

The first of these might be thought of as a principle for maximizing satisfaction. The second might be thought of as a principle of justice, as an aim at giving everything its due. So an asymmetry would remain, but in spite of this it seems that we have here an opposition of practical principles. Each arises from consideration of all the circumstances, problems, and possibilities of life in this world. And if in view of these considerations it is claimed that there is some aim which is the right aim on the whole, then a claim that some other aim is the right aim on the whole must be a rival claim. Two such claims are not jointly acceptable. They are opposed.

Though these are practical utterances, we are verging here again on the suppositions of the practical doctrines with which we began, their suppositions about existents and the conditions of existence. A recommendation of a course of action supposes something about the world in which the course of action would take place. For example, it supposes that the person or persons to whom it is addressed can undertake and carry out the course of action. Otherwise making the recommendation would involve an absurdity. But before we explore further the suppositions of the initial practical doctrines, let us see whether direct oppositions between the following proposals of ends in view can be found.

Aim at attaining nibbāna.
Aim at acting to the glory of God.

Let us suppose that neither of these recommendations is meant to exclude adoption of all other ends in view in the course of life. Suppose that the communities in question encourage or at least permit pursuit of other aims by their members. It seems that ordinarily a religious community, in the course of its teaching activity, recommends a number of aims in life to its members, not just one. Life is very complex, and its members must deal with situations of many different kinds. So consider the following:

Whatever else you aim at, aim at attaining nibbāna.
Whatever else you aim at, aim at acting to the glory of God.

These recommendations as they stand do not even require that other aims should be compatible with the aims they mention. The thought might be that if one holds steadily to the aim at attaining nibbāna or, in the other case, to the aim at acting to the glory of God, then any aims which are incompatible with that aim will undergo transformations.

But if a community holds that its authentic doctrines are consistent with one another, it supposes that any other aims recommended in its authentic doctrines are compatible with the aim recommended here. If the compatibility of some pair of aims is challenged, then the aims must be explained and qualified. Also, unauthentic teachings would have to be weeded out and set aside.

At this point in our attempt to construct an opposition, we should consider priorities as well as compatibilities. There seems no general reason, apart from cases of incompatibility, why a community should not recommend some aim in life and recommend also some other aim in life, without giving either of these a priority over the other. This holds also for courses of action. There seems to be nothing intrinsically objectionable, nothing illogical, in proposing a simple conjunction of aims or of courses of action.

But religious communities often do build priorities into conjunctions of recommendations. It is said in Matthew 23:23 (1) that tithes should be paid on mint, anise and cummin ("these ye ought to have done"). It is also said

(2) that justice, mercy, and faith are required (these ought not to be left undone). Here we have a conjunction of recommendations. In addition, it is said that justice, mercy, and faith are "the weightier matters of the law." Here we have a comparative valuation which issues in a priority of one aim and one course of action over another. In adopting and pursuing one aim, the priority of some other aim should be observed.

There are different patterns of priority. (1) There are teleological priorities. Here some aim in life has priority over some other if the value of attainment of the latter aim is that it conduces to attainment of the former. Thus, for example, it could be said that learning to aim at some end contributes to learning to aim at and attain some other end which is in some way more important to attain. Learning to be a good member of a family or a monastic order or a civil society contributes to attainment of a more important end, to attaining inward freedom or to being a good member of some universal society.

(2) There are also focal priorities. Here some aim in life has priority over some other aim in life if attainment of its end is a condition of the rightness, and also perhaps of the fruitful pursuit, of the other aim. In this case the end of one aim is thought of as more central in life than the end of some other, instead of, as in the teleological pattern, an ulterior end. So this may be spoken of as a focal priority. Some aim is more important than some other aim because the other aim is right only if conditioned by the former aim. Thus, for example, it could be said that an aim at justice, mercy, and faith has a priority over an aim at tithing mint, anise and cummin, because pursuit of the latter is right only if it is conditioned by the former.

Along with such comparative judgments which establish priorities of this or that aim over some other aim, in the bodies of doctrines of religious communities there seem to be cases where the end of some recommended aim is given not just a priority over this or that other aim but a priority over any other aim whatever, that is to say a primacy. So in a search for possible oppositions we should consider such primacy rankings as the following:

Whatever else you aim at, above all else aim at attaining nibbāna.
Whatever else you aim at, above all else aim at acting to the glory of God.

Here an aim at attaining nibbāna is given a priority over any other aim whatever. It is given a primacy among aims in life. So also with the aim at acting to the glory of God. We noticed earlier the contrasting valuations of these ends in view, which these primacy-ranking recommendations of aims reflect.

Now do we have here an opposition? More particularly, do we have here an opposition by virtue of the fact that each of these recommendations assigns a primacy among aims to the aim it mentions? It seems so. It seems that both of these recommendations could not be accepted without absurdity. For each of them would have the effect of deposing the aim recommended by the other from its proposed primacy among aims in life.

Furthermore, this would seem to hold even if different patterns of priority and primacy should be involved. The Buddhist passages suggest that the primacy of the aim at nibbāna has a teleological pattern. Nibbāna is spoken of as the ultimate goal. The Christian passages suggest a pattern of focal priority and primacy. The aim at acting to the glory of God is made central in life rather than ultimate. We might think also of the verse: "Seek ye first his kingdom, and his righteousness, and all these things shall be added unto you." (Matt. 6:33). Some lines from an old hymn are also to the point:

> Hast thou not seen
> How all thy desires e'er have been
> Granted in what He ordaineth?

Still, in spite of the fact that different patterns of priority and primacy seem to be involved in these recommendations, they seem to be opposed by virtue of a primacy among aims in life which each assigns to the aim it recommends.

There seems to be no general reason to suppose that an individual could not adopt and maintain two (or more) aims in life, each with a priority over some aims in life but neither with a priority over the other. Further, it could be that attainment of the end of either of these aims would be compatible with, and even would contribute to, attainment of the end of the other.

Let us grant for the sake of argument that this could happen in the case of a body of doctrines of a religious community. Let us grant that a community might set forth in its teachings various aims in life without assigning to any of them a primacy, that is, a priority over any other aim whatever. But in the case before us there seem to be primacy rankings. And it is this feature of the recommendations which seems to produce the opposition. Further, the passages we have noticed seem to lend some plausibility to the recommendations as doctrines of the communities in question. So, though we are treating this as a hypothetical case, since we have not argued that the recommendations are indeed authentic doctrines of the respective communities, it is not a bare hypothesis.

Now we can turn to the suppositions of the practical doctrines with which we began. Though a recommendation of a course of action is not an assertion, it supposes something about the world in which the course of action would be carried out. So anyone who recommends a course of action ought to be ready and willing to acknowledge the suppositions of the recommendation. Further, he ought to be ready and willing either (1) to stand by its suppositions, to assert them and argue for them if they are not granted by his hearers, or (2) to withdraw the recommendation. Otherwise his recommendation carries no weight.

It seems that the prima facie Buddhist practical doctrine supposes that it is possible for a human being to attain a state in which there are no compulsive attachments, aversions, or confusions, hence no bondage to conditioned existence, and hence no rebirth. And it seems that the prima facie Christian doctrine supposes that God is a present existing reality to which the recommended attitudes are a proper response. Are these suppositions opposed? First let us put each of them in a perspective.

It seems that the Buddhist doctrine supposes it is possible for a human being to discipline his bodily activities, his feelings, and his mind so as to live in this world without suffering, in a steady state of bliss. For such a person, the world would no longer be a vale of tears. The point is not that he will think he has no compulsive attachments, aversions, or confusions, and it is not just that he will feel blissful. Instead the point is that the relevant predicates are true of him, not just true of the way he thinks and feels that he is. One consequence is that he is no longer subject to rebirth. He will never have to repeat the arduous process of winning freedom from conditioned existence.

So when it is supposed that the attainment of nibbāna is possible, something more is supposed than the possibility of enjoying trance states, though such states may be stages in the path to nibbāna. A stronger claim is being made about existents and the conditions of existence.

Does this mean that if there were an ideal observer (an ideal psychiatrist?), this observer, though perhaps no actual observer (except another buddha?), would be in a position to say that someone has no compulsive attachments, aversions, and confusions? And does this mean that an ideal observer (an ideal historian?), though no actual observer, would be in a position to say that someone will never be reborn? Such an observer would know perfectly the circumstances of all future births and he would be equipped with a set of effective criteria of identity.

However that might be, it seems that the Buddhist doctrine supposes that the conditions of existence are such that attainment of nibbāna is not just conceivable but really possible, and that its consequences are real consequences. It seems that what is intended in the doctrine is not just a pious wish but a supposition of a real possibility, that is to say a possibility arising from the way things really are in the world.

It seems also that the prima facie Christian practical doctrine supposes some facts about the real constitution of the world. The attitudes to be embodied in natural activities like eating and drinking are vectors. They are not just emotional accompaniments of the bodily activities; they are responses to a present existing reality, a reality other than the subjects who respond. Furthermore, it seems that they are not responses to a purely transcendent reality wholly beyond the world; they are responses to a reality which operates in the world of everyday life.

This may be brought out by considering a Question in the *Summa Theologica* of Thomas Aquinas.[10] The topic of Part I, Question VIII, is "The Existence of God in Things." In the first article of that Question Aquinas argues that "God is in all things, not, indeed, as part of their essence, nor as an accident, but as an agent is present to that upon which it acts." In the second article he argues that God is everywhere. "He is in all things as giving them being, power and operation; so He is in every place as giving it being and locative power." In the third article he argues that God is everywhere by essence, presence, and power. "God is in all things by His power, inasmuch as all things are subject to His power; He is by His presence in all things, inasmuch as all things are bare and open to his eyes; He is in all things by His essence, inasmuch as He is present to all as the cause of their being." In the fourth article he argues that "To be everywhere primarily and essentially is proper to God," that is to say to God alone.

So it seems that both the supposition of the possibility of attaining nibbāna and the supposition of the real existence of God have to do with the ways things are in the world in which bodily activities take place. Are these suppositions opposed to one another?

The answer to this question is not clear to me. Perhaps the best way to bring out some of the difficulties arising from the disparities and complexities of the relevant bodies of doctrines is to construct some arguments which might be brought forward from the Buddhist side against the Christian supposition, and some arguments from the Christian side against the Buddhist supposition. The point of this is not to help us decide which arguments are stronger; instead it is a device which might help to uncover an opposition, if there is one, between the suppositions.

1. From the Buddhist side, it might be argued that the Christian supposition requires of those who adopt it a compulsive attachment to God. But it is from bondage of just this sort, and of other sorts, that we would be liberated by taking the path to nibbāna. Hence if the Christian supposition requires that this response should be sustained, then attainment of nibbāna would be impossible. Hence the suppositions are opposed.

But it might be replied from the Christian side that the response to God which is called for by his existence as a present reality is not a compulsive attachment. Thanksgiving, praise, and love and service of God are free responses. They are reasonable responses in view of the wisdom, goodness, and power of God. So it seems that along this line of argument the two suppositions, of the possibility of attaining nibbāna and of the existence of God as a present reality, do not meet head on.

10. Pegis, *Basic Writings of Aquinas*, 1: 63–69.

2. Again from the Buddhist side, it might be argued that the attainment of nibbāna is possible only if all existents are conditioned and hence changeable. If we ourselves or any of the things with which we are connected were unchangeable, then the ties which bind us to them would be unbreakable. And, since God is unchangeable, maintaining a relation to God would make attainment of nibbāna impossible. Hence again the suppositions are opposed.

It may be true that on the version of Christian doctrines assumed by this argument—that God is absolutely unchanging and unchangeable in all respects—the argument would indeed lead to an opposition between the Buddhist and the Christian doctrines. But it might be replied from the Christian side that, while God cannot be made to change by any other power, and while in some respects God is unchanging, in other respects he is not. At least, it might be said, his operations in changing things are coordinate with the changes which occur in them. For example, Aquinas says that God cannot make the past not to have been.[11] (*Summa contra Gentiles*, II:75) So what God does on some occasion in the life of a person or in the history of the world will not be the same as what he does on some other occasion. God is not a static absolute; he is a living active being. On this latter version, the way to an opposition with the Buddhist supposition would not be so clear.

3. It might be argued from the Buddhist side that the Christian supposition is unwarranted, that there is no good reason to believe that it is true. Furthermore, explanations of beliefs that it is true might be offered, drawn from analysis of human tendencies to project wishes and confusions onto the face of the world. (It seems that at least some of the elements of such an argument might be drawn from Buddhist doctrines.)

But unless it could be shown that the conclusion of this argument depends on the truth of the supposition that attainment of nibbāna is possible, it is not clear how we could find an opposition between that and the Christian supposition along this line. There is a considerable agreement among scholars that Theravada Buddhism teaches the nonexistence of God, at least by implication. But at this point we are asking only whether the supposition that attainment of nibbāna is possible is opposed to the supposition that God is a present reality.

4. From the Christian side, it might be argued that since God is a present reality, and since his presence and power is a condition of all other existents, nothing can be done without his power. So nibbāna cannot be attained without his power. But this argument does not itself require denial of the supposition that attainment of nibbāna is possible, or of the claim that it has been attained in some cases.

11. Saint Thomas Aquinas, *On the Truth of the Christian Faith (Summa contra Gentiles)*, Book 2, trans. James F. Anderson (Garden City: Doubleday, 1956), p. 75.

5. From the Christian side, it might be argued that there is no good reason to believe that rebirth is a feature of the process of existence. This commonsense objection might be reinforced by an appeal to the Bible, where it is generally supposed that any human being has only one life to live on earth, so that death acquires a decisive significance it would not otherwise have. The conclusion of the argument would be that the Buddhist claim that attainment of nibbāna brings freedom from rebirth is an empty claim.

One question about this line of argument is whether or not the supposition that attainment of nibbāna is possible depends on the claim that rebirth is a feature of human existence on earth. But the main question about it, from the perspective of our present inquiry, is whether objections to belief in rebirth flow from those assertions about God which are supposed by the prima facie Christian practical doctrine we have been studying. Objections to rebirth which are not derived from this supposition, whether or not they are derived from other Christian doctrines, will not lead us toward a decision on whether the Christian supposition is, or is not, opposed to the supposition that attainment of nibbāna is possible. Other objections to rebirth or, more generally, other objections to the possibility of attaining nibbāna would not be to the present point.

So it seems that this exploration of lines of argument about the suppositions of the Buddhist doctrine and the Christian doctrine is inconclusive on the question at issue. That question has been: Are (1) the supposition that attainment of nibbāna is possible, and (2) the supposition that God is a present existing reality opposed? It may be that an opposition of these suppositions can be discovered by some route I have not thought of. Or it may turn out that, though the consistency of these suppositions seems counter-intuitive, they are really not opposed. In any case, one lesson we could learn from this discussion is that it is not always easy to discover logical connections between comparable doctrines of different religious communities.

At some points we do seem to have discovered oppositions between certain developments from the practical doctrines with which we began. These appeared in our developments of recommendations of rules of mindfulness and in our developments of recommendations of aims in life. These may be recalled here:

Carry on bodily activities without valuing bodily powers and worldly objects as good in some way and hence without treating them with respect.

In carrying on bodily activities, value bodily powers and worldly objects as good in some way and accordingly treat them with respect.

In this life on the whole the right aim is an aim at freedom from the tangles of conditioned existence.

In this life on the whole the right aim is an aim at responding positively to the reality which creates the world of conditioned existence and acts in the midst of it.

Whatever else you aim at, above all else aim at attaining nibbāna.

Whatever else you aim at, above all else aim at acting to the glory of God.

So if these are indeed valid developments from the practical prima facie doctrines with which we began, then, since these developments yield oppositions, those initial practical doctrines are opposed to one another. And, if the prima facie Buddhist doctrine with which we began is indeed an authentic doctrine of the Buddhist community, and if the prima facie Christian doctrine with which we began is indeed an authentic doctrine of the Christian community, then we would have discovered an opposition between a practical doctrine of the Buddhist community and a practical doctrine of the Christian community.

If we take these results together with the inconclusive outcome of our discussions of the suppositions of (1) the possibility of nibbāna and of (2) the existence of God, one upshot of this case study is the modest suggestion that there may be oppositions, and more generally logical connections, between different bodies of religious doctrines at some points, but not at other points. Finally, it may need to be said again that showing connections between prima facie doctrines of different religious communities falls short of showing connections between authentic doctrines of different religious communities.

All that has been done in this chapter is to suggest how various kinds of logical connections between comparable doctrines of different religious communities might be studied and, in particular, how intuitions of connections might be tested. Various other lines of philosophical inquiry into doctrines of different religious communities have not been attempted.

One topic is those doctrines of communities which bear on doctrines of other religious communities. That topic will be touched on in later chapters, where we study doctrines about alien claims, including secular claims as well as doctrines of other religious communities. But, going beyond what we do there, the following question could be investigated: What do various communities, taken one by one, teach their members about doctrines of various other religious communities, and especially what sorts of arguments against doctrines of other communities do these communities encourage or permit? But we shall not venture far into that territory.

CHAPTER SEVEN

Doctrines and
Alien Claims I

ALIEN CLAIMS

A claim that what is proposed in some assertion is true, or that some course of action is right, is an alien claim, with respect to some community, if and only if what is proposed in the claim is not an authentic doctrine of that community. So as we study positions a community might take on alien claims, we are dealing with external relations of bodies of doctrines. In contrast, in chapter 3 we were dealing with some internal relations of bodies of doctrines, with relations of members of a body of doctrines to one another, in particular with orderings of them in importance and their consistency.

Some alien claims are doctrines of other religious communities. But it may turn out that what is said in a doctrine of some community is also said in a doctrine of some other religious community. This was argued in chapter 6. So it may happen that what is claimed in a doctrine of some other religious community is not, with respect to the community in question, an alien claim.

Some alien claims are secular claims, claims which are independent of the distinctive doctrines of any religious community. Here again it may happen that what is said in some secular claim is said also in an authentic doctrine of some religious community. So it may be that some secular claim is not, with respect to that community, an alien claim. Natural theology, along with equivalent enterprises in the reflective activities of nontheistic religious communities, is a case in point. In the teachings of some communities it seems to be supposed that some propositions and precepts which are authentic doctrines of the community can be reached also as conclusions of arguments which do not depend on the distinctive norms of any religious community.

So, though some alien claims are doctrines of other religious communities, and some alien claims are secular claims, the essential feature of a claim which is, with respect to some community, an alien claim, is that what is proposed in the claim is not an authentic doctrine of that community. This is not to say that what is proposed in the claim is inconsistent with authentic doctrines of that community; it may be consistent, or it may be inconsistent, with doctrines of that community.

No doubt there are doctrines of religious communities which are opposed to doctrines of other religious communities, though as we found in chapter 6 it is not always easy to locate such oppositions. Also, no doubt some secular claims are opposed to doctrines of various religious communities. Indeed, it would be strange if this were not so. For it is a familiar feature of the teaching activities of the major religious communities that they seem to suppose that they have to contend with various versions of worldly wisdom. They do not seem to take it for granted that the world to which they speak agrees with what they have to say. But the point to be made here is only that though alien claims, with respect to some community, are not doctrines of that community, it is not a part of the concept of an alien claim that an alien claim is inconsistent with doctrines of that community.

Alien claims arise most naturally outside the bounds of a community, in the teachings of other religious communities or in the course of secular inquiries of various sorts. But there is a sense in which claims arising within a community could be regarded as alien claims, if the community decides that what is claimed is not in accord with its principles and rules for authenticity. But these are in the first instance claims to authenticity, which were discussed in chapter 2. Sometimes failed claims to authenticity are treated as alien claims by the community in question. They are explained sometimes as aberrations arising from extraneous sources; for example, more orthodox Christians explained some of Origen's teachings as incursions of Platonism.

With the discussions in chapter 6 in hand, no further introduction to doctrines of different religious communities is needed. But something more should be said about secular claims. Among the topics of secular inquiries are various questions about what exists and the conditions of existence in the world or in some segment of it. In historical study, in the natural and social sciences, and in philosophy such questions are studied in sustained and methodical ways. But such questions occur, and answers to them are sought also in less methodical ways on countless occasions of common experience. A surgeon wants to know whether a scalpel is on the table in the operating room and whether it has been sterilized. A shopper wants to know the weight of a roast. True perceptual judgments and true reports are wanted. And in a multitude of such short and unsystematic inquiries, as well as in more extended and more complex inquiries, the process of finding out what one wants to know is carried on without reference to the distinctive standards of any religious community.

There are also secular inquiries as to the right way to attain some end in view. How does one go about making an efficient plow or maximizing the production of some crop? Rules of thumb may be used, or elaborate technologies may be developed. Furthermore, many practical inquiries have moral dimensions. What ends is it right to aim at in situations of various sorts or in life as a whole? In both sorts of cases practical inquiries often proceed without introducing distinctive norms of religious communities.

MAY THERE BE ALIEN CLAIMS WHICH ARE TRUE OR RIGHT?

Suppose we should set out to study the teachings of some religious community on relations of its doctrines to claims which arise outside its bounds and do not satisfy its criteria of authenticity. A threshold question for us to ask would be: Is the community in a position to grant that some such claims may be true or right even though they are not doctrines of its own? May there be truths and right courses of action which the community is not bound to teach? Could the community grant that there could be sentences such that (1) they do not express authentic doctrines of the community, and (2) what is said in them would turn out to be true or right? Or, on the contrary, would the community have to say that the assertions made in alien claims will turn out to be untrue and the courses of action proposed in practical alien claims will turn out to be not right?

A community's answer to this complex question would be a primary doctrine of that community. It would say something about the world in which the community finds itself; it would say whether a certain state of affairs holds or not. In developing its answer the community would be guided by its principles and rules for developing its doctrines, whatever these may be. They would include its criteria of authenticity, its principles of consistency, and its principles connecting claims to authenticity and claims to truth and to rightness.

First we need to put this question in its place. Notice that this would be a live question for a community only if the community has a doctrine patterned by schema A-T/R, which says that if a sentence is an authentic doctrine of the community, then what is said in that sentence is true or right. An A-T/R doctrine permits, though it does not require, an affirmative answer to our question. If on the other hand a community's position on the relation of authenticity to truth or rightness is patterned by schema T/R-A, then our question would not be a live question for that community. For a doctrine patterned by that schema would say that if what is said in some sentence is true or right, then that sentence expresses an authentic doctrine of that community. With such a doctrine there could be no alien claims which are true or right, for the reason that any sentence which is true or right is an authentic doctrine of the community, hence not an alien claim.

Let us place our question in some other ways. From the point of view of someone who is not a member of the community in question it might seem obvious that there could be many truths and right courses of action which that community could not be reasonably expected to teach. Of course, he might say, there not only may be, there are, many truths and right courses of action which have little or nothing to do with what that, or any other religious community for that matter, is supposed to teach, for example complex geometrical theorems and practical rules for operating computers. But we are not concerned with such reactions of individual persons just now; we want to find out something about doctrines, and options for doctrines, of religious communities themselves on this question.

Members of a religious community might also be surprised and puzzled by our question. Of course, it might be said, we learn many things about the world and about right behavior otherwise than from what our community teaches us. That is only natural. There are many things our teachers do not know. But, again, we are not concerned here with the competence of the teachers of a community or with the effectiveness of its teaching activity.

Furthermore, we would not be asking whether a community is in a position to assert of some particular alien claim that it is true or right. That would be a different and more problematical question. Indeed it seems to lead to a paradox. For it seems that if a community says that some proposition is true, then it is proposing that proposition for acceptance. Hence, it would seem, the proposition is, or is supposed to be, a doctrine of that community. Similarly, if a community says that some course of action is right, then it seems that the community is proposing that, in appropriate circumstances, the course of action should be undertaken and carried out. In a serious proposal the proposer puts his weight behind the proposal. But how could a religious community put its weight behind proposals which do not satisfy its own criteria of authenticity? So it seems that if a community proposes what is said in some claim, then what is being proposed is no longer an alien claim. A condition in our initial question has been annulled.

So we would not be asking whether the community in question is in a position to propose the beliefs and valuations and courses of action put forward in alien claims. We would ask only whether the community could grant that some alien claims may turn out to be true or right. Or, do its principles require it to say that in all cases what is proposed in an alien claim is untrue or wrong?

A community might be in a position to decide whether some alien claim is consistent or inconsistent with its doctrines. If it is known that the alien claim is inconsistent with its doctrines, then, we may suppose, the community would want to say that the claim is not true or right. This, as we will see later, supposes that the community has an extended principle of consistency as a governing doctrine. But if it is known that some alien claim is not inconsistent with doctrines of the community, the community is not thereby placed in a position to judge whether or not the claim is true or right.

In such cases members of the community would be free to judge whether the alien claim is true or right if they are competent to do so, even if the community itself is not in a position to do so. In taking the position we are considering, a community would acknowledge that there are propositions which it does not judge to be true and does not judge to be untrue, and courses of action which it does not judge to be right and does not judge to be wrong. It refrains from those appraisals insofar as alien claims are not inconsistent with its teachings.

If we add in these considerations about consistency, we have a three-cornered question to ask about a community's doctrines. We would be asking whether its principles and rules put the community in a position to grant the possibility of claims which (1) are not authentic doctrines of the community, (2) are not inconsistent with doctrines of the community, and (3) are true or right. Do the doctrines of the community admit a non-empty class of claims which have these features?

VALLA'S DISCOVERY

We need to develop this position further. Then we can return to the point about consistency. For help in developing the position, let us recall Lorenzo Valla's discovery, which we noticed in chapter 2 in a different connection. For a number of centuries Christians and others in western Europe had believed that the Emperor Constantine I had in a certain document, the *Constitutum Constantini*, granted to Pope Sylvester I and his successors temporal authority over western Europe. According to a modern historian this document

> was incorporated in the Pseudo-Isidorean Decretals when this collection was made in the middle of the ninth century. It was cited as authoritative by Ado of Vienne and Hincmar of Rheims. It was accepted in the collections of canon law by Anselm of Lucca, Cardinal Deusdedit, the so-called Ivo of Chartres, Hugo of Fleury, *de regia potestate et ecclesiastica dignitate* and, though omitted by Gratian himself, was soon put in his collection under the "palea." It was referred to as valid or used by many popes, including Leo IX, Urban II, Eugenius III, Innocent III, Gregory IX, Innocent IV, Nicholas III, Boniface VIII, and John XXII. Though Gregory VII apparently did not use it, his representative, Peter Damiani, did so. It may possibly have been in the mind of other popes who exacted oaths from prospective emperors that they would preserve all the rights and possessions granted by all previous emperors to the see of St. Peter, and may also have influenced Hadrian IV.
>
> It was accepted by the great majority of the writers of the Middle Ages, lawyers, historical writers, theologians. Even those who regretted it or denied

its validity, and opposed extension of papal power, for the most part did not question its genuineness. Dante's feelings on the subject were very strong, but he had no thought of denying that the donation had taken place.[1]

Then in 1440 Valla argued that the document was a forgery, and in time it came to be generally agreed by scholars that Valla was right. It is worth noting that in 1448 he was appointed to a position in the papal secretariat.

Our own interest in this matter may be put in the following way: If it should turn out that the doctrines of the Roman Catholic church permit it to grant that there may be alien claims which are true or right, what would be the status of Valla's conclusion relative to the teaching activity of the church?

Let us continue developing the position and its consequences abstractly, but now with the case of Valla in mind. The position can be restated as follows:

There may be sentences such that
(1) what is said in *s* is not an authentic doctrine of the community, and
(2) what is said in *s* is not inconsistent with authentic doctrines of the community, and
(3) what is said in *s* is true or right.

One interpretation of *s* would be Valla's conclusion:

The *Constitutum Constantini* is a forgery.

Another interpretation of *s* would be the practical sentence:

If it is suspected that some document is not what it purports to be, the origin of the document should be investigated.

This would be a maxim guiding Valla's course of action.

Now we ask: If a community takes this position, what would be the consequences for the teaching practices of that community? It seems that from (1) it would follow that the community is not bound to teach what is said in such a sentence. From (2) it seems to follow that the community is not bound to deny what is said in such a sentence. The more puzzling point is what consequences (3) would have for the teaching practices of the community. How should the community take note in its teaching activity of the possibility that such a sentence is true or right? How could the community explain itself on this point?

One line of explanation would run as follows. Presentations of doctrines of the community have objective contexts. Utterances of its doctrines are addressed to various groups of hearers and readers in various particular situations. So in its teaching activities the community has to take account of

1. Christopher Bush Coleman, *Constantine the Great and Christianity* (New York: Columbia University Press, 1914), pp. 178–79.

the objective contexts in which its presentations of its doctrines occur. Otherwise it may fail to convey to hearers and readers what it wants to convey. It has to take account of the stock of beliefs, assumptions, and practical intentions which, in given situations, hearers and readers may be presumed to have, especially those which, in the minds of hearers and readers, have some connection or other with doctrines of the community.

Suppose now that some secular claim such as Valla's conclusion plays a part in objective contexts of the community's teaching activities. In the minds of hearers and readers this claim has some relevance to doctrines of the community. Suppose that from the standpoint of the community this claim may be true or right. It is not inconsistent with doctrines of the community. But the community is not itself in a position to decide that what is claimed is true or right. Then do teachers in the community have some obligation with respect to this claim? It seems that they do.

If the community's position is that the claim may be true or right, then it seems that teachers in the community ought to attend to various obstructions in the minds of hearers and readers to acceptance of what is said in the claim. And it seems that they ought to give special attention to obstructions for which the community is responsible. It seems further that they have an obligation to do what can be done to remove the obstructions which the community has put, or allowed to stand, in the way of acceptance of the claim. This would be a matter of justice.

What would be the ground of this obligation? We are supposing that the community has a doctrine patterned by schema A–T/R. It teaches that if some sentence expresses an authentic doctrine of the community, then what is said in that sentence is true or right. Then does it not have a stake in situations where its own past activities have resulted in obstructions to acceptance of some secular sentence which may be true or right? Would there not be a dissonance between (1) the community's claiming that its own doctrines are true or right and (2) its role in allowing obstructions to acceptance of secular sentences which, it acknowledges, may be true or right? If the community takes its own claims to truth and rightness seriously, should it not treat other claims to truth and rightness with due respect?

Coming back to the Donation of Constantine, one obstruction to acceptance of Valla's conclusion would be an assumption that it is inconsistent with doctrines of the church. The fact that important teachers of the church had accepted the *Constitutum Constantini* as genuine would encourage this assumption. So, in situations where the Donation is mentioned by teachers of the church in the course of their teaching activities, they would have an obligation to make it clear that Valla's conclusion is not inconsistent with doctrines of the church.

In doing so these teachers would be honoring condition (2) of the position which, we are supposing, their community takes. But should they not also go further? For condition (3) does not follow from condition (2) any more than condition (2) follows from condition (2). Just as "s is not inconsistent with doctrines of the community" does not follow from "s is not an authentic doctrine of the community," so "s is true or right" does not follow from "s is not inconsistent with doctrines of the community." So it seems that teachers of the community would have further obligations, going beyond the obligation to make it clear that s is not inconsistent with its doctrines. What would these be? What further obstructions to acceptance of s would they be obligated to consider?

Would historical explanations of obstructions to accepting s be appropriate? Would teachers of the community be obligated to mention arguments for accepting s? (Mentioning arguments is not giving them.) Would accounts of arguments call for appraisals of the arguments? Here a problem might arise. By entering upon such explanations and accounts of arguments, would those teachers be embarking on a course which would end by immersion in secular historical questions or, if s is a practical sentence, in secular moral questions? This question might well trouble a religious community. It might have to take account of limitations on the competence of its teachers in dealing with such questions.

However that may be, if a community recognizes the possibility of truths and right actions which it is not bound to teach, it is obligated to leave room in the minds of hearers and readers for recognition and acceptance of such truths and courses of action, though it does not itself teach them. So we ask again what other obstructions to accepting s there might be besides inhibitions arising from an assumption that s is inconsistent with doctrines of the community.

ARE ONLY THE DOCTRINES OF THE COMMUNITY TRUE OR RIGHT?

One assumption which would need attention is an assumption that only the doctrines of the community are true or right. This assumption, which directly counters the position we are considering, would be a powerful obstruction to recognition and acceptance by its members of truths and right actions which the community is not bound to teach. How could this obstruction be removed or diminished? To put it another way, how could a community's own doctrine which, we are supposing, says that there may be truths and right courses of action which the community is not bound to teach, be further implemented and supported in the face of an assumption, in the minds of hearers and readers, that only the doctrines of the community are true or right?

This assumption is clearly not a commonsense assumption, nor does it arise naturally in the course of any secular inquiry. It arises rightly or wrongly in the experience of members of a community. Since they have learned something of great value from the community, their expectations of what the community can teach them grow beyond the limits set, we are supposing, by the community itself. So the main response of the community to this assumption would have to proceed by explaining limitations on the scope of its teachings.

We shall consider this point, and a problem to which it gives rise—a problem about the comprehensiveness of the teachings of a community, in chapter 8. But before going further in that direction we should pause for a brief reflection. We have been considering, as a possible doctrine of a religious community, the position that there may be truths and right courses of action which the community is not bound to teach. We have been considering some consequences of such a doctrine. But consideration of these consequences does not amount to an argument that religious communities should adopt such a doctrine. Indeed, consideration of these and other consequences might dispose some community to refrain from adopting such a doctrine, or to adopt a position opposed to it. In this matter as in other matters a community has to begin by asking what, in view of its criteria of authenticity, its doctrines ought to be if it is to be true to itself.

So we may suppose that if a community grants that there may be alien claims which are true or right, it has some warrant for teaching this doctrine. Further, we may suppose that its warrant for the doctrine is drawn from the community's sources in accord with its principles. We may suppose that the community has reason to think that the doctrine satisfies its criteria of authenticity, whatever these may happen to be.

We may suppose also that the community could draw upon its primary doctrines for an explanation of the possibility that alien claims may be true or right. Such explanations would have to do with the powers of human minds, with the course of human history, with the status of the natural world as the setting for human life, with the activity of God in the natural world and in human history, or with some other way of explaining how there may be truths and right courses of action which are not authentic doctrines of the community itself.

It may be that a community which grants that there may be such truths and right actions would have to acknowledge that there are criteria of truths and of right actions which are not just its own. We shall explore this point further later in this chapter.

On the other hand it may be that some community would find that these considerations, or some of them, would stand in the way of adopting and maintaining as a doctrine the position that there may be alien claims which are true or right.

NOSTRA AETATE

So far, in developing the position that there may be alien claims which are true or right, we have considered secular alien claims, taking Valla's conclusion as a case in point. But alien claims arise also as doctrines of other religious communities, and these present problems for a religious community which are different from the problems posed by secular alien claims. This may be evident already from our study of the prima facie Buddhist practical doctrine and the prima facie Christian practical doctrine in chapter 6.

Secular alien claims, arising from ordinary experience and commonsense reasoning, from historical studies, from mathematics and logic, from natural and social sciences, from philosophical studies, and otherwise, do not ordinarily confront a religious community with comprehensive patterns of life alternative to its own and with a range and depth comparable to its own. Doctrines of other religious communities do this. They challenge the doctrines of a religious community more directly and more deeply than secular alien claims ordinarily do. So it would not be surprising if a religious community should, in its doctrines bearing on alien claims, discriminate between secular claims and doctrines of other religious communities.

For this reason we ought to consider a case where a religious community puts forward doctrines about the doctrines of other religions. The Second Council of the Vatican has spoken for the Roman Catholic church on this topic in the document *Nostra Aetate,* dated 28 October 1965.[2] The title given in the translation is *Declaration on the Relation of the Church to Non-Christian Religions.* I give the full text, omitting only three footnote references. Then I comment on some points which are relevant to our own inquiry.

> 1. In this age of ours, when men are drawing more closely together and the bonds of friendship between different peoples are being strengthened, the Church examines with greater care the relation which she has to non-Christian religions. Ever aware of her duty to foster unity and charity among individuals, and even among nations, she reflects at the outset on what men have in common and what tends to promote fellowship among them.
>
> All men form but one community. This is so because all stem from the one stock which God created to people the entire earth (cf. Acts 17:26), and also because all share a common destiny, namely God. His providence, evident goodness, and saving designs extend to all men (cf. Wis. 8:1; Acts 14:17; Rom. 2:6–7; 1 Tim. 2:4) against the day when the elect are gathered together in the holy city which is illumined by the glory of God, and in whose splendor all peoples will walk (cf. Apoc. 21:23 ff.).
>
> Men look to their different religions for an answer to the unsolved riddles of human existence. The problems that weigh heavily on the hearts of men are the same today as in the ages past. What is man? What is the meaning and purpose of life? What is upright behavior, and what is sinful? Where does suffering originate, and what end does it serve? How can genuine happiness be found? What happens at death? What is judgment? What reward follows death? And finally, what is the ultimate mystery, beyond human explanation,

2. Trans. Fr. Killian, O.C.S.O., in *Documents of Vatican II,* ed. Austin P. Flannery (Grand Rapids: Eerdmans, 1975), pp. 738–42. Used by permission of the Wm. B. Eerdmans Publishing Company, Grand Rapids, Michigan.

which embraces our entire existence, from which we take our origin and towards which we tend?

2. Throughout history even to the present day, there is found among different peoples a certain awareness of a hidden power, which lies behind the course of nature and the events of human life. At times there is present even a recognition of a supreme being, or still more of a Father. This awareness and recognition results in a way of life that is imbued with a deep religious sense. The religions which are found in more advanced civilizations endeavor by way of well-defined concepts and exact language to answer these questions. Thus, in Hinduism men explore the divine mystery and express it both in the limitless riches of myth and the accurately defined insights of philosophy. They seek release from the trials of the present life by ascetical practices, profound meditation and recourse to God in confidence and love. Buddhism in its various forms testifies to the essential inadequacy of this changing world. It proposes a way of life by which men can, with confidence and trust, attain a state of perfect liberation and reach supreme illumination either through their own efforts or by the aid of divine help. So, too, other religions which are found throughout the world attempt in their own ways to calm the hearts of men by outlining a program of life covering doctrines, moral precepts and sacred rites.

The Catholic Church rejects nothing of what is true and holy in these religions. She has a high regard for the manner of life and conduct, the precepts and doctrines which, although differing in many ways from her own teaching, nevertheless often reflect a ray of that truth which enlightens all men. Yet she proclaims and is in duty bound to proclaim without fail, Christ who is the way, the truth and the life (Jn. 14:6). In him, in whom God reconciled all things to himself (2 Cor. 5:18–19), men find the fulness of their religious life.

The Church, therefore, urges her sons to enter with prudence and charity into discussion and collaboration with members of other religions. Let Christians, while witnessing to their own faith and way of life, acknowledge, preserve and encourage the spiritual and moral truths found among non-Christians, also their social life and culture.

3. The Church has also a high regard for the Muslims. They worship God, who is one, living and subsistent, merciful and almighty, the Creator of heaven and earth, who has also spoken to men. They strive to submit themselves without reserve to the hidden decrees of God, just as Abraham submitted himself to God's plan, to whose faith Muslims eagerly link their own. Although not acknowledging him as God, they worship Jesus as a prophet, his virgin Mother they also honor, and even at times devoutly invoke. Further, they await the day of judgment and the reward of God following the resurrection of the dead. For this reason they highly esteem an upright life and worship God, especially by way of prayer, alms-deeds and fasting.

Over the centuries many quarrels and dissensions have arisen between Christians and Muslims. The sacred Council now pleads with all to forget the past, and urges that a sincere effort be made to achieve mutual understanding; for the benefit of all men, let them together preserve and promote peace, liberty, social justice and moral values.

4. Sounding the depths of the mystery which is the Church, this sacred Council remembers the spiritual ties which link the people of the New Covenant to the stock of Abraham.

The Church of Christ acknowledges that in God's plan of salvation the beginning of her faith and election is to be found in the patriarchs, Moses and the prophets. She professes that all Christ's faithful, who as men of faith are sons of Abraham (cf. Gal. 3:7), are included in the same patriarch's call and that the salvation of the Church is mystically prefigured in the exodus of God's chosen people from the land of bondage. On this account the Church cannot forget that she received the revelation of the Old Testament by way of that people with whom God in his inexpressible mercy established the ancient covenant. Nor can she forget that she draws nourishment from that good olive tree onto which the wild olive branches of the Gentiles have been grafted (cf. Rom. 11:17–24). The Church believes that Christ who is our peace has through his cross reconciled Jews and Gentiles and made them one in himself (cf. Eph. 2:14–16).

Likewise, the Church keeps ever before her mind the words of the apostle Paul about his kinsmen: "they are Israelites, and to them belong the sonship, the glory, the covenants, the giving of the law, the worship, and the promises; to them belong the patriarchs, and of their race according to the flesh, is the Christ." (Rom. 9:4–5), the son of the virgin Mary. She is mindful, moreover, that the apostles, the pillars on which the Church stands, are of Jewish descent, as are many of those early disciples who proclaimed the Gospel of Christ to the world.

As holy Scripture testifies, Jerusalem did not recognize God's moment when it came (cf. Lk. 19:42). Jews for the most part did not accept the Gospel; on the contrary, many opposed the spreading of it (cf. Rom. 11:28). Even so, the apostle Paul maintains that the Jews remain very dear to God, for the sake of the patriarchs, since God does not take back the gifts he bestowed or the choice he made. Together with the prophets and that same apostle, the Church awaits the day, known to God alone, when all people will call on God with one voice and "serve him shoulder to shoulder" (Soph. 3:9; cf. Is. 66:23; Ps. 65:4; Rom. 11:11–32).

Since Christians and Jews have such a common spiritual heritage, this sacred Council wishes to encourage and further mutual understanding and appreciation. This can be obtained, especially, by way of biblical and theological enquiry and through friendly discussions.

Even though the Jewish authorities and those who followed their lead pressed for the death of Christ (cf. John 19:6), neither all Jews indiscriminately at that time, nor Jews today, can be charged with the crimes committed during his passion. It is true that the Church is the new people of God, yet the Jews should not be spoken of as rejected or accursed as if this followed from holy Scripture. Consequently, all must take care, lest in catechizing or in preaching the Word of God, they teach anything which is not in accord with the truth of the Gospel message or the spirit of Christ.

Indeed, the Church reproves every form of persecution against whomsoever it may be directed. Remembering, then, her common heritage with the Jews and moved not by any political consideration, but solely by the religious motivation of Christian charity, she deplores all hatreds, persecutions, displays of antisemitism leveled at any time or from any source against the Jews.

The Church always held and continues to hold that Christ out of infinite love freely underwent suffering and death because of the sins of all men, so that all might attain salvation. It is the duty of the Church, therefore, in her preaching to proclaim the cross of Christ as the sign of God's universal love and the source of all grace.

5. We cannot truly pray to God the Father of all if we treat any people in other than brotherly fashion, for all men are created in God's image. Man's relation to God the Father and man's relation to his fellow-men are so dependent on each other that the Scripture says "he who does not love, does not know God" (1 Jn. 4:8).

There is no basis therefore, either in theory or in practice for any discrimination between individual and individual, or between people and people arising either from human dignity or from the rights which flow from it.

Therefore, the Church reproves, as foreign to the mind of Christ, any discrimination against people or any harassment of them on the basis of their race, color, condition in life or religion. Accordingly, following the footsteps of the holy apostles Peter and Paul, the sacred Council earnestly begs the Christian faithful to "conduct themselves well among the Gentiles" (1 Pet. 2:12) and if possible, as far as depends on them, to be at peace with all men (cf. Rom. 12:18) and in that way to be true sons of the Father who is in heaven (cf. Mt. 5:45).

It becomes evident that the document does not address directly the question we have been raising about doctrines and alien claims. But we can learn something from it, not least from this very fact. A religious community has to go about its business in its own way. Still, we can ask our own questions about what it says. Before we do, notice some other features of the document.

After a preamble it begins with some Christian doctrines. "All men form but one community." Other doctrines are given as reasons why this is so: God's creation of the world, his providence, his goodness, and his saving designs. This already signals that the council wishes members of the church to think first and foremost of the individual persons who are members of other religious communities, and only in second place at most of those communities as organized bodies.

This is particularly noticeable with respect to Muslims and Jews. The Muslim community is not mentioned. The term *Judaism* does not occur in the document, though it occurs in a postconciliar document[3] produced by a commission instituted by the pope "to encourage and foster religious relations between Jews and Catholics." (*Guidelines*, p. 749.) Instead of speaking of the Judaic community or of Israel as a people, *Nostra Aetate* speaks

3. Commission on Religious Relations with the Jews: *Guidelines on Religious Relations with the Jews*, in Flannery, ed., *Documents of Vatican II*, pp. 743–49.

of the stock of Abraham, or of the people of the ancient covenant or, usually, as in the title of the guidelines, of Jews. (There are historical references
to "Jerusalem," which "did not recognize God's moment when it came,"
and to the Jewish authorities and those who followed them.)

Some parts of the document may be characterized as phenomenological
accounts of various forms of religious consciousness and aspirations. There
is also a faint echo of Father Schmidt's theory of a primitive monotheism.
And it speaks of the concepts and language in which religions in advanced
civilizations endeavor to answer religious questions. Hinduism, and Buddhism in its various forms, are mentioned here [2].[4]

The document expresses the Church's high regard for individual members of other religious communities and their ways of life, and in that connection various practical recommendations are addressed to Christians.
Christians are urged to enter into discussion with members of other religious communities, with a view to mutual understanding, and into collaboration with them. The church reproves all religious persecution and
discrimination. It begs Christians to live in peace with all men. These
practical doctrines are all based on Christian grounds.

Throughout it is made clear that the church is in duty bound to proclaim
Christ as the way, the truth, and the life. In him men find the fullness of
their religious life. So in discussions with members of other religious communities, Christians should witness to their own faith and way of life.

But our own concern is what the document has to say about the doctrines of other religious communities, rather than what it has to say about
how Christians should deal with individual members of them. Notice by
the way that the doctrines of other communities with which *Nostra Aetate*
is concerned are their primary doctrines, their doctrines about the setting
of human life and the conduct of life in that setting. It seems that the document does not mention doctrines of other communities about their own
bodies of doctrines, their principles and rules for shaping and regulating
their bodies of doctrines, the doctrines on which we focus in this study.

It is true that in a body of doctrines, primary doctrines and governing
doctrines are related to one another. For example it seems that a primary
doctrine about the Qur'ān, saying that it was sent down by Allah, could
be brought forward in support of Muslim principles of authenticity. This
primary doctrine would support inclusion, among Muslim criteria of authenticity, of the condition that what is said in some sentence in question
is clearly taught in the Qur'ān. Or, the doctrine that the Qur'ān was sent
down by Allah could be advanced in support of a Muslim principle of internal consistency. Taken together with various suppositions, the fact that
the Qur'ān was sent down by Allah would assure the reliability and the

4. Bracketed numerals refer to sections in the text of *Nostra Aetate*.

consistency of doctrines drawn from the Qur'ān. But the distinction between primary doctrines and governing doctrines would still hold.

We can advance our own inquiry by asking a series of questions.

1. Does the document say or imply that some of the doctrines of other religions may be true or right? It seems quite clear that it does. This comes out at a number of points.

The church rejects nothing of what is true and holy in other religions. Their precepts and doctrines often reflect a ray of that truth which enlightens all men [2]. In view of John 1:9, which this seems to allude to but does not mention, it seems fair to suppose that "that truth" refers to the truth revealed in Christ.

Again, Christians should acknowledge, preserve, and encourage the spiritual and moral truths found among non-Christians, also their social life and culture [2]. (Incidentally, does the last phrase hint that some secular claims arising in non-Christian cultures might be true or right?)

The document speaks with evident approval of a number of Muslim beliefs and practices [3]. Also, in a discussion of the historical debts of the church to the Jews, the stock of Abraham, it mentions that the church received the revelation of the Old Testament by way of that people [4].

But is this sufficient to show us a doctrine about the doctrines of other religions which are alien claims? Clearly it is not. For it seems that in every case those doctrines of other religions which are mentioned with approval in the document are also doctrines of the Catholic community. Hence it is possible that "the spiritual and moral truths found among non-Christians" are also Catholic doctrines, hence not alien claims. If so, that phrase would not refer to those doctrines of other religions which are not also Catholic doctrines and hence are, with respect to the Catholic community, alien claims.

2. Does the document say of any of the distinctive doctrines of other religions, doctrines which are not also Catholic doctrines, that it is true or right?

It seems clear that the document does not say of any particular distinctive doctrine of some other religion that it is true or right. But is this surprising? On what basis could a religious community, speaking for itself, say of some sentence which does not satisfy its own criteria of authenticity, and hence is not one of its own doctrines, that what is said in that sentence is true or right?

In any case the position we have been considering does not require this. Granting that there may be alien claims which are true or right does not require a community to go further and single out some alien claim or other as true or right. All the position requires is that the community should leave room for such alien claims.

3. Does the document say that none of the distinctive doctrines of other

religions, doctrines which are not also Catholic doctrines and hence are alien claims, are true or right?

As far as I can see, the document does not explicitly adopt the principle that none of the distinctive doctrines of other religions is true or right. It does not seem to teach that no doctrine of another religion is true or right unless that doctrine is also a doctrine of the Catholic community.

If the document did take this position, then it would clearly exclude the position we have been considering. This would be evidence, whether or not conclusive, that the Catholic community does not grant that there may be alien claims which are true or right, at least not with respect to alien claims which are doctrines of other religions. The document does not seem to give us such evidence.

On this point consider the following. We are told that the "precepts and doctrines" of other religions differ in many ways from the teaching of the church [2]. Now if we had reason to suppose that the fathers of the council thought that all doctrines of other religions which differ from Catholic doctrines are inconsistent with Catholic doctrines, this would give us an answer to our question.

But the document gives us no reason to suppose that the thoughts of the fathers of the council ran in that direction. We are not told that all those doctrines of other religions which differ from Catholic doctrines are inconsistent with them. And there seems no good reason to suppose that the fathers were unaware of the distinction between differences and inconsistencies, or that they were confusing one of these sorts of relations with the other.

Later on we shall have occasion to notice some pronouncements of Vatican II on secular claims. From these it will be clear that the council did not take the position that no secular claims are true or right unless they are also doctrines of the Catholic community. With respect to secular claims, it seems that the council took the position that alien claims of that sort may be true or right. There may be secular alien claims which are not inconsistent with Catholic doctrines. Of such claims, it seems, the council had no special reason to say that they are not true or not right.

We would not be warranted in concluding from the council's pronouncements on secular claims that it would, or that it should, take a parallel position on doctrines of other religions. We have noticed an important difference between the problems posed for a religious community by secular claims and the problems posed by doctrines of other religions.

We have been developing a question which could be asked about bodies of doctrines taken one by one. For each case the question would be whether the doctrines of the community permit it to take a certain position with respect to alien claims. This position would be that there may be claims (1) which are not authentic doctrines of the community, (2) which are not inconsistent with doctrines of the community, and (3) which are true or right.

Nostra Aetate gives us an opportunity to ask our question: Does the document grant, with respect to doctrines of other religious communities, that there may be alien claims which are true or right? What can we conclude from our discussion?

It seems clear that the document does not take the position we have been considering. We are not told that some doctrines of other religious communities which are not also doctrines of the Catholic community may be true or right. It seems clear also that the document does not exclude this position. We are not told that no doctrines of other religious communites are true or right unless they are also doctrines of the Catholic community. So, since the document neither endorses nor rejects the position, it seems to leave the way open for the Catholic community to consider it further. Perhaps the fathers of the council meant to leave the question on the theological agenda of the community.

EXTENDED PRINCIPLES OF CONSISTENCY

If a community takes the position that there may be alien claims which are true or right, then it would need, along with a principle of internal consistency, an extended principle of consistency. We should consider how this is so and what some of its consequences are.

Recall that the schema for principles of internal consistency is as follows:

For any pair of sentences *(s1, s2)*, if
(1) s1 is an authentic doctrine of the community, and
(2) s2 is an authentic doctrine of the community, then s1 and s2 are consistent.
Hence, if s1 and s2 are inconsistent, then
(1) s1 is not an authentic doctrine of the community, or
(2) s2 is not an authentic doctrine of the community, or
(3) neither s1 nor s2 is an authentic doctrine of the community.

Some reminders: "*s* is a doctrine" abbreviates "*s* expresses a doctrine" or "what is proposed in *s* is a doctrine." "*s1* and *s2* are consistent" abbreviates "what is proposed in *s1* and what is proposed in *s2* are consistent."

As we saw in chapter 3, ordinarily doctrines patterned by this schema are supposed, if not explicitly taught, by the teaching practices of religious communities. Ordinarily a community is ready and willing to defend the consistency of its authentic teachings with one another, even though it recognizes that there are problematical cases.

It is evident from the schema that such doctrines deal only with internal consistency. The condition for consistency is the authenticity of the sentences. So these doctrines apply only to cases where, if there are inconsistencies, the problematical element is the authenticity of the sentences.

Notice that the schema does not introduce the expression "true or right." This expression was introduced in chapter 4, where we considered principles which connect claims to authenticity with claims to truth or rightness. And now in this chapter, supposing that some community adopts the principle that its authentic doctrines are true or right, we have been considering, as a further possible doctrine of such a community, the position that there may be truths and right courses of action which are not authentic doctrines of the community but alien claims. There may be alien claims which are true or right.

As we have seen, a community could not be expected to adopt this position unless it holds that, if some alien claim is true or right, then what is proposed in the claim is consistent with its authentic doctrines. So, to cover such cases, an extended principle of consistency is required. A principle of internal consistency would not cover such cases, for in cases where alien claims are involved, if inconsistencies occur, the authenticity of the sentences would not be the only problematical element; the truth or rightness of the sentences would also be a problematical element. So in this respect the schema for extended principles of consistency would have to be more complex than the schema for principles of internal consistency.

The schema for extended principles of consistency would have to be as follows:

For any pair of sentences *(s1, s2)*, if
(1) *s1* is an authentic doctrine of the community (hence true, or right), and
(2) *s2* is not an authentic doctrine of the community, then if *s2* is true, or right, *s1* and *s2* are consistent.
Hence, if *s1* and *s2* are inconsistent, then
(1) *s1* is not an authentic doctrine of the community, or
(2) *s2* is not true, or right, or
(3) both (1) and (2) hold.

To put this principle in perspective, consider some conditions under which a community would have no need for it. Suppose (a) that a community refuses to take notice, in the course of its teaching activity, of doctrines of other religious communities or of secular claims. Thus it does not take notice of alien claims. Then it seems that the only claims which would concern it would be claims that various sentences express, or do not express, authentic doctrines of the community, and these claims about authenticity would have to be judged by reference to the community's principles and rules for identifying its doctrines. Then the only principle of consistency it would need would be a principle of internal consistency.

Or suppose (b) that a community holds and teaches a doctrine which says that all alien claims are untrue or not right. Then it would have no need of an extended principle of consistency. The cases to which an extended principle of consistency would be relevant would have been decided already by a short cut, by its doctrine that all alien claims are untrue or not right.

Or suppose (c) that a community does not claim that its own doctrines are true or right. It claims only that they are authentic. It does not adopt an A-T/R doctrine. Then again it would have no need for an extended principle of consistency.

So a religious community needs an extended principle of consistency, along with a principle of internal consistency, only if (1) it takes notice in its teaching activity of doctrines of other religions which differ from its own, or of secular claims which differ from its own doctrines, and (2) it grants that there may be alien claims which are true or right, and (3) it claims that its own doctrines are, if they are authentic, true or right. This last condition has been built into the schema: "(hence true or right)".

This helps to explain an obvious contrast between the schema for principles of internal consistency and the schema for extended principles of consistency. The terms *true* and *right* do not occur in the schema for principles of internal consistency; they do occur in the schema for extended principles of consistency.

Clearly doctrines which express extended principles of consistency rely on general principles of consistency. General principles of consistency do not depend on the distinctive standards of any religious community. They are secular claims. Some such principles could be stated as follows:

For any pair of sentences *(s1, s2)*
(1) If *s1* expresses a proposition, and that proposition is true, and *s2* expresses a different proposition, and that proposition is true, then *s1* and *s2* are consistent.
(2) If *s1* expresses a proposal for a course of action, and that course of action is right, and *s2* expresses a proposal for a different course of action, and that course of action is right, then *s1* and *s2* are consistent.
(3) If *s1* expresses a proposition, and that proposition is true, and *s2* expresses a proposal for a course of action, and that course of action is right, then *s1* and *s2* are consistent.

Do doctrines which embody principles of internal consistency also depend on such general principles of consistency? It is not clear that they do. It is reasonably clear that a religious community could give reasons in support of its principle of internal consistency, but it is not clear that in doing so it would have to rely on such general principles of consistency as these.

For example, in the passage from the *Mahāparinibbānasutta* we studied in chapter 2, one of the conditions for acceptable reports of sayings of the Buddha was that a reported saying must be consistent with what the Buddha is already known to have said. This seems to suppose that genuine sayings of the Buddha, and hence authentic doctrines of the Buddhist community, are consistent with one another. This would be a principle of internal consistency. But would the Buddhist community have to appeal to a general principle of consistency as a reason for adopting this principle? A different reason would lie nearer at hand: the Buddha would not teach something inconsistent with what he has otherwise taught.

Similarly, a principle of internal consistency seems implicit in Muslim teachings about traditions as to what Muhammad said and did (hadīth). Confronted with apparently inconsistent traditions, a Muslim scholar would have to examine the provenance of the traditions and their relation to what is said in the Qur'ān, to see whether they are genuine or not. The most natural reason for the Muslim community to give for the principle of internal consistency which is supposed here would be that the Prophet could be relied on not to speak inconsistently.

Again, when it is held that the teachings of the Bible are consistent with one another, and hence that those doctrines of the Judaic community which are rightly derived from the Bible are consistent with one another, it is not clear that this position would have to be supported by general principles of consistency. A reason is more immediately available: the Bible contains the Word of God, and the Word of God cannot be opposed to itself.

In contrast, it seems that doctrines which embody extended principles of consistency, patterned by the schema set out above, do depend on general principles of consistency. The schema covers both consistencies of (1) sentences which express doctrines of religious communities and (2) sentences which express alien claims. So general principles of consistency seem to be supposed. Hence the kinds of reasons given for principles of internal consistency, in the cases we have noticed, would not be sufficient for doctrines which give extended principles of consistency.

Though a doctrine patterned by the schema for extended consistency would depend on general principles of consistency, it would not be generated by such principles. As we have seen, such doctrines depend also on doctrines which grant that there may be alien claims which are true or right. And they depend also on claims by communities that their authentic doctrines are true or right, that is to say, on A-T/R doctrines. So, even though a doctrine of extended consistency depends on general principles which can be defended as secular claims, this doctrine does not follow from those principles alone. It depends also on doctrines of the community which are not secular claims. The motive for adoption of a principle of extended consistency is generated by the community's own principles.

A similar point can be made about doctrines which express principles of internal consistency. Even if it could be shown that a community's doctrine about the consistency of its doctrines depends on general principles of consistency, it could not be shown that the doctrine is generated by such principles. For, though the notion of authenticity is essential for a doctrine of internal consistency, general principles of consistency do not speak of authenticity at all. Even with general principles of consistency, a community would still need the principle that its authentic doctrines are consistent with one another. General principles of consistency could not displace principles of internal consistency.

Consider further the dependence of doctrines of extended consistency on A-T/R doctrines, which say that authentic doctrines of a community are true or right. Suppose that a community, instead of adopting an A-T/R doctrine, adopts a doctrine patterned by schema T/R-A, which says that all sentences which are true or right are authentic doctrines of that community. Then it seems that an explicit principle of internal consistency would not be needed. If members of the community know, on the basis of general principles of consistency, that all truths and right courses of action are consistent with one another, that is all they need to know in order to be assured that the doctrines of the community are consistent with one another.

Also, it seems, this would leave no application for an extended principle of consistency. For, as we have seen, it would follow from a T/R-A doctrine that claims which are not authentic doctrines of the community are not true or not right. There could be no alien claims which are true or right. But the point of a doctrine of extended consistency is to put a community in a position to deal with consistencies and inconsistencies between its authentic doctrines and alien claims which may be true or right.

We should consider an objection against reliance by a religious community on general principles of consistency, hence against adoption of an extended principle of consistency, and hence against the position that there may be alien claims which are true or right. Related objections have hovered over our earlier discussions at various points, and they will be studied further as we go along, though it is not our own business to resolve them. Issues such as these would have to be resolved, insofar as they can be resolved, by particular religious communities speaking for themselves. Our own business is to investigate the issues and to consider some relevant arguments.

Spokesmen for some religious community might argue as follows. It seems that general principles of consistency are alien claims; they are not authentic doctrines of the community. So if the community adopts an extended principle of consistency, which depends on general principles of consistency, it places itself in a false position. It would be relying, indirectly, on principles not given in its sources. Thus it would go beyond its own limitations on the scope of its doctrines. It would make itself responsible for a position which it is not qualified to defend. So, to free itself from this false position, the community should cut the roots which produce this unwanted branch.

One root would be cut if the community should refuse to mention alien claims in the course of teaching its doctrines. Then there would be no occasion to say anything about them. The community would restrict itself to expounding its own doctrines without relating them to alien claims, and alien claims would not come into view in the course of teaching activities. Then the only principle of consistency needed would be a principle of internal consistency.

Or the community might take a different tack. Consideration of alien claims would be said to be worthless or even harmful. For example, it might be said that they distract the mind from following the path to enlightenment. No arguments would be offered against alien claims. For dialectical arguments against alien claims, to show they are self-inconsistent, would themselves rely on worldly principles; inductive arguments against them would have to begin with natural facts; and in arguments against them based on doctrines of the community, it seems that an extended principle of consistency would have to come into play. Thus arguments against alien claims would have the effect of enforcing the entanglement of the mind in worldly affairs, which is just what the wise man should seek to avoid.

Or the community might apply the blade to a still deeper root of what its spokesmen take to be a false position. It abstains from claiming that its doctrines are true or right in any sense which would hold also of alien claims. It thinks that authenticity is the most it can claim for its doctrines, and that this is enough. One consequence, which it would welcome, is that it would not have to apply general criteria of truth or rightness to its doctrines. It could still freely use the terms *true* and *right* and their equivalents in such ways as the following:

> This is the true doctrine.
> Beware of false teachers.
> Keep to the right way and do not turn aside from it.

But it would be understood that in the context of its teaching activities, "true" and "right" have the force of "authentic," and "false" and "wrong" have the force of "inauthentic."

This is not to say that the community would have to give some other semantic characterization of the force of its doctrines. It would not need to say, for example, that its doctrines only express feelings, attitudes, or convictions. The point is only that it abstains from characterizing them as true or right in any sense which goes beyond saying that they satisfy the community's criteria of authenticity. Then would the A-T/R principle, that if some sentence expresses an authentic doctrine of the community, then it is true or right, turn into a tautology, though perhaps a useful one?

The position would be that the community has its own criteria of authenticity, and these are all it needs. If it entangles itself in general criteria of truth and of rightness it will be led to stand on ground that is not its own. Adopting an extended principle of consistency would result in a confusion at the heart of its body of doctrines. Its doctrines would become mixed with alien elements which would weaken their force. If, in the case of a community which accepts the Bible as a source of its doctrines, opponents of this position should refer to the passage in Exodus about spoiling the Egyptians, defenders of the position would draw a lesson from the worship of the golden calf in the wilderness and ask: How does a community keep its doctrines from being corrupted by these spoils?

Now consider a different way a community might be able to look on its doctrines. This would involve a correction of the estimate of the initial situation from which the position laid out just above takes its start. That position supposes that the general principles of consistency are alien to the community. Hence reliance on them draws the community into a false position, a position which it is not authorized to defend and which it is incompetent to defend.

But, a community might be able to argue, is that supposition correct? Are the general principles of consistency really alien claims? Though they can be supported on grounds which are independent of the distinctive doctrines of the community, independent also of the distinctive doctrines of any other religious community, they are not alien to the community. Just as doctrines of other religious communities are not always alien to the community, since some doctrine of another community may happen to be an authentic doctrine of this community also, what is proposed in some secular claim may also happen to be an authentic doctrine of the community. Though it may be advanced as a secular claim, it may also be advanced as a doctrine of the community, since it satisfies the community's criteria of authenticity.

There are at least two ways in which general principles of consistency might be, so to speak, authenticated, two ways in which such secular claims might turn out to be authentic doctrines of a community also, and hence, with respect to that community, not alien claims. In such cases they would still be secular claims, since they could be defended without reference to the distinctive doctrines of any religious community, but they would not be, with respect to the community in question, alien claims. It might be argued that general principles of consistency have a basis in the sources of the community's doctrines. Or it might be argued that they are necessary suppositions of the community's teaching practices. Arguments of these different sorts may be compatible with one another.

(1) As a community studies the sources of its doctrines, i.e., its scriptures, the sayings of its learned and respected teachers, and whatever other sources of its doctrines it recognizes, it may discover that some general principle of consistency has been taught in them. Or it may discover that teachings derivable from its sources suppose this general principle of consistency and thus require it. Or it may discover that the teaching practices

of its founder or other authoritative teachers suppose this principle. Hence such principles are not alien to the community; they are part of its own heritage.

Or, (2) as the community reflects on its own past and current teaching practices, it may find that some general principle of consistency is a supposition of those practices. It might reason in this way: The community has been commissioned to teach its doctrines, not just to receive, contemplate, and reflect on them. Now the practices which are necessary to teach its doctrines suppose some general principle of consistency. The community cannot discharge its responsibility to teach its doctrines without relying on this principle. So the principle is thereby legitimated as a doctrine of the community.

If a community is in a position to authenticate general principles of consistency in either or both of these ways, then the obstacle to adopting an extended principle of consistency would be removed.

Also, a theistic community might defend an extended principle of consistency more directly in the following way. The sources of its teaching say that some truths about the natural world, and the rightness of some courses of action, can be apprehended independently of the distinctive doctrines of that or any other religious community. The explanation of this possibility is that God is the creator of the world, including human beings, and that he has endowed human beings with these abilities. So it seems that what human beings can learn about the natural world and about right actions by the right use of these abilities, independently of the distinctive doctrines of the community, must be consistent with the distinctive doctrines of the community. This seems to imply that if there are claims which are not authentic doctrines of the community, and these claims are true or right, then they are consistent with the authentic doctrines of the community. Perhaps there could be nontheistic arguments to a similar effect.

So, if a community is in a position to offer arguments such as these, then it could say that in adopting a doctrine which expresses an extended principle of consistency the community is not being drawn into a false position; it is being true to itself.

INCONSISTENCIES OF DOCTRINES AND ALIEN CLAIMS

In our discussions of principles of internal consistency in chapter 3 we considered problematical cases, cases where sentences which are taken to be authentic doctrines of a community appear to be inconsistent with one another. Now we are dealing with doctrines which express extended principles of consistency. So we must consider inconsistencies between doctrines and alien claims.

Suppose a community confronts a situation of the following sort: What is said in some sentence *(s1)*, which is taken to be an authentic doctrine of the community, and what is said in some other sentence *(s2)*, which is taken to be an alien claim, appear to be inconsistent. Suppose further that the community claims that its authentic doctrines are true or right, and that it has an extended principle of consistency. Then for this community the possible outcomes of the situation would be as follows:

I. The inconsistency of the sentences is only apparent. The sentences are really consistent with one another; both could be true or right.
II. The sentences are really inconsistent with one another. It could be that one or the other is true or right, or that both are untrue or not right. But it could not be that both are true or right. So either
   (a) *s1* is not an authentic doctrine of the community, or
   (b) *s2* is untrue or not right, or
   (c) both (a) and (b) hold.

For if *s1* is indeed an authentic doctrine of the community, the community is bound to say that it is true or right. And if it is also the case that *s2* is true or right, then the community would be bound to hold that *s1* and *s2* are consistent with one another. This would be in accord with a general principle of consistency which is built into the community's extended principle of consistency. So, if *s1* and *s2* are really inconsistent, not just apparently so, it must be that *s1* is not an authentic doctrine of the community, or that *s2* is not true or right, or that both of these are the case.

Notice that the schema for extended principles of consistency specifies that one of the sentences in question is an authentic doctrine of the community and that the other is not. One of the sentences is an alien claim. But we should take account of the possibility that some sentence might be misidentified as an alien claim. It might happen that a sentence which has been taken to be an alien claim would turn out to be an authentic doctrine of the community. In that case an extended principle of consistency would not apply. Both the sentences in question would be authentic doctrines of the community. So what would be needed then would be a principle of internal consistency.

Often a community may not be in a position to decide whether the members of a pair of sentences are really inconsistent. Suppose the community is not in a position to decide whether a sentence is an authentic doctrine of the community. Suppose, for example, it is not clear whether the sentence can be rightly derived from the sources of the community's doctrines. Or perhaps there is not a clear consensus of the community on the authenticity of the sentence, one way or the other. Then the community would not be in a position to decide whether there is an inconsistency between an authentic doctrine and an alien claim.

Or, suppose, as it often happens, that the community is not in a position to decide whether or not some alien claim is true or right. Suppose, for example, that the alien claim is a complex theory in modern physics. Would the community be competent to decide whether the theory is true? In many such cases the best a community can do is to deal with the apparent inconsistency indirectly and hypothetically. It might be in a position to say that some other sentence (s3) is indeed inconsistent with its doctrines and hence, it must say, untrue or not right. So if, but only if, s3 follows from the alien claim, then the alien claim would be inconsistent with its doctrines. But if the community is not in a position to decide directly whether the alien claim is true or right, then it is not in a position to say outright whether, on that score, there is an inconsistency between a doctrine and the alien claim. Incidentally, notice that if a community takes this hypothetical tack it is granting tacitly that the alien claim may be true or right.

Another consequence of an extended principle of consistency should be noticed. If there is a real inconsistency between a sentence taken to be a doctrine of the community (s1) and a sentence taken to be an alien claim (s2), the inconsistency can be explained and, we might say, resolved, just as well by a conclusion that s1 is not an authentic doctrine of the community as by a conclusion that s2 is not true or not right. An extended principle of consistency does not tip the scale in favor of either conclusion. A community which confronts a situation of this sort has to weigh (1) what can be said for the authenticity of s1 against (2) what can be said for the truth or rightness of s2. But a community's adoption of an extended principle of consistency as a doctrine does not itself determine which way the community will cope with the inconsistency.

BELLARMINE AND THE COPERNICAN THEORY

Some passages in a letter from Robert Cardinal Bellarmine (1542–1621) to Paolo Antonio Foscarini, dated April 12, 1615, are relevant to some of these points. Foscarini, a Carmelite priest and a disciple of Galileo, had sent to Bellarmine an essay and a covering letter. In the essay Foscarini defended the Copernican theory of the relation to the earth of the sun. He argued that the theory is consistent with Christian doctrines. Bellarmine's reply (in full) was as follows.

> I have gladly read the letter in Italian and the essay in Latin that Your Reverence has sent me, and I thank you for both, confessing that they are filled with ingenuity and learning. But since you ask for my opinion, I shall give it to you briefly, as you have little time for reading and I for writing.
> First. I say that it appears to me that Your Reverence and Sig. Galileo did prudently to content yourselves with speaking hypothetically and not positively, as I have always believed Copernicus did. For to say that assuming the earth moves and the sun stands still saves all the appearances better than eccentrics and epicycles is to speak well. This has no danger in it, and it suf-

fices for mathematicians. But to wish to affirm that the sun is really fixed in the center of the heavens and merely turns upon itself without traveling from east to west, and that the earth is situated in the third sphere and revolves very swiftly around the sun, is a very dangerous thing, not only by irritating all the theologians and scholastic philosophers, but also by injuring our holy faith and making the sacred Scripture false. For Your Reverence has indeed demonstrated many ways of expounding the Bible, but you have not applied them specifically, and doubtless you would have had a great deal of difficulty if you had tried to explain all the passages that you yourself have cited.

Second. I say that, as you know, the Council (of Trent) would prohibit expounding the Bible contrary to the common agreement of the holy Fathers. And if Your Reverence would read not only all their works but the commentaries of modern writers on Genesis, Psalms, Ecclesiastes, and Joshua, you would find that all agree in expounding literally that the sun is in the heavens and travels swiftly around the earth, while the earth is far from the heavens and remains motionless in the center of the world. Now consider whether, in all prudence, the Church could support the giving to Scripture of a sense contrary to the holy Fathers and all the Greek and Latin expositors. Nor may it be replied that this is not a matter of faith, since if it is not so with regard to the subject matter, it is with regard to those who have spoken. Thus that man would be just as much a heretic who denied that Abraham had two sons and Jacob twelve, as one who denied the virgin birth of Christ, for both are declared by the Holy Ghost through the mouths of the prophets and apostles.

Third. I say that if there were a true demonstration that the sun was in the center of the universe and the earth in the third sphere, and that the sun did not go around the earth but the earth went around the sun, then it would be necessary to use careful consideration in explaining the Scriptures that seemed contrary, and we should rather have to say that we do not understand them than to say that something is false which had been proven. But I do not think there is any such demonstration, since none has been shown to me. To demonstrate that the appearances are saved by assuming the sun at the center and the earth in the heavens is not the same thing as to demonstrate that in fact the sun is in the center and the earth in the heavens. I believe that the first demonstration may exist, but I have very grave doubts about the second; and in case of doubt one may not abandon the Holy Scriptures as expounded by the holy Fathers. I add that the words *The sun also riseth, and the sun goeth down, and hasteth to the place where he ariseth* (Ecclesiastes 1:5) were written by Solomon, who not only spoke by divine inspiration, but was a man wise above all others, and learned in the human sciences and in the knowledge of all created things, which wisdom he had from God; so it is not very likely that he would affirm something that was contrary to demonstrated truth, or truth that might be demonstrated. And if you tell me that Solomon spoke according to the appearances, and that it seems to us that the sun goes round when the earth turns, as it seems to one aboard ship that the beach moves away, I shall answer thus. Anyone who departs from the beach, though to him it appears that the beach moves away, yet knows that this is an error and corrects it, seeing clearly that the ship moves and not the beach; but as to the sun and earth, no sage has needed to correct the error, since he clearly experiences that the earth stands still and that his eye is not deceived when it judges the sun to move, just as he is likewise not deceived when it judges that the moon and the stars move. And that is enough for the present.[5]

Bellarmine grants it is "excellent good sense" to say that "the celestial appearances" are explained better by the Copernican theory than by the Ptolemaic theory. Taking the theory as a hypothesis runs no risk of conflict with the Scripture. (In the usage Bellarmine was following, *hypothesis* connotes a disavowal of a claim to physical truth.) And taking it this way "suffices for mathematicians," as indeed Pierre Duhem would argue three hundred years later. (Bellarmine was misled into thinking that Copernicus proposed his theory only as a hypothesis. He was misled by a preface to the *De Revolutionibus* which, as it turned out later, and as Galileo was already convinced, was not written by Copernicus.)

If on the other hand the theory should be claimed to be true in fact, this would have the effect of "making the sacred Scripture false." For then the theory would be inconsistent with what is said in the Bible. The situation would be like those we have been discussing; there would be an inconsistency between a doctrine of a religious community and a claim which is not itself a doctrine of that community, between a doctrine and an alien claim. But, it would have to be said, this depends on whether the sentence with which the Copernican theory would be inconsistent is indeed an authentic doctrine of the Christian community. And that would depend on how the Bible is to be interpreted.

Bellarmine chides Foscarini for not applying to particular Scripture passages the methods of interpreting the Scriptures which, Foscarini had claimed, would show that the Copernican theory was consistent with Christian doctrines. The rule of interpretation to which Bellarmine appeals here is that an exposition of the Bible must not be contrary to a consensus of the fathers of the church. And, he says, the fathers do agree that the Bible teaches that the earth is motionless, the sun traveling around it.

Notice two comments on this point. One is from Galileo's *Letter to the Grand Duchess Christina,* which was written in 1615 but not published until 1636:

> Either the Fathers reflected upon this conclusion [i.e., the mobility of the earth] as controversial, or they did not; if not, then they cannot have decided anything about it even in their own minds, and their incognizance of it does not oblige us to accept teaching which they never imposed, even in intention. But if they had reflected upon and considered it, and if they judged it to be

---

5. *Discoveries and Opinions of Galileo,* trans. Stillman Drake (Garden City: Doubleday, 1957), pp. 162–64. Parenthetical phrases in brackets are supplied by the translator.

erroneous, then they would long ago have condemned it; and this they are not found to have done. [Drake, p. 203]

The other comment is by James Broderick, S.J., in his thoroughly revised biography of Bellarmine: "It would obviously be anachronistic and unfair to judge St. Robert Bellarmine's views on Scripture and the Fathers of the Church by the standards of modern Catholic biblical criticism, especially as developed since the publication of Pope Pius XII's encyclical *Divino Afflante Spiritu*, in 1943, curiously the fourth centenary of the publication of *De Revolutionibus Orbium Caelestium*."[6]

In a letter written in May 1615 to one of his friends Galileo said: "To me, the surest and swiftest way to prove that the position of Copernicus is not contrary to Scripture would be to give a host of proofs that it is true and that the contrary cannot be maintained at all; thus, since no two truths can contradict one another, this and the Bible must be perfectly harmonious." (Drake, p. 166)

Here Galileo appeals to a general principle of consistency: no two truths can contradict one another. And Bellarmine, in the final paragraph of his letter to Foscarini, seems to agree. Indeed he is so deeply convinced that proven truths are consistent with the teaching of the Scriptures that, he says, if there were a true demonstration that the earth goes around the sun, "then it would be necessary to use careful consideration in explaining the Scriptures that seemed contrary, and we should rather have to say that we do not understand them than to say that something is false which had been proven." (Drake, p. 164)

Clearly this grants that the Copernican theory may be true, and hence that there may be alien claims which are true, or right. The theory is not being ruled out from being true on the score that it is a secular claim. Nor is it being ruled out on the score that it is not a Christian doctrine but an alien claim. Bellarmine is sure that it is not a Christian doctrine, yet he seems to grant that it may be true. He even seems to grant that the Copernican theory could be demonstrated to be true, though he thinks there is not yet such a demonstration, "since none has been shown to me."

Furthermore, Bellarmine seems to grant that if the theory should turn out to be true it would be consistent with authentic Christian doctrines. His position seems to suppose an extended principle of consistency. Now a practical consequence of this principle would be as follows: if the theory is true, and if the Christian community has taught propositions contrary to it on the basis of what the Scriptures had been thought to say, then the community ought to re-examine those teachings to see whether they are indeed authentic Christian doctrines. In particular, the community ought

6. James Broderick, S.J., *Robert Bellarmine, Saint and Scholar* (London: Burns & Oates, 1961), p. 363.

to reconsider its principles and rules for interpreting the Scriptures. Bellarmine seems to agree to this. But he does not see how to understand what the Scriptures say if the Copernican theory is true and hence consistent with what the Scriptures say. In that case, perhaps as a last resort, we would have to confess that we do not understand the Scriptures.

In speaking of the stability of the earth and the motion of the sun, do the Scriptures propose theses in astronomical physics? Or do they sum up conclusions from ordinary perceptual experience? Apart from an allusion to Solomon's reputed learning in the human sciences Bellarmine does not address this pair of questions directly and explicitly. But he rejects the suggestion that Solomon spoke (only) "according to the appearances," and he defends the validity of ordinary perceptual experience of the sun in relation to the earth. He says that an ordinary observer "clearly experiences that the earth stands still and that his eye is not deceived when it judges the sun to move." His eye is not deceived. Just so, his opponents could say, adding that for an informed judgment on the Copernican theory other considerations have to be taken into account as well.

This case study illustrates some features of the argument which has been developed in this chapter. The argument may be restated as follows:

1. Suppose that among the governing doctrines of a community there is a doctrine which says that the authentic doctrines of the community are true or right.

2. Suppose that among the governing doctrines of this community there is also a principle of internal consistency which says that the authentic doctrines of the community are consistent with one another. So if there is a real inconsistency between the members of some pair of sentences, then both sentences cannot be authentic doctrines of the community.

3. Suppose that among the primary doctrines of the community there is a doctrine which says that there may be alien claims which are true or right. Thus there may be truths and right courses of action which the community is not bound to teach, since they are not authentic doctrines of the community.

4. Then it seems that this community would need to have, among its governing doctrines, an extended principle of consistency. This principle would say that if some alien claim is true or right, then what is said in the claim would be consistent with authentic doctrines of the community.

5. From an extended principle of consistency it would seem to follow that if there is a real inconsistency between the members of some pair of sentences, then it is not the case that one of the sentences is an authentic doctrine of the community and that the other sentence is an alien claim which is true or right.

Now suppose that this community is confronted with an apparent inconsistency between the members of a pair of sentences. One of the sentences, *(s1)*, has been taken to express an authentic doctrine of the community. The other sentence, *(s2)*, has been taken to express an alien claim and, let us suppose, does indeed express an alien claim; it is not an authentic doctrine of the community.

Then the community ought to distinguish and take note of both of two questions. The questions are: (1) whether or not what is said in *s1* is indeed an authentic doctrine of the community and (2) whether or not what is said in *s2* is indeed true or right.

The community would deal with the first question by considering and reconsidering its doctrines, including its governing doctrines. Among other points, it would consider its criteria of authenticity, its identification of the sources of its doctrines, and its principles and rules for interpreting what is said in the sources.

It would be spurred to these considerations and reconsiderations by the possibility, which it grants, that the alien claim may be true or right and by its acknowledgment, in its extended principle of consistency, that if the alien claim is true or right, then it is consistent with the authentic doctrines of the community. Hence the community would have a stake in questions about whether the alien claim is true or right.

But its stake in such questions would be limited. If the alien claim is not inconsistent with its authentic doctrines, it may be that the community itself would have no obligation arising from its own doctrines to go further, though it may have an obligation, arising from its primary doctrines, to encourage its members to employ their talents in inquiries to discover whether or not the claim is true or right. This last point will be discussed in the next chapter.

CHAPTER EIGHT

Doctrines and
Alien Claims II

LIMITS ON THE SCOPE OF PRIMARY DOCTRINES

In the last chapter we considered, as an option for doctrines of religious communities, the position that there may be truths and right courses of action which the community is not bound to teach: that there may be alien claims which are true, or right. A consequence would be that there are limits on the scope of the primary doctrines of the community. This consequence could be embodied in a principle which a community could adopt as a norm to guide the development of its body of doctrines: the scope of its primary doctrines is limited.

We considered a closely connected consequence in our discussion of Valla and the Donation of Constantine, a practical consequence for the teaching activities of a community. If a community grants that there may be alien claims which are true, or right, then teachers of that community would have an obligation to leave room for such claims in the minds of its members. In particular, if members of the community have assumed that only the authentic doctrines of the community are true or right, and hence that no alien claims are true or right, then these teachers ought to challenge that assumption. Now we return to that assumption to consider some responses which teachers of a community could make to it. Then later, since these responses imply limits on the scope of the primary doctrines of a community, we should consider an important objection to such limitations. The objection is that a community ought to develop a comprehensive pattern of life.

Against an assumption (perhaps naive) on the part of members of a community that there are no truths or right courses of action except those which are taught in the authentic doctrines of their community, various arguments could be advanced. Notice that both the assumption and the arguments against it have consequences for a community's doctrines about its doctrines. An underlying question is what a community's governing doctrines on the point at issue should be.

1. The community has a definite aim. It nurtures its members in a certain pattern of life. Built into this pattern is a certain end in view for human life, or more than one, for example liberation from worldly bonds, compassion for other beings, obedience to God, salvation from sin. There may be other ends which could be aimed at consistently with aiming at the end or ends the community proposes, but the community does not direct its members to those ends.

To attain the end or ends the community proposes it is necessary to know certain truths which are set forth in the proposals for belief and proposals of valuations which are constituents of its pattern of life. Likewise, it is necessary to undertake certain courses of action included in the pattern. But it is only those beliefs, valuations, and courses of action which are necessary to attain the end or ends presented in its pattern of life that the community is bound to teach.

Hence, the argument would go on to say, there may be true beliefs and valuations which the community is not bound to teach and its members are not bound to accept, for accepting those beliefs and valuations is not necessary to living out the pattern of life the community teaches. Likewise, there may be courses of action which are right, in general or in particular circumstances, which the community is not bound to teach. It is possible to live out the pattern without undertaking those courses of action.

For example, consider the *avyakata* questions, the questions the Buddha refused to answer, such as whether the world is eternal or not. "And why, Māluṅkyāputta, has this not been explained by me? It is because it is not connected with the goal, is not fundamental to the Brahma-faring, and does not conduce to turning away from [the world], nor to dispassion, stopping, calming, super-knowledge, awakening nor to nibbāna. Therefore it has not been explained by me, Māluṅkyāputta."[1] The reason given here for not answering the question is not that the Buddha was ignorant. Indeed, it is taught in some traditions that the Buddha was omniscient. The reason given is that knowing the answer would not conduce to attaining nibbāna. It follows that knowing the answer is not necessary to attaining nibbāna.

For another example, among the five categories of actions in Muslim law with respect to their religious significance there is the category of actions which are indifferent *(mubah* or *murakhkhas)*. Carrying out such courses of action is not necessary to living out the pattern of life taught by the Muslim community.

In the cases mentioned, the point is that knowing certain truths or carrying out certain courses of action would not contribute positively to living out the pattern of life taught by the community. But a community might develop its doctrine on this point further. It might be in a position to say

---

1. *The Collection of the Middle Length Sayings,* vol. 2, trans. I. B. Horner (London: Pali Text Society, 1957): 101.

that even if knowing some truth or carrying out some course of action would, as it happens, contribute positively to living out its pattern of life in the case of some individuals in some circumstances, it would not follow that knowing that truth or carrying out that course of action is necessary to living out the pattern. The pattern can be lived out without knowing that truth and without carrying out that course of action. Hence the community is not bound to teach that truth or to instruct its members in carrying out that course of action.

It may be that a community would have no reason to discourage its members from learning truths it is not bound to teach or carrying out courses of action in which it is not bound to instruct them, provided that these truths and courses of action are consistent with the doctrines it is bound to teach. It may even be that a community could encourage its members, or some of them, to do so.

Consider, for example, truths of modern physics and the activity of investigating physical phenomena. Let us suppose that the community holds and teaches that if there are truths of physics, these are not inconsistent with the truths it is bound to teach, and that the courses of action which are necessary for physical investigations are not incompatible with the courses of action proposed in its own practical doctrines.

Suppose now that one of the community's practical doctrines is that one ought to do one's work well. Suppose the community gives the following reason for this: By doing one's work well one shows gratitude to God for the talents one has been given. Then, if one's work is to be a physicist or an engineer, knowing physics would contribute positively to doing one's work well. Hence for that person it would contribute positively to living out the pattern of life the community teaches, though many people may do their work well and show gratitude to God for their talents without knowing modern physics.

There could be another reason for learning physics. Suppose the community teaches that the phenomena studied in physics are a feature of God's creation, and that through physical investigations one can become aware of the power and wisdom of God, though many people become aware of the power and wisdom of God in his creation without studying modern physics. Then learning physical truths could be encouraged even though it would not follow that the community would be bound to teach such truths.

Consider a different kind of reason for encouraging the study of physics. Suppose a community teaches that the illusions about the world which are generated in perceptual experience by our wishes and aversions hinder us from attaining enlightenment. And suppose that for some people the study of physics helps to dispel some such illusions. Then for these people the study of physics would contribute positively to living the pattern of life the community teaches, in which the end in view is enlightenment, though many people attain enlightenment without knowing truths of modern physics. Then that community would have no good reason to object to, and might even encourage, the study of physics, though it would not be bound to teach truths of modern physics.

So, even though a religious community might for some reason or other encourage some of its members to learn physical truths, it could, consistently, say that to live a life in accord with the pattern of life it teaches it is not necessary to know modern physics. So the community is not bound to teach physical truths or to instruct its members in methods of physical investigation.

Hence, this line of argument would run, the truths the community teaches are not the only truths there are. And the courses of action in which it instructs its members are not the only right courses of action there are. The business of the community is to set forth those truths and right courses of action which are necessary to living in accord with its pattern of life.

2. A different but complementary line of argument would run as follows. In its teaching activities, as in its other activities, the community has only a limited authority. It has been commissioned to teach certain truths and to propose and foster certain courses of action, namely those which are to be found in the sources of its doctrines. Though there may be other truths and other courses of action which are right in general or in some circumstances, and even though these other truths and right courses of action are not inconsistent with those it is authorized to teach, the community is bound not to extend the scope of its teaching beyond the limits of its authorization. It is thus bound not to teach as true or as right what is said in sentences which are not authentic doctrines of the community. For example, Christian theologians have at times warned that on points on which the Scriptures are silent the church is bound not to speak.

Both this and the preceding line of argument are broached in Article VI ("Of the Sufficiency of the Holy Scriptures for Salvation") of the (Anglican) *Articles of Religion*. This article, which was introduced for another purpose in chapter 2, begins as follows: "Holy Scripture containeth all things necessary to salvation: so that whatsoever is not read therein, nor may be proved thereby, is not to be required of any man, that it should be believed as an article of the Faith, or be thought requisite or necessary to salvation."

Consider another example. At the beginning of chapter 8 of book 4 of his *Institutes,* John Calvin discusses the spiritual power which belongs to the church. With respect to doctrine this consists in its authority to lay down articles of faith and to explain them. The end for which this authority has been given to the church is "for upbuilding and not for destruction." He continues:

> Now the only way to build up the church is for the ministers themselves to endeavor to preserve Christ's authority for himself; this can only be secured if what he has received from his Father be left to him, namely, that he alone is the schoolmaster of the church. For it is written not of any other but of him alone, "Hear him" (Matt. 17:5).

The power of the church is therefore to be not grudgingly manifested but yet to be kept within definite limits, that it may not be drawn hither and thither according to men's whim. For this reason it will be of especial benefit to observe how it is described by the prophets and apostles. For if we simply grant to men such power as they are disposed to take, it is plain to all how abrupt is the fall into tyranny, which ought to be far from Christ's church.

Accordingly, we must here remember that whatever authority and dignity the Spirit in Scripture accords to either priests or prophets, or apostles, or successors of apostles, it is wholly given not to the men personally, but to the ministry to which they have been appointed; or (to speak more briefly) to the Word, whose ministry is entrusted to them. For if we examine them all in order, we shall not find that they have been endowed with any authority to teach or to answer, except in the name and Word of the Lord. For, where they are called to office, it is at the same time enjoined upon them not to bring anything of themselves, but to speak from the Lord's mouth. And he himself does not bring them forth to be heard by the people before teaching them what to speak: they are to speak nothing but his Word.[2]

Calvin's own application of this principle in chapter 8 is an argument against "that power by which those spiritual tyrants who have falsely called themselves bishops and prelates of religion have commended themselves now for some centuries among the people of God" (p. 1158). He proceeds then to examine the authority of church councils.

But this principle, or one analogous to it, could be brought to bear by a religious community against an assumption that there are no truths or right courses of action other than those the community has been authorized to teach. Calvin does not do this in chapter 8. In that chapter he does not show the slightest interest in our question about relations of doctrines to alien claims. Still it is clear that he thought the teachings of his own community were, as he says, "to be kept within definite limits." Ministers of the word have no authority "to teach or answer, except in the name and Word of the Lord." From this it seems to follow that if there are inquiries which cannot be answered in that name and from that word, but can be answered otherwise, then there may be truths and right courses of action which the Christian community is not bound to teach.

Elsewhere in the *Institutes,* Calvin has a good deal to say about such inquiries and the claims to which they give rise. In book 1, chapter 5, commenting on Psalm 19 and Romans 1:19–20, he considers how the wisdom of God can be known from our experience of the created world. He says,

There are innumerable evidences both in heaven and on earth that declare his wonderful wisdom; not only those more recondite matters for the closer observation of which astronomy, medicine, and all natural science are intended, but also those which thrust themselves upon the sight of even the most untutored and ignorant persons, so that they cannot open their eyes

2. Calvin, *Institutes of the Christian Religion,* pp. 1150–51 (vol. 2).

without being compelled to witness them. Indeed, men who have either quaffed or even tasted the liberal arts penetrate with their aid far more deeply into the secrets of the divine wisdom. Yet ignorance of them prevents no one from seeing more than enough of God's workmanship in his creation to lead him to break forth in admiration of the Artificer. To be sure, there is need of art and of more exacting toil in order to investigate the motion of the stars, to determine their assigned stations, to measure their intervals, to note their properties. As God's providence shows itself more explicitly when one observes these, so the mind must rise to a somewhat higher level to look upon his glory. Even the common folk and the most untutored, who have been taught only by the aid of the eyes, cannot be unaware of the excellence of divine art, for it reveals itself in this innumerable and yet distinct and well-ordered variety of the heavenly host. It is, accordingly, clear that there is no one to whom the Lord does not abundantly show his wisdom. Likewise, in regard to the structure of the human body one must have the greatest keenness in order to weigh, with Galen's skill, its articulation, symmetry, beauty, and use. But yet, as all acknowledge, the human body shows itself to be a composition so ingenious that its Artificer is rightly judged a wonder-worker. [pp. 53–4]

In book 2, chapter 2, Calvin discusses the power of human understanding. Though human understanding is weakened by dullness and vanity, a theme which he treats amply both here and in other parts of the *Institutes,* yet

> When we so condemn human understanding for its perpetual blindness as to leave it no perception of any object whatever, we not only go against God's Word, but also run counter to the experience of common sense. For we see implanted in human nature some sort of desire to search out the truth to which man would not at all aspire if he had not already savored it. Human understanding then possesses some power of perception, since it is by nature captivated by love of truth. [p. 271]

A little later he introduces a distinction which, it should be said, he does not always maintain with perfect clarity,

> that there is one kind of understanding of earthly things; another of heavenly. I call "earthly things" those which do not pertain to God or his Kingdom, to true justice, or to the blessedness of the future life; but which have their significance and relationship with regard to the present life and are, in a sense, confined within its bounds. I call "heavenly things" the pure knowledge of God, the nature of true righteousness, and the mysteries of the Heavenly Kingdom. The first class includes government, household management, all mechanical skills, and the liberal arts. In the second are the knowledge of God and of his will, and the rule by which we conform our lives to it.
>
> Then follow the arts, both liberal and manual. The power of human acuteness also appears in learning these because all of us have a certain aptitude. But although not all the arts are suitable for everyone to learn, yet it is a certain enough indication of the common energy that hardly anyone is

to be found who does not manifest talent in some art. There are at hand energy and ability not only to learn but also to devise something new in each art or to perfect and polish what one has learned from a predecessor. [pp. 272–73]

Next he comes to the sciences:

> Whenever we come upon these matters in secular writers, let that admirable light of truth shining in them teach us that the mind of man, though fallen and perverted from its wholeness, is nevertheless clothed and ornamented with God's excellent gifts. If we regard the Spirit of God as the sole fountain of truth, we shall neither reject the truth itself, nor despise it wherever it shall appear, unless we wish to dishonor the Spirit of God. For by holding the gifts of the Spirit in slight esteem, we contemn and reproach the Spirit himself. What then? Shall we deny that the truth shone upon the ancient jurists who established civic order and discipline with such great equity? Shall we say that the philosophers were blind in their fine observation and artful description of nature? Shall we say that those men were devoid of understanding who conceived the art of disputation and taught us to speak reasonably? Shall we say that they are insane who developed medicine, devoting their labor to our benefit? What shall we say of all the mathematical sciences? Shall we consider them the ravings of madmen? No, we cannot read the writings of the ancients on the subjects without great admiration. [pp. 273–74]

It seems fair to conclude that in Calvin's view: (1) the authentic teachings of the Christian community are limited in scope, and (2) there may be truths and right courses of action which that community is not bound to teach. Indeed, his evident respect for the liberal and the manual arts and for the natural sciences, and his admiration of various achievements in these secular arts and sciences, suggest that he thought there not only may be, there are, such truths and right courses of action. Further, since he purports to speak as a Christian theologian, it seems that (3) he is proposing that the teaching of the church should include positive valuations of secular arts and sciences. This is evident also in the theological explanation of their achievements he proposes, that (4) they are due to the grace of God. Hence we should be grateful for them. We shall come back to these two latter points about doctrines and secular claims later on.

Our own immediate interest is in the first two points, and especially in a reason for the first point which can be drawn from what Calvin says. The teachings of the church are "to be kept within definite limits." Ministers of the word have no authority "to teach or answer, except in the name and Word of the Lord." So, it seems, if there are inquiries which cannot be answered in that way, then there may be truths and right courses of action which the Christian community is not bound to teach.

The conclusion of an argument of this type is that there may be theoretical and practical questions which the community has no warrant to undertake to answer. If it should do so it would be unfaithful to the charter which regulates its existence. Hence there may be truths and right courses of action which it is not bound to teach.

3. Consider another line of argument against an assumption that only those propositions which are authentic doctrines of a community are true and that only those courses of action which are authentic doctrines of the community are right. This assumption would be strengthened by another assumption which, like it, may be implicit and may be naive. The latter assumption is that the community is competent to decide all the issues which arise for thought or for practice. So, if the teachers of the community wish to counter the former assumption, they might wish to speak to the latter assumption also.

Perhaps they would be in a position to argue that the community's sources do not warrant saying that its competence is unlimited, or perhaps they could bring forward warrants from the sources for saying there are claims to truth and to rightness which the community is not competent to judge. An auxiliary argument would run as follows. The community must be concerned about the effectiveness of its teaching activities. If it extends the range of its teachings beyond the limits of its competence, this would diminish the force of its teachings on points where it is competent to speak.

It seems clear that these arguments would lend support to the earlier arguments against an assumption that only the teachings of the community are true or right. Conversely, one reason which could be given for accepting the incompetence of the community to speak on some point is that it is not necessary for the community to speak to that point. Attaining the aims set forth by the community does not require settling that point. Another reason would be that the community is not authorized by its sources to speak on that point. But further reasons could be given. Consider two types of cases.

There are claims which arise in the course of various technical inquiries, for example in civil law, in economics, and in physics. In such inquiries claims are often tied tightly to procedures which a community may not have at its disposal. It may be that a community does not have the equipment, the experience, or the knowledge to be in a position to judge whether some claim is true or not or right or not. It could be responded that competence in these matters can be acquired if necessary. It is true that members of a community can acquire competence in such technical inquiries, and their competence may help a community to avoid going beyond its own competence in its teaching activities. But the main question is whether in all cases technical competence in such inquiries is necessary to the community itself in its own teaching activities. Here a community would have to consider the pattern of life it aims to nurture in its members, its ends in view for human life, and the sources of its teachings. It seems that at this point the other lines of argument we have considered would have to come into play.

In other cases, the argument might run, where moral claims are concerned the specificity of the community's teaching must be limited. The community is not in a position to know all the circumstances of a particular course of action carried out by some individual, and it cannot know with certainty all the motives and intentions of the individual which bear on the course of action. It can present principles and rules bearing on the course of action, and it may legislate on the ground of probabilities with respect to circumstances, motives, and intentions. But there are limits to what it can teach as to what people should do. In a theistic community it could be said that the community cannot know all the circumstances of a course of action as God knows them, and that it cannot know the heart of the agent as God knows it. Thus the competence of the community in its teachings about specific courses of action by specific persons is limited.

In these ways and perhaps others a community may have to recognize limits on its competence. The community itself does not have the resources to decide all the questions which may arise in the course of life. Hence there may be truths and right courses of action, answering to various theoretical and practical questions, which are beyond the bounds of its competence. It might be that in some cases the competence of the community would extend at most to decisions on whether some proposition or some course of action is consistent with its authentic doctrines. If what is claimed is inconsistent with its doctrines, and if the community holds that its doctrines are true or right, then the community would have to judge that what is claimed is untrue or not right. But the consistency of a proposition or a course of action with its doctrines would not warrant a decision that the proposition is true or that the course of action is right.

4. Another consideration could be brought forward by a community against an assumption which overestimates its competence. It may happen in some particular historical situation that the mind of a community is not yet made up on some question. The time is not yet ripe for the community to speak clearly and firmly, even on questions which seem to fall within the bounds of its competence. At the time, the theoretical and practical implications of some proposition or some course of action have not yet been worked out. So it is not yet clear how it is relevant to the doctrines of the community and whether it is inconsistent or not with authentic doctrines of the community.

These matters would have to be pondered, and sometimes the pondering goes slowly, especially when consensus is an important criterion of authenticity, or when a doctrine of some other religion or some secular claim introduces unfamiliar concepts or depends on unfamiliar procedures. The histories of religious communities show good reasons for tempering tendencies to give quick answers to complex questions.

Hence at particular times it may be that just what a community is bound to teach on some topic is not yet clear to it. At such times, it seems, the position of a community has to include an envisagement of the possibility that there may be truths and right courses of action which it is not bound to teach.

We have been considering some lines of argument available to a community which adopts the position that there may be alien claims which are true or right. These arguments would counter an assumption, which some of its members might be tempted to make, that the truths and right courses of action which it is bound to teach are the only truths and the only right courses of action there are. Against this assumption the community could argue that there are limitations on the scope of its teachings, limitations deriving from the definiteness of its aims, or the warrants for its teaching authority, or the quality of its competence, or from its existence as a social body under historical conditions. The community could argue that it is neither omniscient nor omnicompetent, and that the process of bringing its resources to bear on changing circumstances in the world around it takes time.

We might say that the scope of the teachings of such a community would be different from the scope of study and teaching in an ideal university. An ideal university, let us say, would aim at studying and teaching all subjects in which truths may be found, as well as all the arts, all those activities in which proficiency may be acquired. In contrast, a religious community which takes the position we have been considering would accept limits on the scope of its teaching. Though it might well encourage the discovery of truths and right courses of action which it is not bound to teach, even perhaps by founding or supporting universities, it would not itself set out to teach all possible truths and right courses of action.

So a conspectus of the doctrines of such a community would be unlike a universal encyclopedia. It might well be that many commonsense truths, many historical truths, many logical and mathematical truths, and many truths of physics and other natural and social sciences would not be included in such a conspectus. Also, directions for such activities as building bridges and computers, performing on musical instruments, removing appendices and gall bladders, producing plays, and many other sorts of activities would not be included in the conspectus.

Also, it might well be, a conspectus of the teachings of the community would not include many of the rights and duties instituted in codes of civil law, codes of conduct adopted by various professions, for example by the legal profession, the medical profession, labor unions and business associations, and various other rights and duties which are otherwise built into the structure of the society within which the community exists and functions. The community may recognize the legitimacy of some of these rights and obligations and relate them to its own code of conduct. But it would still remain true that in these cases the community is recognizing the possible rightness, in various circumstances, of courses of action which the community itself does not teach as its own authentic doctrines. This would hold both for cases where the community has a less comprehensive code than the highly developed codes of traditional Hinduism, traditional Judaism, and traditional Islam, and also for cases where a traditional community has not, not yet anyway, sufficiently developed its principles and rules of right action in response to changing circumstances.

Here we have considered some reasons a community might give for recognizing limits on the scope of its body of doctrines. These reasons would count against an assumption by its members or by others that the teachings of the community are all-embracing, if that should be taken to mean that the truths and right courses of action which the community is bound to teach are the only truths and right courses of action there are.

Such a community would not have to say that the claims which its body of doctrines does not include are inconsistent with its doctrines. It could hold and teach, as a doctrine about its doctrines, an extended principle of consistency: If an alien claim is true, or right, then what is said in that claim is consistent with authentic doctrines of the community. Also, it would not follow that the community's doctrines have no positive bearing on alien claims. Later we shall explore this point at some length and in detail.

COMPREHENSIVE PATTERNS OF LIFE

Consider now an objection on the part of some community to saying that the scope of its doctrines is limited. For there seems to be a deep-seated tendency in the major religious communities to develop a comprehensive pattern of life, a pattern of life which bears on all human interests (and thus indirectly on the objects of those interests) and on all the situations in which human beings find themselves. Thus the pattern might order life as a whole. This aim might be adopted as a guiding principle embodied in a doctrine of a community about its doctrines: The community should develop a comprehensive pattern of life.

Now if a community means to teach and nurture in its members a comprehensive pattern of life, so the objection would run, it cannot recognize limitations on the scope of its teachings. It would have to undertake to teach all truths whatever and all those courses of action which, in general or in some circumstances, are right. Otherwise the pattern of life it teaches would not be comprehensive. Two points are relevant to this interpretation of the comprehensiveness of a pattern of life.

   1. If a religious community is an integral, perhaps a dominant, feature

of a traditional society, there is a tendency for the community to claim that other features of the society including its laws, its arts, and its sciences derive from the sources of the community's doctrines. Hence there is a tendency to look on all the truths and right courses of action which are embodied in the society's institutions as authentic doctrines of the community, not as alien claims. In such situations there would be, in principle, no problems about the comprehensiveness of the pattern of life taught by the community.

But this tendency does not always prevail. At least in some periods of their histories, the major religious communities have found themselves in societies of a different type, societies in which secular interests, inquiries, and claims are important, if not indeed dominant. In such situations religious communities are under pressure to consider whether there may be truths and right courses of action which are not authentic doctrines of the community. Also, even in traditional societies variants of the tradition occur, sometimes even in early periods of the history of the community. Consider, for example, the various schools of Hindu thought and practice which developed in Indian society. The occurrence of these variants and disputes among their spokesmen raise questions within the community as to whether or not various sentences do indeed express authentic doctrines of the community. And this may lead on to questions whether various sentences, for example Pāṇini's grammatical rules (which we return to in a later section), are really secular alien claims, however valuable the religious community may still judge them to be.

2. Suppose a community could adopt and sustain, as a doctrine about its doctrines, the principle of schema T/R-A, that if what is said in some sentence is true or right, then it is an authentic doctrine of the community. Then the interpretation of comprehensiveness we are considering would be fully implemented and the objection to limits on the scope of the community's doctrines would be decisively reinforced. For with the T/R-A principle there could be no truths or right courses of action which are not authentic doctrines of that community, hence no truths or right courses of action which that community is not bound to teach. In that case, there would be no limits on the scope of its teaching deriving from its aim or from the warrants for its teachings. All truths and right courses of action would fall within the scope of its teachings. They would all be authentic doctrines of the community. Hence with respect to that community there could be no alien claims which are true or right.

But, for reasons brought out in chapter 4, the viability of the T/R-A principle as a doctrine of a religious community about its doctrines is doubtful. So we ought to consider whether a pattern of life taught by a community which does not adopt that principle might still be comprehensive. Are there other ways of construing comprehensiveness than the interpretation developed in the objection?

Recall here that, in a pattern of life taught by a religious community, the elements of the pattern are the beliefs, valuations, and courses of action which are proposed in its primary doctrines. The community nurtures its members in understanding the elements of the pattern and in living out the pattern in their conduct.

It could be said that a pattern of life is comprehensive if for any occasion in the course of human life, some elements of the pattern are relevant to that occasion. Then it could be said that, for any occasion of human life, the pattern covers the occasion, and it could be said that the pattern is occasion comprehensive.

We can limit the occasions with which we are concerned to occasions of human activity. We can leave out any events which are not shaped to some extent by human interests. So it is only to occasions of human activity that elements of a pattern would be said to be relevant or not, and only with respect to such occasions that a pattern of life would be said to be comprehensive or not.

The interests which shape human life are so multifarious that it is not worthwhile here to attempt an all-purpose classification of them. The main point to notice is that many occasions of human activity are shaped, more or less, by interests which are not religious interests. It is true that in many occasions of human activity religious interests are present and effective. But if we consider human life at large and on the whole face of the globe, and if we should allow ourselves to speculate on quantitative proportions, we might be tempted to think that nonreligious interests preponderate in human activities.

At any rate, speculations aside, it seems that, if a pattern of life is to be comprehensive, it must cover in some way or other that vast multiplicity of occasions of human activity which are shaped to some extent if not entirely by nonreligious interests. Furthering this development of the notion of occasion comprehensiveness, let us ask: How does a pattern of life cover an occasion of human activity? An occasion of human activity occurs in a setting, the actual world of that occasion (as Whitehead would say). In this setting there are various interrelated existents, including nonhuman existents, of which the activity in the occasion must take account. The activity is thus conditioned by the setting. So some elements of a pattern would be relevant to an occasion by way of characterizing various features of its setting. Thus some doctrines propose various beliefs about the setting of human life and valuations of features of the setting. Other elements of a pattern would be relevant in a different way. Some doctrines propose courses of inward and outward action in response to the settings of occasions of human activity, with various motives and intentions, and various ends in view.

So, if a religious community should aim at teaching an occasion-comprehensive pattern of life, the community would not have to include, as elements of the pattern, all truths and right courses of action whatever. The community would have only to see to it that (1) for any occasion of human activity, some elements of the pattern of life it teaches are relevant to that occasion, and that (2) the elements of the pattern are consistent with one another and, directly or indirectly, connected with one another.

Such a community could grant that there may be truths and right courses of action which it is not bound to teach. It could and would, we may suppose, also have a doctrine about its doctrines embodying an extended principle of consistency, which would say that truths and right courses of action which it is not bound to teach are consistent with the doctrines it is bound to teach.

It is clear enough that various religious communities include, as elements of the patterns of life they teach, beliefs and practices which are relevant to wide ranges of occasions of human activity. We studied some such practical doctrines in the latter part of chapter 6. The prima facie Buddhist precept we studied there may be summarized as:

In carrying out all the bodily activities in which you engage, be mindful, as a step toward enlightenment.

And the comparable prima facie Christian precept we studied there may be summarized as:

In carrying out the bodily activities in which you engage, do all to the glory of God.

Such general precepts are implemented, among other ways, by sets of ritual observances which mark a wide variety of occasions in human life. The observances are enjoined, explained, and regulated by sets of theoretical and practical doctrines. The significances of the occasions are thereby brought to mind and integrated into the pattern of life taught by the community.

Thus daily events such as arising from sleep, sunrise, meals, sunset, and going to sleep are occasions for meditations, prayers, and recitations of verses from scriptures. Events in the cycle of a life such as birth, puberty, marriage, and death are occasions for reminders of their importance in life and of the responsibilities they bring with them. Various weekly or monthly or seasonal or annual occasions are marked by reminders of transitions in the course of nature or of important events in the history of the community. There are times for celebration, times for self-examination and repentance, and times for reflection on the conditions and limitations of human life, all of which are meant to reinforce such responses at other times as well.

Furthermore, religious communities, some more than others, develop codes which cover not only ritual observances but also behavior in many other sorts of situations, for example the Hindu *dharmashāstra*, the Buddhist *vinaya,* the Judaic *halakah,* Roman Catholic canon law, and Muslim *shari'a.* Along with detailed regulations for personal life, family life, and public life, courts and procedures are provided for adjudicating disputed cases. In such ways also religious communities aim to make their teachings immediately relevant to many types of occasions in the lives of their members.

Consider the following passages as expressions of a tendency in the teaching activities of a religious community to bring its teachings to bear on a wide range of occasions of human activity. We may begin with a brief introduction to midrash in Judaism, taken from an article in an encyclopedia, as a stepping stone.

> *Midrash:* From the Hebrew *dorash* which means probing. Rabbinic exposition of scripture aiming not alone at the simple elucidation of the Biblical text, but also at the discovery within Scripture of general norms which would have universal application. The inspiration for the Midrash was, on the one hand, the need for continued clarification of the Bible, and, on the other hand, the desire to order life in accordance with Biblical prescriptions. Since the changed circumstances prevailing in post–Biblical times had made the simple code of the Bible insufficient in itself to direct life, the rabbis sought to probe more penetratingly into the Biblical text in order to discover implications, not always apparent on the surface, that might offer the required guidance.[3]

The theme is deepened and enriched by Judah Goldin. Discussing the rabbinic understanding of God's Torah, he says, "Here is a text that is never outdated." Soon after he goes on to say: "However, what is another way of saying 'it is never outdated?' It is always relevant. But how are an ancient text and its contents kept relevant? To meet this assignment Judaism adopts not the neutral and descriptive terms of change and adaptation, but a view of revelation which is permanently at work through an activity called 'Midrash.' " He explains how this activity is not just a matter of change and adaptation to change. In Midrash, "though the pressure of the immediate is keenly appreciated (otherwise, why Midrash at all?), attention must *also* be directed to the original, classical patterns which have given the community its particular features." Attention must be directed to the past.

> Midrash, however, is not mere reference to the past: it is the enlistment of the past in the service of the present. Even more specifically, it is a reinsertion into the present of the original divine Word, "memory/making past present" (Marianne Moore), but a supernatural Word that is not simply the primitive hierogram: that Word is given definition and repeated application by men. Without man, without the scholar, there can be no Midrash. Theoretically, he is not free to invent meanings or implications independently of the Word.

3. Ben Zion Bokser, in *An Encyclopedia of Religion,* ed. Virgilius Ferm (New York: Philosophical Library, 1945), p. 490.

Therefore, from the first the divine word consists of layers upon layers of intentions and instructions. And when the sage offers his interpretation he is making one more disclosure, he is laying bare one more implication, he is exposing to view still another radiance hitherto covered up. Since the Word is the word of the Living God, it never ceases to make contact with the human world. The Word does not change, but it fulfils itself through disclosures and interpretations of the scholars. And if the world changes, the Word has been prepared for all contingencies from the outset. The permanent and the fluid, if I may say so, are not two opposed features, or even sharply distinguished from each other. The Word is continuously directed to the world and the world is shaped by the Word through the instrumentality of the Sages.

It is therefore not with change and adaptation as such that the rabbis are preoccupied; this is not their fundamental orientation. It is with the preservation of that intimate relationship between the inexhaustible Word and human society that they are concerned. Since that relationship cannot be sustained without active human performances, commentary never ceases, and each generation's interpretations become, as it were, additional promptings to be reflected on in turn. And since, despite all their aspirations, human beings cannot escape being affected by what takes place in their own times, they keep interpreting the old in terms that grow directly from their own experiences.[4]

Notice that this position is neither defensive, nor, on the other hand, relaxative. The world is neither being fended off, nor is it a matter of giving way to the world. Notice particularly the point that there is much in the teaching which would not be realized if the teaching were not brought to bear on what comes to be known in and about the world. One might say that there is an aim here at making a body of doctrines comprehensive with respect to times.

But we still need to raise a further and more specific question. Recall that the position we began to consider in chapter 7 envisages the possibility of sentences which (1) are not authentic doctrines of the community in question (they are alien claims), (2) are not inconsistent with authentic doctrines of that community, and (3) are true or right. Among such sentences, let us suppose, are some doctrines of other religious communities and some secular claims. For the time being let us concentrate on the secular alien claims. Much of what can be said about these will apply also to alien claims which are doctrines of other religious communities.

Then the further question is: How could a religious community which grants that there may be such sentences bring its doctrines to bear on them? How could a pattern of life cover those occasions of human activity in which secular inquiries are carried on by members of the community or

4. Judah Goldin, "Of Change and Adaptation in Judaism," *History of Religions* 4/2 (Winter 1965): 269–94. ©1986 by the University of Chicago. All rights reserved. Quotations are from pp. 276–78, by permission of the University of Chicago Press, with the approval of the author.

by others? How could the pattern be particularized in relation to inquiries in which success is not measured by the standards of any religious community?

We should keep a perspective on this topic. A community which adopts the position is not thereby committed to accepting all secular claims as true or right. (Indeed, very often secular claims are inconsistent with one another.) For example, the Buddhist precept we studied in the latter part of chapter 6 does not give permission to engage in all sorts of bodily activities. And this is true also of the codes of other religious communities. Likewise, it is taught in various religious communities that various alien claims are untrue. For example, the Buddha denied fatalism; the early Christian fathers denied astrological determinism; Shankara opposed perceptual realism; and Ramanuja opposed atheism.

In these cases claims about certain practices and theories are held to be inconsistent with authentic doctrines of the community. So it is not a live question whether a body of doctrines could be comprehensive, if this should be taken to mean that a community would have to accept all secular alien claims as true or right. At most it would mean that the community should find ways of honoring, so to speak, the possibility that some secular alien claims are true or right.

We are now supposing that an aim at a comprehensive pattern of life is an aim at making the pattern relevant to all occasions of human activity, including those occasions of human activity in which secular alien claims to truth or rightness are arrived at or proposed or argued. So we now ask how a religious community might bring its doctrines to bear on occasions of human activity of that sort.

VALUATIONS OF SECULAR ALIEN CLAIMS

Among the primary doctrines of a religious community there may be proposals of valuations of secular alien claims. We are not concerned here with valuations of the motives or the intentions of those who make such claims. Instead, we are concerned with valuations of knowing truths proposed in such claims (supposing that what is proposed is true) and with valuations of knowing how to carry out courses of action proposed in such claims (supposing that the proposed courses of action are right). Such valuations are one way the doctrines of a community which recognizes limits on the scope of its doctrines could be brought to bear on claims which arise beyond those limits.

Some such valuations are positive; some are negative. A positive valuation of a secular alien claim would say that it is good, for one reason or another, to know the truth proposed in the claim, or that it is good, for one reason or another, to know how to carry out the course of action proposed in the claim. A negative valuation of a secular alien claim would say that it is not worthwhile to know what is proposed in the claim even if it is true, or to know how to carry out the course of action proposed in the claim even if it is in some way right. Or it may say that it is harmful, in one way or another, to pay attention to the claim or to occupy oneself with it. Mainly we will deal with positive valuations, but something will be said about negative valuations later on.

JOHN COTTON

Now with this preliminary explanation in hand, let us come to cases. We begin with the Puritan notion of Christian vocations "in our outward and temporal life." John Cotton (1584–1652), son of a struggling lawyer in Derby, was a student at Trinity College, Cambridge, and later a fellow of Emmanuel College, where he had his first religious awakening. After about twenty years as vicar of St. Botolph's in Boston (Botolph's Town), Lincolnshire, he set out for New England in 1633 with Thomas Hooker and others. Soon after his arrival in the Massachusetts Bay colony he was elected by the members of the first church in Boston as their teacher, and he continued in that post to the end of his life.

In a treatise probably composed in England before 1633,[5] Cotton begins at one point (p. 436) by saying, "Having done with shewing how wee live the inward and spiritual life of grace by faith," and then continues, in Miller's transcription, as follows:

> We are now to speak of living by faith in our outward and temporal life. Now, our outward and temporal life is twofold, which we live in the flesh: it is either a civil or a natural life; for both these lives we live, and they are different the one from the other. Civil life is that whereby we live as members of this or that city or town or commonwealth, in this or that particular vocation and calling.
>
> Natural life I call that by which we do live this bodily life. I mean, by which we live a life of sense, by which we eat and drink, and by which we go through all conditions, from our birth to our grave, by which we live and move and have our being. And now both these a justified person lives by faith.
>
> To begin with the former: A true believing Christian, a justified person, he lives in his vocation by his faith.
>
> Not only my spiritual life but even my civil life in this world, all the life I live, is by the faith of the Son of God: He exempts no life from the agency of His faith; whether he lives as a Christian man, or as a member of this or that church or commonwealth, he doth it all by the faith of the Son of God.

5. John Cotton, "The Life of Faith," in *The way of Life*, . . . *foure several Treatises on foure Texts of Scripture*, (London, 1641), pp. 255–481. I give below some passages from Perry Miller's transcription of pp. 436–51 of this treatise. Miller's heading for his selection from the treatise is "Christian Calling." *The American Puritans, Their Prose and Poetry*, ed. Perry Miller (Garden City: Doubleday, 1956), pp. 172–82.

Now, for opening of this point, let me show you what are those several acts of faith which it puts forth about our occasions and vocations, that so we may live in God's sight therein:

First: faith draws the heart of a Christian to live in some warrantable calling. As soon as ever a man begins to look towards God and the ways of His grace, he will not rest till he find out some warrantable calling and employment. . . . This the clean work of faith, he would have some employment to fill the head and hand with.

Now more particularly, faith doth warily observe the warrantableness of its calling.

Three things doth faith find in a particular calling:

1. It hath a care that it be a warrantable calling, wherein we may not only aim at our own, but at the public good. That is a warrantable calling: "Seek not every man his own things, but every man the good of his brother" (I Cor. 10.24). . . .

2. Another thing to make a calling warrantable, is, when God gives a man gifts for it, that he is acquainted with the mystery of it and hath gifts of body and mind suitable to it. . . . He would have his best gifts improved to the best advantage.

3. That which makes a calling warrantable is, when it is attained unto by warrantable and direct means, when a man enterprises not a calling but in the use of such means as he may see God's providence leading him to it. . . .

Secondly: another work of faith, about a man's vocation and calling, when faith hath made choice of a warrantable calling, then he depends upon God for the quickening and sharpening of his gifts in that calling. . . .

Thirdly: we live by faith in our vocations, in that faith, in serving God, serves men, and in serving men, serves God. . . . And therefore—that which follows upon this—he doth it all comfortably, though he meet with little encouragements from man, though the more faithful service he doth, the less he is accepted; whereas an unbelieving heart would be discontented that he can find no acceptance. . . .

Fourthly: another act of faith about a man's vocation is this: It encourageth a man in his calling to the most homeliest and difficultest and most dangerous things his calling can lead and expose himself to. If faith apprehend this or that to be the way of my calling, it encourages me to it, though it be never so homely and difficult and dangerous. . . .

Fifthly: another act of faith by which a Christian man lives in his vocation is that faith casts all the failings and burthens of his calling upon the Lord; that is the proper work of faith; it rolls and casts all upon Him. . . .

Sixthly: faith hath another act about a man's vocation, and that is, it takes all successes that befall him in his calling with moderation; he equally bears good and evil successes as God shall dispense them to him. . . . It is the same act of unbelief that makes a man murmur in crosses which puffs him up in prosperity. Now faith is like a poise: it keeps the heart in an equal frame; whether matters fall out well or ill, faith takes them much what alike; faith moderates the frame of a man's spirit on both sides.

Seventhly: the last work which faith puts forth about a man's calling is this: faith with boldness resigns up his calling into the hands of God or man;

whenever God calls a man to lay down his calling when his work is fin-
ished. . . .

It is likely that Cotton had foremost in mind such callings as those of
merchants, farmers, blacksmiths, household servants, clerks, and lawyers.
But in times to come there would be other occupations by which men and
women made their livings in Lincolnshire and in Massachusetts. There
would be, for example, historians and physicists. So it would be fair to
ask whether principles analogous to Cotton's would apply to occupations
such as these.

Consider then how the pattern of life taught by some religious community might cover various occasions in the life of a historian. On some
occasions he is deciphering manuscripts or assessing conflicting accounts
of some event with a view to finding out what, probably, happened. On
other occasions he is reflecting on his activities as a historian, on his motives
and aims in his historical work. In what ways might the doctrines of a
religious community be relevant to occasions of these sorts?

We may suppose that, though the historian may have religious interests
of his own, and though he may have a religious perspective on his work
as a historian, though indeed he may have such a perspective as the one
John Cotton was offering his readers, still, in producing his historical conclusions he is controlled more or less by the standards of his profession.
If we may suppose that Cotton would have expected a blacksmith in his
congregation to aim at being a good blacksmith, then there would be an
analogy between the blacksmith and the historian. Each would set out to
do well, by the standards of his profession—though perhaps not only by
those standards—the work he has in hand.

Let us suppose further, not unreasonably, that some of the standards by
which the blacksmith's work is judged, by himself and by other blacksmiths, to be well done, are not dependent on the standards of any religious
community. And let us suppose that some of the standards by which the
historian's work is judged, by himself and other historians, to be well done,
are likewise not dependent on the teachings of any religious community.
Then in these respects both the blacksmith and the historian would be engaged in secular activities.

There are right ways of making a plowshare, and there are right ways
of giving a historical account of an election. Now it seems plausible that
some of the technical procedures for making a plowshare or producing an
account of an election are not dependent for their rightness on the distinctive
doctrines of any religious community; it seems plausible that some of the
directions for these procedures are secular claims. Also, it seems plausible
that, with respect to some religious community, some of these directions
are not given in authentic doctrines of that community; with respect to
that community they would be alien claims.

Further, it is plausible that whether a historian's account is true does not depend on the distinctive doctrines of any religious community, and hence is a secular claim. Also, it is plausible that some secular historical claims are alien claims with respect to that community; they do not fall within the scope of the primary doctrines of the community.

Yet it seems essential to being a good blacksmith that an apprentice should learn the technical standards and procedures for making plows and shoeing horses, and that he should learn to make good judgments in particular cases. Also, learning technical standards and procedures and learning to make good judgments in particular cases are essential to becoming a good historian.

It seems clear that a perspective developed from John Cotton's treatise would be relevant to the activities of a blacksmith or a historian, whether or not the blacksmith or the historian adopts that perspective, and relevant also to the activities of those engaged in various other arts and sciences. That is to say, a pattern of life developed from that perspective would be comprehensive of those activities. Recall some of the principles Cotton proposes.

A Christian should seek an employment to fill his head and hand. He should ask whether this or that calling is fitted to the gifts of body and mind God has given him. Further, he should improve those gifts to the best advantage of himself and other men. Thus he should do well the work he is called to do even when the work is homely or difficult or dangerous. In all this he should rely on God, who has given him his gifts, who leads him to his calling by various signs, who can quicken and sharpen his gifts, and who encourages him to use them in his calling. This faith is a poise to keep him from being puffed up by pride and from being cast down by despair. Finally it enables him to be content when he must lay down his calling.

Let us draw this perspective to a sharper focus on the secular aspects of a calling and on the alien claims encountered in the course of doing the work of a calling. It is taught in Puritan doctrines, let us say, that Christians should do their work well. Now it happens that, in some callings at least, to do their work well persons have to learn the standards and procedures of their callings, and learn to make good judgments in the course of their work. So it would seem that there should be doctrines of the Puritan community which would encourage its members to learn these standards and procedures and to learn how to make good judgments in the course of their work. Otherwise the recommendation to do the work well would not connect with the realities of the situation. Now we may suppose that some of these standards and procedures, and the knack of making good judgments as a blacksmith or as a historian, are not taught in authentic Puritan doctrines. Then it seems there ought to be Puritan doctrines which express positive valuations of learning these standards and procedures, and of acquiring these abilities, even though these standards, procedures, and abilities are not themselves taught in authentic Puritan doctrines.

To bring out further the reasoning here, consider the following. First suppose that the Puritan community holds and teaches as a governing doctrine that if some sentence is an authentic doctrine of the community, then what is said in that sentence is true or right (an A–T/R doctrine). Suppose also that the Puritan community grants that there may be alien claims which are true or right. Then consider the following sentences and schemas.

(1) A Christian should have a warrantable calling in his civil life.
(2) A Christian should do the work of his calling well.

Suppose that (1) and (2) are authentic practical doctrines of the Puritan community.

(3) To do well the work of some warrantable calling (C1) it is necessary to know how to carry out some courses of action (A1).
For C1: blacksmithing, historical study, etc.
For A1: making a plow, deciphering a document, etc.

Suppose that some of the practical claims which fit this schema—claims about right ways of carrying out courses of action—are secular claims. Their rightness does not depend on the distinctive doctrines of any religious community. Suppose also that some such secular claims are not authentic doctrines of the Puritan community; with respect to that community they are alien claims.

A reminder: To say that a claim is an alien claim with respect to some community is not to say or imply that the claim is inconsistent with doctrines of that community.

(4) It is good to know how to do A1.

This is a positive valuation of knowing how to carry out a particular course of action. It seems that the Puritan community ought to accept it and teach it as an authentic doctrine if (1) and (2) are authentic doctrines of the community and if a sentence patterned by (3) is true.

(5) To know how to carry out A1 it is necessary to know some set of truths (T1).
For T1: some properties of metals, Latin grammar, etc.

Suppose that some set of truths which fit into this schema is a set of secular claims. The truth of these claims does not depend on the distinctive doctrines of any religious community. Suppose also that relative to the Puritan community these are alien claims. They are not authentic doctrines of that community.

(6) It is good to know T1.

This is a positive valuation of knowing some set of truths. It seems that the Puritan community ought to accept it and teach it as an authentic primary doctrine of the community if (4) is an authentic doctrine of the community and if a sentence patterned by (5) is true.

Whether or not John Cotton would have approved this development from his remarks is not to the point. The object of the construction is to explain one way in which the relevance of the doctrines of a community would extend to coverage of those occasions of human activity in which alien claims are encountered. This would be so if among the doctrines of the community there are positive valuations of knowing what is said in alien claims, supposing that what is said in them is true or right. Such doctrines would have the effect of sanctioning and motivating inquiries as to right courses of action, and as to truths, which the community itself is not bound to teach. The valuations would be authentic doctrines of the community, but what is said in the alien claims would not be authentic doctrines of the community.

In this case practical inquiries come first. Truths are introduced insofar as they need to be known in order to carry out the courses of action proposed in practical doctrines. But valuations of knowing alien truths arise in other ways also. The introduction of valuations of knowing alien truths may be more direct, as we may see by considering a passage from the writings of a seventeenth-century natural historian.

JOHN RAY

John Ray (1627–1705) studied at Trinity College, Cambridge, nearly half a century after John Cotton. He has been called the father of English natural history. In the course of many journeys he went through most of Great Britain, and he spent several years of travel in Europe, observing, collecting, and making notes on plants, trees, animals, fish, birds, and insects. He was admitted to the Royal Society in 1667. The title of his first paper for the Society, two years later, was "Experiments Concerning the Motion of Sap in Trees." In 1660 he was ordained as a clergyman in the Church of England. In 1662 he refused to subscribe to the Act of Uniformity and gave up his Trinity College fellowship.

Most of his published writings are detailed accounts in Latin of various kinds of living things and their environments. His first publication in natural history was his *Catalogus Plantarum circa Cantabrigiam Nascentium,* a handbook for amateur botanists, at Cambridge in 1660. The object, he said, "was in general to illustrate the glory of God in the knowledge of the works of nature or creation; then to enhance the reputation of my Alma Mater, the University of Cambridge, which must suffer abroad if its equipment in this field were defective; and finally to enrich the common life and extend the advantages which such studies can bestow."[6] His later publications in natural history were more comprehensive and more systematic.

A passage in *The Wisdom of God Manifested in the Works of the Creation* (London, 1691) suggests a different line of doctrinal development from the one we constructed starting from John Cotton's treatise. In this case doctrines which propose beliefs, in contrast with practical doctrines, are introduced more directly. The passage runs as follows.

> Some Reproach methinks it is to Learned men, that there should be so many Animals still in the world, whose outward shape is not yet taken notice of, or described, much less their way of Generation, Food, Manners, Uses, observed. If Man ought to reflect upon his Creator the Glory of all his works, then ought he to take notice of them all, and not to think any thing unworthy of his Cognizance. Let us then not esteem any thing contemptible or inconsiderable, or below our notice-taking; for this is to derogate from the Wisdom and Art of the Creator, and to confess our selves unworthy of those Endowments of Knowledge and Understanding which he hath bestowed on us. [p. 130]

Now, as in the case of the Puritan community, let us suppose that the Anglican community holds and teaches as a doctrine about its doctrines that its authentic doctrines are true or right. Suppose also that it grants that there may be truths and right courses of action which are not authentic doctrines of the community. Then, setting out from this passage, we can construct the following line of thought without supposing that Ray would have approved it

(1) God is the creator of the world.
(2) Human beings ought to reflect back on their creator the glory of all his works. They ought to praise him for his power, wisdom, and goodness, which can be discerned in the creation.
(3) Praise of God should be intelligent and discriminating. He should be praised with the mind as well as from the heart.

Suppose that (1), (2), and (3) are authentic doctrines of the Anglican community.

(4) To praise God for all his works with intelligence and discrimination it is necessary to have detailed knowledge of the natural world.

Should we suppose that (4) is an authentic doctrine of the Anglican community? Would a community hesitate to put in its catechism questions calling for detailed knowledge of the natural world? How much such knowledge is required for rightly praising God? Still, a community could say "as much as possible under the circumstances" and "the more the better." So let us suppose that, with suitable qualifications, (4) is an authentic doctrine of the Anglican community.

(5) Hence it is a good thing to know not only the outward shapes of living creatures but also the processes through which they have come to be as they are and the habits by which they sustain and reproduce themselves. Knowing such features of living things is good in that it enables us to understand more clearly, and to appreciate more discriminatingly, the power, wisdom, and goodness of God.

This is a positive valuation of knowing truths of a certain kind about living creatures of various sorts, a valuation of having detailed knowledge of them. This valuation would follow from (4), it seems, and hence we may suppose that it would also be an authentic doctrine of the Anglican community.

(6) To learn such features of living things it is necessary to study them by way of observations and experiments (that is to say, in effect), by way of secular inquiries. It would not be enough to read what the Scriptures or other texts say about them.

Suppose that (6) is true independently of distinctive Anglican doctrines and also independently of distinctive doctrines of other religious communities. Suppose it is a secular truth. Suppose also that (6) is not an authentic doctrine of the Anglican community. Suppose that though it is not inconsistent with Anglican doctrines it is, with respect to the Anglican community, an alien claim.

(7) Hence it is a good thing to carry out secular inquiries about plants and animals and other creatures and thus to learn secular truths about them, truths which are independent of doctrines of religious communities, including truths which are not doctrines of the Anglican community and thus are, with respect to that community, alien claims.

This is a positive valuation of secular inquiries of a certain kind and of knowing truths which are discovered in these inquiries including truths which are expressed in secular alien claims.

It seems that (7) would follow from (5) taken together with (6). We are supposing that (5) is an authentic doctrine of the Anglican community, though (6) is not. It seems that (6) does not depend on (5). So we may suppose that (7) might be deri ed from (6) taken together with some valuation other than (5), as well as from (5) taken together with (6).

So we can ask whether (7) could be an authentic doctrine of the Anglican community even if one of its premises, i.e., (6), is with respect to the Anglican community a secular alien claim. It seems that this could be so unless the criteria of authenticity of the Anglican community include a provision that no doctrine of the community is authentic if it depends on an alien claim.

We may suppose that one point of such a provision would be to keep the community from having to argue for some alien claim in the course of arguing in support of a doctrine. For if the doctrine depends on the alien claim, then the alien claim would have to be supported, it seems. It might be thought that the community is not competent to argue for the claim, or that its sources do not warrant its doing so. But in the present case this difficulty could be avoided by reformulating (7) as follows: If (6) is true then it is a good thing to carry out secular inquiries about plants and animals, etc. Thus this objection to taking (7) as an authentic doctrine would be removed.

The situation might turn out a different way. In chapter 5 we considered various rules for arguments in support of doctrines. Recall that a rule of type II would permit substantive reasons in support of a doctrine even if these reasons are not authentic doctrines of the community. So if the Anglican community should have as a governing doctrine a rule of that type, then a subordinate argument supporting (6) in the course of an argument for (7) would be permitted, even if the subordinate argument depends on a secular alien claim.

But even if (7) should turn out to be an authentic doctrine of the Anglican community, this would not imply that the Anglican community itself should undertake such inquiries, that it should plan and carry out research programs in botany and zoology. It would imply only that the community should encourage its members to engage in such inquiries.

The main point of this construction is to show how the relevance of a pattern of life could extend to coverage of occasions of human activity in which secular inquiries are confronted or engaged in. This is one way a community could give effect to an aim at a comprehensive pattern of life. Here the focus is on valuations of knowing secular truths, including secular alien truths, and engaging in secular inquiries.

Of course it might be said that such valuations, insofar as they might be supposed to generate motivations for secular inquiries, are superfluous. There is plenty of natural curiosity, and there are in our society plenty of active and wide-ranging scientific interests, generated, sustained, and channeled not only by scientific institutions but also by educational, political and economic institutions.

But if we consider the pressures under which human beings live and the variations in their levels of energy and their moods, it seems that natural curiosity is subject to fluctuations. And if we survey the changing scene of human history, it seems that scientific interests and scientific institutions are not altogether immune from changes in the societies in which they function. (The same could be said of historical and other studies.)

So it seems that such valuations as those we have been considering may not be negligible as reinforcements, to say the least, of natural curiosity and scientific interests, and as motives for secular inquiries such as those in which John Ray was engaged. This consideration gains added force from the fact that these valuations would be either consequences or constituents of patterns of life which are meant to be both consistent and comprehensive.

NEGATIVE VALUATIONS OF SECULAR ALIEN CLAIMS

Since the cases of valuations of secular alien claims we have considered so far, and some we consider later, are cases of positive valuations, some points about negative valuations should be noticed.

1. Insofar as the comprehensiveness of a pattern of life is concerned, it does not matter whether a valuation of knowing what is said in some secular alien claim is positive or negative. In either case the valuation would bring the teachings of the community to bear on the claim and thus on those occasions of human activity in which the claim is encountered. Valuations of both sorts extend the import of a body of doctrines to cover occasions of human activity which are impinged on by worldly concerns.

2. Proposing negative valuations of secular alien claims is compatible with the position that there may be alien claims which are true or right. In the negative valuations the immediate point is not whether some claim is true or right. Without denying that some alien claims are true, and without denying that some courses of action proposed in alien claims are right, it is judged and taught that such truths are not worth knowing, or that it is not worth knowing how to carry out such courses of action. Such theoretical or practical knowledge would not contribute to living out the pattern of life which the community teaches. Or it may be judged and taught that knowing such truths or knowing how to carry out such courses of action would distract one from living out the pattern of life the community teaches and thus be harmful, a hindrance to attaining the aims set forth by the community.

Consider a passage in the Brahma-Gāla Suttanta.[7] The Buddha is speaking to a group of monks about how they should react to dispraise and to praise of himself, of the Doctrine, or of the Order. "It is in respect only of trifling things, of matters of little value, of mere morality, that an unconverted man, when praising the Tathāgata, would speak" (p. 3). Then he goes through a long list of such items of little value, of which an unconverted man would speak in praising the Buddha, including the following:

Or he might say: "Whereas some recluses and Brahmans, while living on

7. *Dialogues of the Buddha,* Part 1, trans. T. W. Rhys Davids.

food provided by the faithful, continue addicted to such low conversation as these:

Tales of kings, of robbers, of ministers of state; tales of war, of terrors, of battles; talk about foods and drinks, clothes, beds, garlands, perfumes; talks about relationships, equipages, villages, town, cities, and countries; tales about women, and about heroes; gossip at street corners, or places whence water is fetched; ghost stories; desultory talk; speculations about the creation of the land or sea, or about existence and non-existence—

Gotama the recluse holds aloof from such low conversation." [pp. 13–14]

The list of topics of "low conversation" in the main paragraph occurs at a number of other places in the Pali scriptures. In some of these contexts such conversation is called "worldly talk" (literally, "animal talk"). The immediate point of the passage is that it is no great praise of the Buddha to say that he holds aloof from low conversation—that is no great achievement—and that such praise misses the main point of his life and teaching. It seems clear that the Buddha shares a negative valuation of such topics of conversation.

The underlying negative valuation of worldly talk is not because what is said in it is not true. Instead, worldly talk is disvalued because it reflects interests which do not contribute to liberation from bondage to the world; indeed, it distracts the mind from the path to nibbāna.

3. So teaching a negative valuation of some secular alien claim is different from teaching that what is proposed in the claim is not true or not right. Suppose a community takes the position that no alien claims are true or right. We have noticed two ways in which the thought expressed in this position might occur: (1) There may be an assumption (perhaps implicit, perhaps naive) on the part of members of a community, which comes to be taught explicitly by the community as a doctrine about its doctrines, that only the authentic doctrines of the community are true or right. Or, (2) if a community should adopt the T/R-A principle as a way of connecting claims to authenticity with claims to truth and rightness, it would follow from this principle that if some sentence is not an authentic doctrine of the community, then what is said in the sentence is not true or right. In other words, no alien claims are true or right. If a community should come to take this position by either of these routes there would be no occasion for it to teach either a positive valuation or a negative valuation of knowing something, or of knowing how to do something, which is proposed in an alien claim. The community's position would then not permit it to teach such valuations.

It is only with respect to those claims in which what is said may be true or right that questions arise as to whether what is said in a claim is worth knowing. Of course it could be said that it is worth knowing whether what is said is true or right. But that is not the point here. If it has been decided that no alien claims are true or right, then the question whether what is said in some alien claim is or is not worth knowing does not arise. In that case, we might say, there is nothing to be known, or nothing to be (rightly) done.

If a community's position is that no alien claims are true or right, the community could point out that what is asserted in some alien claim is untrue or that a course of action proposed in some alien claim is not right, if the community is competent to do this. Also, perhaps the community could explain why what is proposed is untrue or not right, if it is competent to do this. Perhaps, for example, it could show how what is proposed is inconsistent with its own authentic teachings. Further, the community might try to explain how the claim came to be made and thus develop an object lesson on how to avoid making claims which are not true or not right.

But all this would be a far cry from teaching the members of the community to make negative valuations of knowing some actual or possible truth proposed in a claim, or negative valuations of knowing how to carry out some actually or possibly right course of action proposed in a claim.

4. If one looks for cases of negative valuations of secular knowledge which are both clear and strong, one is hampered somewhat by a concern to present plausibly authentic cases. Radical disvaluations of secular knowledge, theoretical or practical, are more likely to occur in eddies or diversions than in the mainstreams of religious communities. Further, it would not be sufficient to find examples of unworldly attitudes and judgments. Indifference to worldly knowledge would not be enough to generate negative valuations of having worldly knowledge.

5. The negative valuations we have been considering are a special case of negative valuations. Our attention has been on negative valuations of knowing truths proposed in alien claims and negative valuations of knowing how to carry out right courses of action proposed in alien claims. Quite apart from these valuations of secular knowledge, there is plenty of room for a community to teach negative valuations of various sayings and doings of its own members and of various features of its natural and social environment. Consider for example the denunciations of the Roman empire in the New Testament book, the Revelation of John.

GRAMMAR

The scriptures of the major religious communities are written in natural languages, languages which are not artificially constructed, for example Sanskrit, Pali, Hebrew, Greek, and Arabic. Hence it seems that something may be learned about the vocabularies and grammars of the languages of their scriptures not only by studying the scriptures themselves but also otherwise, for example by studying the natural histories of the languages, by studying cognate languages, and perhaps in other ways.

Suppose now that a community accepts this feature of the language in which a scripture is written, or at least that its doctrines do not deny that something about the language can be learned otherwise than by studying the scripture itself. Then that community might take account in some way or other of secular claims about the vocabulary and grammar of the language, claims which do not depend on distinctive doctrines of any religious community. Furthermore, it is plausible that some such claims are, with respect to that community, alien claims, claims which are not authentic doctrines of that community. So we should consider the possibility of valuations of knowing what is said in such secular alien claims.

In a passage where he is arguing for a thesis about the date of the Indian grammarian Pānini (the fifth century B.C.), Theodor Goldstücker discusses some of the great commentators on the Vaidika (Vedic) texts, like Mādhava-Sāyana. He goes on to say:

> But it would be utterly erroneous to assume that a scholar like Sāyana, or even a copy of him, like Mahīdhara, contented himself with being the mouthpiece of the predecessors or ancestors. They not only record the sense of the Vaidika texts and the sense of the words of which these texts consist, but they endeavour to show that the interpretations which they give are *consistent with the grammatical requirements of the language itself*. And this proof, which they give whenever there is the slightest necessity for it—and in the beginning of their exegesis, even [if] there is no apparent necessity for it, merely in order to impress on the reader the basis on which they stand,—this proof is the great grammatical element in these commentatorial works.
>
> In short, these great Hindu commentators do not merely explain the meanings of words, but they justify them, or endeavour to justify them, on the ground of the *grammar* of Pānini, the *Vārtikas* of Kātyāyana, *and the Mahābhāshya of* Patañjali.[8]

In passing it is worth noticing that a contemporary linguist, Murray Fowler, says: "Pānini's grammar has been through two thousand years repeatedly called the best grammar of the Sanskrit language." Fowler quotes Leonard Bloomfield (*Language,* p. 11) as follows: "This grammar . . . is one of the greatest monuments of human intelligence. It describes, with the minutest detail, every inflection, derivation, and composition, and every syntactic usage of its author's speech. No other language, to this day, has been so perfectly described."[9]

As an instance of the reliance of Hindu commentators on truths of grammar, take a remark by Rāmānuja (eleventh century) in his comments on the first of the vedānta-sutras. The first sutra is:

8. Theodor Goldstücker, *Pānini,* ed. S. N. Shāstri (Varanasi: Chowkhamba Sanskrit Series, 1965), pp. 262–63. Originally published in London, 1860. The emphasis is the author's.

9. Murray Fowler, "How Ordered Are Pānini's Rules?" *Journal of the American Oriental Society* 85 (1965): 44.

Then therefore the enquiry into Brahman.

Rāmānuja comments as follows:

> In this Sūtra the word "then" expresses immediate sequence; the word "therefore" intimates that what has taken place (viz. the study of the kar-makāṅda of the Veda) constitutes the reason (of the enquiry into Brahman). For the fact is that the enquiry into (lit. "the desire to know") Brahman— the fruit of which enquiry is infinite in nature and permanent—follows immediately in the case of him who, having read the Veda together with its auxiliary disciplines, has reached the knowledge that the fruit of mere works is limited and non-permanent, and hence has conceived the desire of final release.
>
> The compound "brahmagigñāsā" is to be explained as "the enquiry of Brahman," the genitive case "of Brahman" being understood to denote the object; in agreement with the special rule as to the meaning of the genitive case, Pāṇini II, 3, 65. It might be said that even if we accepted the general meaning of the genitive case—which is that of connexion in general—Brah-man's position (in the above compound) as an object would be established by the circumstance that the "enquiry" demands an object; but in agreement with the principle that the direct denotation of a word is to be preferred to a meaning inferred we take the genitive case "of Brahman" as denoting the object.[10]

The auxiliary disciplines of the Veda are the *vedangas,* including pho-netics, meter, grammar, and etymology. So it is clear that Rāmānuja thinks that knowing grammar and other such disciplines would contribute to un-derstanding the sutras on which he is commenting. Similar valuations occur in the histories of other religious communities.

The fourteenth-century Muslim scholar Ibn Khaldūn, in a discussion of the Bedouin Arabic of Muhammad's time, says:

> (Now,) the Qur'ān was revealed in (the language of the Mudar), and the Prophetical traditions were transmitted in it, and both the Qur'ān and the traditions are the basis of Islam. It was feared that, as a result of the dis-appearance of the language in which they were revealed, they themselves might be forgotten and no longer be understood. Therefore, a systematic treatment of its laws, a presentation of the analogical formations used in it, and the derivation of its rules were needed. (Knowledge of Arabic) thus be-came a science with subdivisions, chapters, premises, and problems. The scholars who cultivated that science called it grammar and Arabic philology. It became a discipline known by heart and fixed in writing, a ladder leaning up to the understanding of the Book of God and the Sunnah of His Prophet.[11]

This is very strong positive valuation of knowing the grammar of a lan-guage.

10. *The Vedānta Sūtras,* pp. 3–4.
11. Ibn Khaldūn, *The Muqaddimah,* trans. Franz Rosenthal (New York: Pantheon, 1958), 3: 346–47. Rosenthal's glosses are in parentheses.

So our next question is whether in some cases the grammatical knowledge which is thus valued by spokesmen for religious communities is secular knowledge. Are some of the claims which are made in grammars of languages in which scriptures are written secular claims? Are they claims which do not depend, for their truth or rightness, on the distinctive doctrines of any religious community? And are those grammatical claims, or some of them, alien claims with respect to the community in question?

To an ordinary reader of Renou's translation of the sutras of Pānini[12] it seems clear that Pānini constructs his rules of Sanskrit grammar, and argues for them, as one would expect a secular grammarian to do, without introducing any distinctively religious doctrines in support of them. Further, Kielhorn has argued that later respected Indian grammarians, though they were followers and judicious admirers of Pānini, felt free to disagree with Pānini's rules for grammatical reasons and to correct them.[13] This suggests that these grammarians did not regard Pānini's rules as authentic doctrines of the Hindu community.

At one point in his commentary on Jaimini's Pūrva Mīmāmsā Sūtras, the modern commentator Ganganath Jha gives two traditional but opposed interpretations of the status of grammatical rules in relation to the Vedas. One interpretation is that grammatical rules are themselves Vedic:

> . . . we actually find Vedic injunctions supplying the basis for every one of the six factors of grammar:—*viz.*, the etymology of words, the correct forms of words, the necessity of using the correct forms of words, the actual use of such words, the prohibition of the using of words not shown to be correct by the rules of grammar, and the actual avoidance of such words. And all these injunctions being Vedic, these must be regarded to be as eternal as the injunctions laying down the use of kuśa and such other things at sacrifices.
>
> Thus then, the rules of grammar, being all based upon the Vedic grammar, must be allowed the same regard as all other Smritis, that is to say, they must be accepted as having an authoritative bearing upon dharma, specially as the chief use of grammar has been held to lie in the laying down of certain restrictions which help in the fulfilment of dharma. For instance, the restrictions that Grammar lays down are—(1) that one should use only the correct forms of words, the knowledge and use of such words leading the speaker to heaven and helping him to accomplish the Vedic sacrifices; and (2) that "such and such words are correct"—and without the rules of grammar it would not be possible to distinguish correct from incorrect words. Thus then the rules of grammar, being that part of the Vedic dharma which consists of the use of the duly discriminated correct forms of words, serve the purpose of pointing out such correct wordforms as are really expressive.

The other interpretation is as follows:

---

12. Louis Renou, *La Grammaire de Pānini* (Paris: Ecole Française d'Extrême-Orient, 1966.)
13. F. Kielhorn, *Kātyāyana and Patanjali: Their Relation to Each Other and to Pānini* (Varanasi: Indological Book House, 1963), pp. 46–56.

According to Prabhhākara, it is necessary to enquire into the trustworthy character of Grammar, not because it is a Smriti, but chiefly because if the science of grammar were not trustworthy, the whole fabric of Vedic dharma would be jeopardised; that is to say, that a certain word denotes a certain thing and not any other is ascertained finally by the rules of grammar alone; consequently, if these were untrustworthy, there would be no certainty in regard to the meaning of words; and in that case the meaning of all Vedic texts would be doubtful and vague; and this would shake the authority and trustworthy character of the entire Veda.[14]

It seems clear that according to the first interpretation grammatical rules are not, with respect to the Hindu community, alien claims; they are based on the Vedas themselves. They are part of the Vedic dharma, the Vedic instructions for conduct. Whether grammatical rules are secular, though not alien, claims, is not so clear in this interpretation. Here the question would be whether, though they are based on the Vedas and hence are authentic doctrines of the Hindu community, they could be discovered or constructed independently of the Vedas. In the latter case they would be secular claims which are also authentic doctrines of the community. Grammatical rules are not alien claims; whether they are secular claims is not so clear.

According to Prabhhākara's interpretation, grammatical rules are not dependent on the Veda. Instead, the trustworthiness of (our understanding of?) the Veda depends on the trustworthiness of grammar. (Here we should notice in passing a connection with our discussion of general principles of consistency in chapter 7. It seems that at this important point Prabhhākara is not afraid of relying on a general principle of intelligibility. He does not seem to fear that this would threaten the integrity of the body of doctrines of his community.) Now we may suppose that if the trustworthiness of grammar is not dependent on the authority of the Veda, then it is not dependent on the distinctive doctrines of any other religious community either. Hence grammatical rules would be secular claims. On this interpretation, what is not so clear is whether grammatical claims are also alien claims. For, as we have noticed in a number of earlier discussions, not all secular claims are alien claims with respect to the community in question.

It seems that Prabhhākara grants that grammar is a smriti (a work which has secondary authority for the Hindu community insofar as it agrees with the Vedas), though he says the trustworthiness of grammar does not depend on that. And he does not deny that grammatical rules are in accord with the Veda. So, it seems, he does not deny that grammatical rules are authentic doctrines of the Hindu community.

So some points in these passages seem clear enough, though others are

---

14. *The Pūrva Mīmāmsā Sūtras of Jaimini, Chapters I–III,* trans, with an original commentary by Ganganath Jha (Allahabad: Panini Office, 1916), pp. 90–91.

not so clear. But we do not need to settle the uncertain points. For our purpose it is enough to notice that, even if some claim about the language in which a scripture is written is both a secular claim and an alien claim, a community might hold and teach strong positive valuations of knowing what is said in the claim. Even if the accuracy and adequacy of a set of grammatical rules can be established by reference to grammatical facts and by grammatical reasoning without essential reference to the distinctive doctrines of the community, and even if the grammatical rules, or some of them, do not satisfy the community's criteria of authenticity (suppose that in the case above, grammar did not have the status of a smriti), it would still be possible for that community to have a high estimation of the importance of grammar for understanding a scripture. So we would need a distinction between the status of grammatical principles and rules themselves and the status of a community's estimation of their importance. Its valuations of a grammar may be authentic doctrines of the community, even if the grammatical principles and rules themselves are not.

A community's positive valuations of knowing the grammar of a language in which a scripture is written may be tempered by various considerations. A community may wish to avoid making grammatical learning a universal requirement for reading and understanding a scripture. It may be said that while it is good to have grammatical learning available to the community, still the essential lessons which the scripture teaches can be understood by those who have no special grammatical knowledge.

There may also be negative valuations of grammatical learning. It may be said that knowing the grammar of the language of a scripture, except insofar as this is obvious to an ordinary reader, is of no real worth. Or it may be said that grammatical learning, along with other arts and sciences, is spiritually harmful. Such learning distracts the mind from concentration on the plain truths and injunctions which the scripture is meant to convey.

Now consider two cases drawn from recent times, which bear on the comprehensiveness of patterns of life taught by religious communities and on valuations of secular alien claims.

VATICAN II

The following passages are drawn from translations of documents of the Second Council of the Vatican (1962–65).[15] These passages are relevant to our study because they express (1) an aim at developing a comprehensive pattern of life and (2) some judgments about secular inquiries and claims, theoretical and practical.

In the *Dogmatic Constitution on the Church (Lumen Gentium)*, lay people

15. Austin P. Flannery, ed., *Documents of Vatican II* (Grand Rapids: Eerdmans, 1975).

are urged to spread the kingdom of Christ, the kingdom of truth and justice. Lay people are said to enjoy a principal role in the fulfillment of this task.

> Therefore, by their competence in secular disciplines and by their activity, interiorly raised up by grace, let them work earnestly in order that created goods through human labor, technical skill and civil culture may serve the utility of all men according to the plan of the creator and the light of his word. [par. 36, p. 393]

A similar theme is developed in the *Decree on the Apostolate of Lay People (Apostolicam Actuositatem)*:

> That men, working in harmony, should renew the temporal order and make it increasingly more perfect: such is God's design for the World.
>
> All that goes to make up the temporal order: personal and family values, culture, economic interests, the trades and professions, institutions of the political community, international relations, and so on, as well as their gradual development—all these are not merely helps to man's last end; they possess a value of their own, placed in them by God, whether considered individually or as parts of the integral temporal structure: "And God saw all that he had made and found it very good" (Gen. 1:31). This natural goodness of theirs receives an added dignity from their relation with the human person, for whose use they have been created. And then, too, God has willed to gather together all that was natural, all that was supernatural, into a single whole in Christ, "so that in everything he would have the primacy" (Col. 1:18). Far from depriving the temporal order of its autonomy, of its specific ends, of its own laws and resources, or its importance for human well-being, this design, on the contrary, increases its energy and excellence, raising it at the same time to the level of man's integral vocation here below. [par. 7, pp. 773–74]

The following passage, under the heading: "Rightful Autonomy of Earthly Affairs," is from the *Pastoral Constitution on the Church in the Modern World (Gaudium et Spes)*:

> There seems to be some apprehension today that a close association between human activity and religion will endanger the autonomy of man, of organizations and of science. If by the autonomy of earthly affairs is meant the gradual discovery, exploitation, and ordering of the laws and values of matter and society, then the demand for autonomy is perfectly in order: it is at once the claim of modern man and the desire of the creator. By the very nature of creation, material being is endowed with its own stability, truth and excellence, its own order and laws. These man must respect as he recognizes the methods proper to every science and technique. Consequently, methodical research in all branches of knowledge, provided it is carried out in a truly scientific manner and does not override moral laws, can never conflict with the faith, because the things of the world and the things of faith derive from the same God. The humble and persevering investigator of the

secrets of nature is being led, as it were, by the hand of God in spite of himself, for it is God, the conserver of all things, who made them what they are. We cannot but deplore certain attitudes (not unknown among Christians) deriving from a shortsighted view of the rightful autonomy of science; they have occasioned conflict and controversy and have misled many into opposing faith and science. [par. 36, p. 935]

A footnote referred to at the end of this passage mentions Pius Paschini, *Vita e opere di Galileo Galilei,* 2 vol., Vatican, 1964.

The next passage occurs later in the same document:

In their pilgrimage to the heavenly city Christians are to seek and relish the things that are above: this involves not a lesser, but rather a greater commitment to working with all men towards the establishment of a world that is more human. Indeed, the mystery of the Christian faith provides them with an outstanding incentive and encouragement to fulfill their role even more eagerly and to discover the full sense of the commitment by which human culture becomes important in man's total vocation.

By the work of his hands and with the aid of technical means man tills the earth to bring forth fruit and to make it a dwelling place fit for all mankind; he also consciously plays his part in the life of social groups; in so doing he is realizing the design, which God revealed at the beginning of time, to subdue the earth and perfect the work of creation, and at the same time he is improving his own person: he is also observing the command of Christ to devote himself to the service of his fellow men.

Furthermore, when man works in the fields of philosophy, history, mathematics and science and cultivates the arts, he can greatly contribute towards bringing the human race to a higher understanding of truth, goodness, and beauty, to points of view having universal value; thus man will be more clearly enlightened by the wondrous Wisdom, which was with God from eternity, working beside him like a master craftsman, rejoicing in his inhabited world, and delighting in the sons of men (Proverbs 8:30–31). As a consequence the human spirit, freed from the bondage of material things, can be more easily drawn to the worship and contemplation of the creator. Moreover, man is disposed to acknowledge, under the impulse of grace, the Word of God, who was in the world as "the true light that enlightens every man" (Jn. 1:9), before becoming flesh to save and gather up all things in himself. [par. 57, p. 961]

We can ask whether these passages teach that it is right to engage in theoretical and practical secular inquiries, inquiries in which success is not measured by the distinctive standards of any religious community. The answer seems to be yes. One reason why this is right is that secular truths do not conflict with the doctrines of the church (p. 935). This seems to suppose, as a doctrine of the community about its doctrines, an extended principle of consistency, a doctrine to the following effect: If what is said in some sentence *(s1),* which is not an authentic doctrine of the community, is true, or right, and if some other sentence *(s2)* expresses an authentic doctrine of the community, then *s1* and *s2* are consistent. Further, it seems that a primary doctrine of the community, that "the things of the world and the things of faith derive from the same God," would be a reason in support of the extended principle of consistency.

Another reason that it is right to engage in secular inquiries is that the demand for the autonomy of earthly affairs, in the discovery and ordering of the laws and values of matter and society, is perfectly in order.

Indeed, it seems that it is not only right to engage in theoretical and practical secular inquiries; there is an obligation to do so. Competence in secular disciplines contributes to spreading Christ's kingdom of truth and justice (393), to renewal of the temporal order (773), to perfecting the work of creation (961). So if there is an obligation to use available means to such good ends, it seems there is an obligation to engage in secular inquiries.

Furthermore, work in philosophy, in history, in mathematics, in the natural sciences, and in the arts contributes toward enlightenment by the wondrous wisdom which was with God from eternity, working beside him as a master craftsman (961). This is a very strong valuation indeed!

It is plausible that some of the secular claims which are valued in these documents are alien claims with respect to the Roman Catholic community. It is plausible that some of these valuations are valuations of knowing truths which the community itself is not bound to teach, or valuations of knowing how to carry out right courses of action which the community is not bound to teach. But we cannot assume this. Recall the similar point we had to deal with in chapter 7 when we considered the treatment of doctrines of other religions in *Nostra Aetate*.

On this question notice especially the references in the documents to technical skill and civil culture (393), to trades and professions (773), to technical means, and to the fields of philosophy, history, mathematics, and science and the arts (961). It does seem plausible that some of the claims to truths and to right procedures in these fields of investigation and practice are claims which the Roman Catholic community itself is not bound to teach. But this will not be argued here. It is enough to point to a possibility.

KARL BARTH

Here is another case in point, which may bring with it some surprises. In Karl Barth's *Church Dogmatics* he expounds the theme that Jesus Christ is the light of life.[16] He says there are other "lights, words, truths" which are distinct from the light of Jesus Christ himself. He gives extended discussions of the relation of these other "lights, words, truths" to Jesus

16. Karl Barth, *The Doctrine of Reconciliation* (*Church Dogmatics*, vol. 4 [3.1]), trans. G. W. Bromiley (Edinburgh: T. & T. Clark, 1961), pp. 38–164.

Christ, who is *the* light of life. We should concentrate on some points which bear directly on our own inquiry.

Some of these "lights, words, truths" are (1) words of the Bible which witness to Jesus Christ, and some of them are (2) words of the Christian community proclaiming Jesus Christ (p. 110). But some of these "good words" (3) may be "spoken in the secular world and addressed to the community from it" (p. 116), even from a world which "is not yet or no longer attached to any religion" (p. 119). It seems that the passage we shall mainly attend to is meant to apply to words of this third class, and we shall take the passage in that application. Barth says that he refrains from giving concrete examples of words of this class because that would distract from his main point (p. 135).

There are some indications that the possible truths spoken in the secular world include moral truths as well as theoretical truths. For example, he speaks of "the sobriety of a scholarly or practical and everyday investigation of the true state of affairs" (p. 125). This might be taken also as an endorsement of secular inquiries. And he speaks of "a humanity which does not ask or weigh too long with whom we are dealing in others, but in which we find a simple solidarity with them and unreservedly take up their case" (ibid.).

It seems that in considering this third class of words Barth has secular truths and practices mainly in mind. There is no explicit mention of doctrines of other religions in this connection. But he does not seem to rule out the possibility that some of these "lights, words, truths" are doctrines of other religions.

Then he considers how "these true words can and should be made fruitful in and for the community" (p. 134), that is to say, the Christian community. He goes on as follows:

> If they are really true, and we have certainly to reckon with this possibility, why should they not do this without being given any canonical or dogmatic status? Their work will consist in leading the community at all times and places, and in all its members, more deeply into the given word of the Bible as the authentic attestation of the Word of Jesus Christ Himself. They will make a contribution to the strengthening, extending and defining of the Christian knowledge which draws from this source and is measured by this norm, to the lending of new seriousness and cheerfulness to the Christian life and new freedom and concentration to the delivery of the Christian message. We may let them do this work without the pretension of acquiring from them new tables or of being empowered and obligated by them to proclaim such tables. They do not need this to accomplish what they can and should accomplish. Why should not those to whom it is given to receive these true words confess them with gratitude, sincerity and resolution, yet also with the humility which is required at this point too? Why should they have to claim them as revelations and make of them a law for themselves

and others? Is it not enough if they are actually heard and followed? To be sure, those who receive them should stand by their insight to the extent that they are sure of their ground. They should not keep it to themselves. They should hold it up as an invitation and summons to others, to the whole community, to share it with them. But they should do this in such a way that they allow the fact of the instruction received from them to speak for itself. They should show themselves to be such as have heard a true word and been radically smitten by it. They should bring forth the appropriate fruits. And then, with a readiness to be corrected, they should leave it to the power of this true word, by the ministry (and not the assertive claim) of its confession, to cause its truth to shine to others and to awaken its recognition and confession in them too. If it is a true word, the time will inevitably come sooner or later when it can make its way and do its work in and to the whole community. As it is really spoken in world history, and in the measure that it is really received in the community, it will certainly do this work in and to it. The more certain the community or individuals within it are of their knowledge of such a word, the greater should be their confidence in its own power, and the more boldly yet also the more modestly will they make known their knowledge. For in these circumstances it will definitely not have been spoken or received in vain. [pp. 134–35]

Notice some features of this passage, drawing on other passages as we go.

Taking them as they come, the "lights, words, truths" of which Barth is now speaking are not Christian doctrines. In the terms we have been using they are alien claims. Yet they may be true or right. So it seems clear that Barth is proposing for his own community the position we considered in chapter 6, that there may be truths and right courses of action which the community itself is not bound to teach.

Further, the passage implies in its rhetorical questions, there is no good reason to adopt them as doctrines of the community. They do not need to be baptized, so to speak, into the body of Christian doctrines. Earlier, Barth has said, "the sphere of the Bible and the Church" is a "narrower and smaller" sphere than the sphere of the dominion of Jesus Christ. Those who have their place and task in the sphere of the Bible and the church "can and must expect that His voice will also be heard" outside this sphere. "In the narrow corner in which we have our place and task we cannot but eavesdrop in the world at large" (p. 117).

Incidentally, we should notice Barth's claim that the position he takes here does not depend on natural theology. He says:

It will be seen that, in order to perceive that we really have to reckon with such true words from without, we have no need to appeal either for basis or content to the sorry hypothesis of a so-called "natural theology" (i.e., a knowledge of God given in and with the natural force of reason or to be attained in its exercise). Even if this were theologically meaningful or practicable (which it is not), it could not provide us with what is required. By way of natural theology, apart from the Bible and the Church, there can be attained only abstract impartations concerning God's existence as the Supreme Being and Ruler of all things, and man's responsibility towards Him. But these are not what we have in view. What we have in view are attestations of the self-impartation of the God who acts as Father in the Son by the Holy Ghost, which show themselves to be such by their full agreement with the witness present in Scripture and accepted and proclaimed by the Church, and which can be materially tested by and compared with this witness. What we have in view are words which like those of the Bible and the Church can be claimed as "parables of the kingdom". Natural theology would belie its very name if it had any interest in words of this type, while we for our part have no interest in what it thinks it can advance as true words concerning God and man in general. [p. 117]

Members of the community who receive and accept these secular "lights, words, truths" should stand by their insights to the extent that they are sure of their ground. And they should not keep these insights to themselves. They should hold them up as invitations to others, to the whole community, to share them. But they should allow the instruction received from these words to speak for itself.

It seems clear that the passage supposes an extended principle of consistency. It is supposed that if these words, which are not Christian doctrines, are really true or right, then what is said in them is not inconsistent with authentic doctrines of the Christian community.

The passage has another surprise in store for those who come to it with some of the author's earlier writings in mind. Going far beyond the supposition that true alien claims are consistent with authentic Christian doctrines, it says that if these words from the secular world are really true they will lead the Christian community more deeply into the given word of the Bible. These secular words will make a positive contribution to understanding the Bible, and to strengthening, extending, and defining the Christian knowledge which draws from the Bible. This may be a thought for Christian theologians not only to wonder at but to ponder as they consider what their community ought to teach about alien claims.

So it seems clear that, among other points Barth is making, he is proposing (1) that the Christian community should grant that there may be truths and right courses of action which the community is not bound to teach, and (2) that the Christian community should teach positive valuations of knowing such truths and of knowing how to carry out such courses of action.

SOME SCHEMAS OF VALUATIONS OF ALIEN CLAIMS

Now let us develop some schemas of primary doctrines which would propose valuations of alien claims. Let s stand for some claim or other which, with respect to the community which proposes the valuation, is an alien claim.

1. Supposing that what is asserted in *s* is true, it would be good to know that feature of the world because . . . (Reasons for the valuation such as the following could replace the dots, and similarly for the other schemas to come.)

knowing that feature of the world would conduce to liberation from aversions, adversions, and confusions which hinder attainment of enlightenment. (For example, suppose this is said of a detailed physiological account of the human body.)

knowing that feature of the world would conduce to more intelligent and discriminating praise of the creator.

2. Supposing that what is said in *s* is true, it would not be good to know that feature of the world because . . .

knowing that feature of the world would distract one from following the path to enlightenment.

knowing that feature of the world would be a temptation to intellectual pride.

3. Supposing that the course of action proposed in *s* is right, it would be good to know how to carry out that course of action because . . .

knowing how to carry out that course of action would enable one to do well the work of one's calling and thus to put one's faith into practice.

knowing how to carry out that course of action would conduce to better understanding of the scriptures. (For example, suppose this is said of studying the grammar of the language of the community's scriptures.)

4. Supposing that the course of action proposed in *s* is right, it would not be good to know how to carry out that course of action because . . .

knowing how to carry out that course of action would encourage trivial pursuits instead of searching for wisdom. (For example, suppose this is said of games and sports.)

knowing how to carry out that course of action would conduce to possessiveness and greed. (For example, suppose this is said of commercial transactions.)

A PERSPECTIVE

Our question has been: How could the pattern of life taught by a community be comprehensive even if the community acknowledges that there may be truths and right courses of action which it is not bound to teach and hence that the scope of its body of doctrines is limited?

Several considerations were brought forward. First, instead of aiming at teaching all truths whatever and all right courses of action whatever, a community would aim at developing a pattern of life which would have a bearing on any occasion of human activity. The comprehensiveness at which it would aim would be occasion comprehensiveness.

Second, among the elements of the pattern of life the community teaches there would be beliefs and valuations which could be particularized so as to bear on wide ranges of the settings of occasions of human activity. Likewise, among the courses of action which are elements of the pattern there would be general courses of action which would bear on wide ranges of responses to these settings, along with a multiplicity of specific precepts, developed perhaps into a comprehensive code of conduct.

We have concentrated on another part of an answer to our question, one which bears more directly on the specifics of the question, since it deals with the relevance of a pattern to occasions in which secular alien claims are encountered. A pattern of life would include among its elements valuations of inquiries which the community is not bound to undertake and valuations of truths and right courses of action which the community is not bound by its criteria of authenticity to teach. This would amplify the range of significance of the pattern. It would extend the range of the pattern to cover the multiplicity of occasions of human activity in which truths and right courses of action which lie beyond the bounds of the community's own body of doctrines are reckoned with.

Recall the generic features of a secular alien claim:

1. It is a claim that some existential or valuational proposition is true or that some course of action is right.

2. Whether the proposition is true or the course of action is right does not depend on the distinctive doctrines of any religious community. The claim is a secular claim.

3. What is proposed in the claim is not an authentic doctrine of the community in question. With respect to that community the claim is an alien claim.

A valuation of a claim that some proposition is true is a judgment that it is good, in some certain way and for some reason or other, to know that the proposition is true, supposing it is indeed true. Or the valuation is a judgment that it is not good to know that the proposition is true.

A valuation of a claim that some course of action is right is a judgment that it is good, in some certain way and for some reason or other, to know how to carry out the course of action, supposing it is indeed right. Or the valuation is a judgment that it is not good to know how to carry out that course of action.

We have been concerned with valuations which are elements of patterns of life taught by religious communities. In such doctrines a community proposes to its members that they should judge the claims they encounter in one or another of these ways and that they should live in accord with these judgments. In particular, we have been concerned with proposals by religious communities of valuations of secular alien claims.

These proposals of valuations would be primary doctrines of religious communities. They would not be doctrines of a community about its own doctrines. Instead they are directly about a feature of the social environment of a community, namely secular claims which, with respect to that community, are alien claims.

Such doctrines, we may suppose, could be firmly embedded in the body of doctrines of a community. They would be required by some other doctrines of the community, and substantive reasons for making the proposed judgments could be drawn from other primary doctrines of the community, as we have noticed at a number of points.

But, though these valuational doctrines would be authentic doctrines of a community, what would be valued or disvalued would be knowledge of some truth which is not taught in authentic doctrines of the community, or practical knowledge of some course of action which is not taught in authentic doctrines of the community. The authenticity of the valuation would not confer authenticity on what is said in the alien claim. We might say that in such cases authenticity is intransitive. These would be cases where claims which are not themselves authentic doctrines of a community would be given an import (though not authenticity) by authentic doctrines of that community.

Though we have concentrated on doctrines which propose valuations of secular alien claims, much that has been said of them could also be said of doctrines which propose valuations of alien claims which are doctrines of other religious communities. This latter topic deserves much more attention than it has been given here.

CHAPTER NINE

A General Perspective

The primary doctrines of a religious community, its doctrines about the setting of human life and the conduct of life in that setting, include proposals for belief about existents and the conditions of existence, proposals of courses of outward and inward action, and proposals of valuations of various features of the setting of human life and of human activities. In these doctrines taken together a community proposes a pattern of life to its members. It aims to nurture its members in living in accord with this pattern.

A case has been made for saying that, along with their primary doctrines, religious communities also hold and teach doctrines of a different kind. We have been speaking of these as doctrines of religious communities about their doctrines, or as governing doctrines. These doctrines are not directly about the world and conduct in the world, as the primary doctrines are. Instead, they are meant by a community to guide and govern its own teaching activities.

Of course the teaching activities of a community are in the world, and they can be reflected on and studied by the community itself as well as by secular historians, anthropologists, sociologists, and others including philosophers. From such studies a community might learn something about itself. But in developing its doctrines about its doctrines a community sets out not just to describe or to analyze its teaching activities, as secular studies might do, but to develop its norms for its teaching activities. It works out principles and rules for governing the formation and development of its body of doctrines.

So the intent of a community's presentations of its governing doctrines differs from the intent of its presentations of its primary doctrines. Like other human beings the members of a community need to find their way in the world. In its primary doctrines a community presents to them a pattern of life, which may be addressed to nonmembers of the community as well. But unlike nonmembers of the community, its members are in a position to contribute responsibly both to the community's exposition of its doctrines and to the community's reflection on its doctrines. In saying and showing what they have learned from the community—from those who have educated them in the life of the community, from the sources of its doctrines, and otherwise—they have a part in the teaching activities of the community. This is so whether or not they have special vocations as teachers of the community. Also, their own reflections on what they have learned contribute to the further shaping of the community's doctrines, including its doctrines about its doctrines.

Nonmembers of the community are not in the same position, so the community's presentations of its governing doctrines are not addressed to nonmembers of the community in the same way they are addressed to its members. We might say that a community's doctrines about its doctrines are presented to nonmembers of the community, in response to requests for explanations of its body of doctrines, for example, but not proposed to them. In contrast, a community's primary doctrines, or some of them, may just as well be proposed to nonmembers of the community as to its members.

Certainly a community's doctrines about its doctrines are not proposed to other religious communities as principles and rules for governing the teaching activities of those communities. A community's doctrines about its doctrines are meant to govern its own teaching activities. So a community's doctrines about its doctrines do not pose direct challenges to the governing doctrines of some other religious community in the way the community's primary doctrines might pose challenges to the primary doctrines of some other religious community.

In earlier chapters, some types of doctrines about doctrines have been introduced and discussed. Now it is time to look again at these and to reflect further on some of their connections and consequences. First, a list of these types of doctrines:

Principles and rules of a community for judging whether what is proposed in some sentence is an authentic doctrine of the community.

Principles and rules of a community for orderings of its doctrines in importance.

Principles and rules of a community on consistency: principles of internal consistency and extended principles of consistency.

Principles and rules of a community which connect claims to authenticity and claims to truth, or rightness.

Principles and rules of a community for deriving and arguing for its doctrines.

Principles and rules of a community on the scope and the comprehensiveness of its primary doctrines, that is to say, of the pattern of life in which it nurtures its members.

It has been argued in a general way that religious communities need doctrines to govern the formation and development of their bodies of doctrines, as well as doctrines about the world and conduct in the world. And it does seem clear that a community which reflects on its doctrines needs criteria of authenticity and a principle of internal consistency.

But it has not been argued that all religious communities ought to hold and teach governing doctrines of all the types on the list. And it has not been argued, with respect to any particular community, that the community ought to hold and teach a certain governing doctrine of some type instead of some other governing doctrine of that type. (Though it was indeed argued in chapter 4 that doctrines which fit the pattern of schema T/R-A are problematical.)

Instead, as explained in chapter 1 and elsewhere, my main argument is in this and in other respects hypothetical. The argument is designed to show some suppositions and consequences of holding and teaching governing doctrines of the types listed. Whether or not some community is in a position to hold and teach a certain doctrine of one or another of these types depends on that community: on what the sources of its doctrines happen to be, on its primary doctrines, and on its other governing doctrines. Furthermore, it has not been claimed that this list of types of governing doctrines is complete. It may be that there are communities which hold and teach governing doctrines of types which are not on the list.

Now some comments on the types of doctrines which have been introduced, taking the types one by one.

AUTHENTICITY

Recall the account given in chapter 2. A principle of a community for judging the authenticity of what is said in some sentence would fit the pattern of a schema such as the following, where s stands for what is proposed in some sentence:

s is an authentic doctrine of the community only if . . . (or only if . . . and . . . ; or only if . . . or. . . ; or only if . . . unless . . .).
s is an authentic doctrine of the community if . . . (or if . . . and. . . ; or if . . . or. . . ; or if . . . unless . . .).

Some examples were given of conditions which, depending on the community in question, could be substituted for ellipsis points in the schemas, such as the following:

s is a clear teaching of the scriptures of the community.
s has not been denied by respected teachers of the community.
s follows from an authentic doctrine of the community.

We have spoken of such conditions as specific criteria of authenticity or simply as criteria of authenticity. So criteria of authenticity are embedded in the frameworks of principles of authenticity. To implement such a principle rules are developed (as in the passage from the Mahāparinibbānasutta) for judging whether some such condition holds in a particular case.

A further point about conditions of authenticity was brought out in chapter 4. Suppose a community has among its governing doctrines a principle which says that its authentic doctrines are true or right (an A-T/R doctrine). Then the truth or rightness of what is said in some sentence would also be a condition of its authenticity.

But this condition of authenticity is different from those discussed in chapter 2, that is to say from criteria of authenticity. Criteria of authenticity have a heuristic value this condition does not have. This condition does not guide judgments as to which true or right sentences are authentic doctrines of the community. To find this out, criteria of authenticity would be needed.

Two further comments: (1) Though it is hard to see how a reflective community could do without principles of authenticity of some sort or other, the discussion in chapter 2 does not limit the range of a community's criteria of authenticity. It leaves open the question what a particular community's criteria of authenticity should be. (2) If a community has principles of authenticity for its doctrines, these would apply to the authenticity of governing doctrines as well as to the authenticity of primary doctrines.

ORDERINGS OF DOCTRINES

Principles and rules of this type would govern a community's assignments of priorities among its authentic doctrines, though it has not been argued that a community ought to assign priorities among its doctrines. Some such doctrines were discussed in the early part of chapter 3. Doctrines of this type have not played an important part in the main argument; no doubt they deserve more attention than has been given them.

CONSISTENCY

Governing doctrines on the internal consistency of a body of doctrines were discussed in chapter 3. The schema given there for principles of internal consistency was as follows:

For any pair of sentences $(s1, s2)$, if
(1) $s1$ is an authentic doctrine of the community, and
(2) $s2$ is an authentic doctrine of the community, then $s1$ and $s2$ are consistent.

Hence, if $s1$ and $s2$ are inconsistent, then
(1) $s1$ is not an authentic doctrine of the community, or
(2) $s2$ is not an authentic doctrine of the community, or

(3) neither *s1* nor *s2* is an authentic doctrine of the community.

Notice that, with a governing doctrine which fits the pattern of this schema, the only cases where sentences would be said to be consistent would be cases where both sentences of some pair are authentic doctrines of the community in question. This suggests that a principle of internal consistency does not depend on general principles of consistency. Also it reminds us again of the prominence of principles of authenticity among the types of doctrines about doctrines we have been considering.

Extended principles of consistency are unlike principles of internal consistency with respect to their coverage. Principles of internal consistency cover cases where the issue is the consistency of doctrines of the community with one another. Extended principles of consistency cover cases where the issue is the consistency of an authentic doctrine of the community and an alien claim. These principles were introduced in chapter 7, where the following schema for them was given:

For any pair of sentences *(s1, s2)*, if
(1) *s1* is an authentic doctrine of the community (hence true or right), and
(2) *s2* is not an authentic doctrine of the community, then, if *s2* is true or right, *s1* and *s2* are consistent.

Hence, if *s1* and *s2* are inconsistent, then
(1) *s1* is not an authentic doctrine of the community, or
(2) *s2* is not true or not right, or
(3) both (1) and (2) hold.

The terms *true* and *right* did not occur in the schema of principles of internal consistency, but they are needed here to link together doctrines and alien claims.

The expression "hence true, or right" signals that a principle of extended consistency supposes that the community claims that its authentic doctrines are true or right. That is to say, if a community holds and teaches an extended principle of consistency, this supposes that the community holds and teaches that its authentic doctrines are true or right (an A-T/R doctrine). For if a community should fail to claim that its authentic doctrines are true or right, how could its doctrines be linked with alien claims in such a way as to be consistent or inconsistent with them?

Consider another sort of connection. In chapter 7 we considered primary doctrines which would grant that there may be alien claims which are true or right. Now it seems that a community could not grant that some alien claim may be true or right unless it supposes that what is said in the claim is consistent with authentic doctrines of the community. So it seems that the position taken in such a primary doctrine would call for an extended principle of consistency to cover such cases.

It seems evident that an extended principle of consistency would have to rely on a general principle of consistency, which would say that, for any pair of claims to truth or rightness, if each member of the pair is true or right, then the members of the pair are consistent with one another.

It has not been argued that a community must have an extended principle of consistency. Suppose a community is concerned at most with the consistency of its doctrines with one another. Suppose that in its teaching activities it can ignore those doctrines of other religious communities and those secular claims which do not also belong to its own body of doctrines. Suppose it can insulate the teaching of its own doctrines from alien claims.

Then it seems that a principle of internal consistency would be sufficient for that community. It would not need to concern itself with the consistency or inconsistency of alien claims with its doctrines. So it could do without a governing doctrine which would fit the pattern of the schema for extended principles of consistency.

But if a community should extend its concern to the consistency or inconsistency of alien claims with its doctrines, it would need an extended principle of consistency, and therewith it would need to rely on a general principle of consistency.

AUTHENTICITY AND TRUTH OR RIGHTNESS

Doctrines about doctrines which would connect claims to authenticity and claims to truth or rightness were discussed in chapter 4, beginning with the following schemas:

Schema T/R-A
For any sentence (s), if what is proposed in s is true or right, then what is proposed in s is an authentic doctrine of the community.
Hence if what is proposed in s is not an authentic doctrine of the community, then what is proposed in s is not true or not right.

Schema A-T/R
For any sentence, if what is proposed in s is an authentic doctrine of the community, then what is proposed in s is true or right.
Hence, if what is proposed in s is not true or not right, then what is proposed in s is not an authentic doctrine of the community.

It became evident that the consequences of doctrines which fit the patterns of these schemas are far reaching. They would have consequences for other governing doctrines of a community and for primary doctrines of the community, especially for its primary doctrines about alien claims. Much depends on the way a community connects claims to authenticity with claims to truth or (for practical claims) rightness.

But we noticed that neither of these principles is strictly indispensable for a community. Suppose a community holds and teaches as a governing doctrine that its doctrines must be derivable from its authentic sources. We have spoken of this as the guarding principle. And suppose further that neither of these principles is derivable from the authentic sources of that community. Then it seems that the community would have reason enough to abstain from embodying either principle in a doctrine about its doctrines.

DERIVING DOCTRINES FROM SOURCES

For this purpose various kinds of principles and rules would be needed. A community would need principles and rules for identifying its authentic sources. It would need principles on whether to order its sources in importance, and if so, how and why. It would need hermeneutical principles for interpreting its sources. And it would need logical principles and rules to guide conclusions as to whether the sources warrant some doctrine.

ARGUING FOR DOCTRINES

We considered, as doctrines about doctrines, the following types of rules to govern arguments in support of a community's doctrines.

I. Doctrines of the community are supportable only by arguments for their authenticity.
II. Doctrines of the community are supportable by direct arguments for their truth, or rightness, as well as by arguments for their authenticity.
III. Substantive reasons advanced in direct arguments for the truth, or rightness, of doctrines of the community must themselves be authentic doctrines of the community.

The consistency and the connections of these rules for arguments with the A-T/R principle (that authentic doctrines of the community are true or right), with the guarding principle and with one another, were discussed in detail. This was an opportunity to explore some interrelations among doctrines about doctrines of different types.

THE SCOPE AND THE COMPREHENSIVENESS OF A PATTERN OF LIFE

We can sum up the discussion of these points in chapter 8 by comparing the following principles taken as governing doctrines.

A There are no limits on the scope of the primary doctrines of the community; the community aims at making its pattern of life topic comprehensive.

Notice incidentally that this principle would follow from a T/R-A doctrine which would say that, for any sentence, if what is proposed in the sentence is true or right, then the sentence expresses an authentic doctrine of the community.

From principle A it would follow that, for any topic of inquiry in perceptual experience, in historical study, in the natural and the social sciences, and in other inquiries, if there are evident or discoverable truths on that topic, then the community ought to aim at teaching those truths. Also, for any topic of practical inquiry in arts, crafts, moral conduct, or other activities, if there are right courses of action which are evident or discoverable, the community ought to aim at teaching those courses of action.

B There are limits on the scope of the primary doctrines of the community; it does not aim at making its pattern of life topic comprehensive.

We considered several lines of argument a community might advance in support of this principle. It could argue that it is bound to teach only those truths and right courses of action which are necessary to attainment of the end or ends set forth in its pattern of life. There may be truths and right courses of action which are not necessary to such attainment.

Or a community might argue that it is bound not to extend the scope of its primary doctrines beyond the limits of its authorizations. Its warrants for its teachings come from the authentic sources of its doctrines. There may well be truths and right courses of action which the community is not warranted to teach.

Or a community might argue that there are claims to truth or to rightness which it is not competent to judge. There are issues to which its competence does not extend. A related point would be that there are issues on which the community has not yet resolved what its judgment should be.

Or a community might advance more than one of these lines of argument for limitations on the scope of its primary doctrines.

C The community aims at making its pattern of life occasion comprehensive, so it would be capable of being brought to bear on any occasion of human activity.

Occasion comprehensiveness was explained as follows: a pattern of life is occasion comprehensive if, for any occasion of human activity, some elements of the pattern are relevant to that occasion. So occasion comprehensiveness does not require topic comprehensiveness.

A pattern of life could be relevant to the activity of a historian, a physicist, a blacksmith, or a theatrical director even if some of the topics reflected on in the activity are not treated in the pattern. It may be that the community is not in a position to offer the agent all the theoretical and practical knowledge needed to carry out the activity. But if some elements of the pattern are relevant to the setting of the activity, to its motives and its ends in view, or to its consequences, the pattern would still cover the occasion.

Principle *A* and principle *B* are incompatible alternatives. Each speaks to the range of topics of the primary doctrines of a community. Principle *A* says the range of topics is not limited; principle *B* says the range is limited. Principle *C* does not speak to the range of the topics of primary doctrines; instead it speaks to the range of relevance of primary doctrines to occasions of human activity. So principle *C* is compatible with principle *B*; it is compatible with acceptance of limitations on the range of the topics of primary doctrines of the community.

In many occasions of human activity claims are entertained, investigated, or proposed which, with respect to some community, are alien claims. How could the pattern of life of that community be relevant to such occasions? The pattern of life a community teaches its members would be directly relevant to alien claims, and thus relevant to occasions of activity in which they are ingredients, if the pattern includes positive or negative valuations of knowing truths proposed in alien claims, or of knowing how to carry out right courses of action proposed in alien claims.

These valuations would be authentic elements in the pattern of life the community teaches, though as it happens the claims themselves would not be authentic doctrines of the community. Such valuational doctrines were discussed in the latter part of chapter 8 with a number of examples.

A valuation taught in such a doctrine is not a judgment that what is proposed in the alien claim is true or right. Instead it is a judgment that, if what is proposed in the alien claim is true or right, it would be good (or, detrimental) in some way to have that theoretical or practical knowledge.

So a condition for a community's teaching such valuational doctrines is that among its other primary doctrines it teaches that there may be alien claims which are true or right. And if a community grants this it would need to have among its governing doctrines an extended principle of consistency, which would say that if some alien claim is true or right, it is consistent with authentic doctrines of the community.

At a number of points we have noticed that primary doctrines of a community have consequences for its governing doctrines, and that a community's governing doctrines have consequences for its primary doctrines. Now one more remark on this topic.

Suppose a community has criteria of authenticity built into the frameworks of principles of authenticity. Suppose also that it has a principle of internal consistency. Suppose now that in the course of the community's reflections on its doctrines it appears that (a) some primary doctrine, which the community has been teaching under the impression that it is authentic, and (b) some governing doctrine, which the community has been teaching under a similar impression, appear to be inconsistent with one another.

Then something or other has gone wrong. Consider possible outcomes of this situation.

One outcome would be that after further reflection the community comes to see that the inconsistency is only apparent, not real. One of the doctrines or both have been misleadingly expressed. Or, consistency has been confused with the stronger relation coherence. Or some other mistake has been made in coming to the conclusion that the primary doctrine and the governing doctrine are inconsistent with one another.

But suppose the inconsistency is not just apparent; it is a real inconsistency. How then could the community reckon with it? From the community's principle of internal consistency it would follow that (1) the primary doctrine is not an authentic doctrine of the community, or (2) the governing doctrine is not an authentic doctrine of the community, or (3) neither is an authentic doctrine of the community.

At this stage in the reflections of the community its principle of internal consistency would be of no further help. That principle would leave the options just mentioned on an equal footing. It would not exempt either the primary doctrine or the governing doctrine from further scrutiny of its authenticity. It would not tell the community just where something has gone wrong.

So it seems that the community would then have to review its criteria of authenticity, the sources to which those criteria point, and its principles and rules for deriving its doctrines from its sources. There may not be just one point in its body of doctrines it would have to attend to, somewhat as there is not just one point at which a tent is anchored to the ground against storms and other disturbances.

This shows us something about the standings of primary doctrines and governing doctrines in a body of doctrines. It also shows that an inconsistency is not necessarily a disaster. And it would help to explain how rethinkings and reshapings of bodies of doctrines sometimes occur.

No doubt the formation and development of a community's body of doctrines is conditioned by events and processes the community does not control. Indeed, in many cases the community is not even clearly aware of these events and processes. But if a community is healthy and vigorous, it will respond to the conditions of its existence in its own way. When new questions about its doctrines arise, it will study its sources anew; it will reflect on the decisions about its doctrines it came to in its past, and on the problems those decisions were meant to settle; and it will face again the question what it ought to teach on the point at issue.

In a reflective community one feature of the activity to which it is stirred by such situations is the development of norms for its doctrines. It aims to develop consistent and adequate principles and rules to guide its decisions about what it ought to teach in this or that kind of situation, or in general, and to guide its everyday teaching activities. We have taken some steps toward studying such principles and rules.

In the past two centuries there has been a tendency for philosophers of religion to take the religious reflections of individuals as their subject matter. One reason is that in this period the ties of individuals to religious communities have often been loosened or broken. So individuals who continue to have active religious interests have tended to look elsewhere than to their own communities for inspiration and guidance. In response, many philosophers of religion have undertaken to offer inspiration and guidance to such individuals in their religious reflections. So a good deal of what has been produced under the auspices of philosophy of religion has been religious philosophy.

This investigation has moved in a different direction. In the first place, instead of taking religious reflections of individuals as its subject matter, it has dealt with bodies of doctrines of religious communities. Second, instead of offering an alternative to doctrines of religious communities, it has asked what philosophers could learn by studying bodies of doctrines.

To develop some of the possibilities it studies some principles and rules which would function as norms for bodies of doctrines. It asks what their suppositions would be, and what consequences they would have for a community's doctrines and teaching practices. Also it explores some positions a community could take on claims which are not themselves authentic doctrines of the community but, with respect to the community, alien claims. These would include those doctrines of other religious communities which are not also doctrines of the community. And they would include alien claims which are independent of the distinctive doctrines of any religious community, that is to say secular alien claims.

Thus the investigation is aimed at opening up not only a way to learn something about the internal structure of a body of doctrines but also a way to learn something about how a community faces the world around it.

How much philosophers can learn about doctrines of religious communities, and what they can learn, depends on the questions they bring to their subject matter, though they may be prompted to their questions by what they find in their subject matter. There are analogies here with philosophical studies of scientific inquiries and scientific institutions, with philosophical studies of law and legal institutions, and with philosophical studies of politics and political institutions.

Such subject matters for philosophical inquiries, we might say, do not wear on their sleeves what philosophers would like to know about them. Teachers of religious communities, scientists, lawyers, and statesmen do not always ask the questions philosophers find it interesting and important to ask.

Whether a philosophical question about doctrines of religious communities is a good question to ask depends on (1) whether the question is framed with some reasonably clear distinctions of a philosophical kind in mind, and (2) whether there is something in the subject matter on which the question can take hold.

The array of principles and rules displayed here is like a pattern on a transparent overlay which could be placed on maps of various territories. The territories would be the bodies of doctrines of the major religious communities. The features of the bodies of doctrines from which the maps would be constructed would be learned from the histories and the literatures of the communities, taken one by one, and from what their present members have to say about them.

By applying the overlay, someone who knows some such territory well would be in a position to ask questions which may not have arisen otherwise. Are there similarities and contrasts between features of the pattern on the overlay and features of the map? Does the pattern fit the map? In what respects is there a fit, and in what respects not? Just as much could be learned by finding that the pattern does not fit as by finding that it fits. If the pattern is well constructed, and if the map is accurate, something can be learned either way.

No maps of such territories have been given here. Bodies of doctrines taken one by one have not been discussed as wholes or even introduced. Instead, hypothetical questions have been explored. Though the principles and rules presented here are not purported or argued to be authentic doctrines of any particular religious community, they are not purely imaginary constructions. The passages given at many places in the argument strongly suggest that they have some applications. A number of points about them are logically interesting, but the main object is to show how light could be shed on doctrines of religious communities.

Finally, some remarks about further philosophical investigations this study might encourage and contribute to. We have concentrated on governing doctrines of certain types. Governing doctrines of other types deserve more attention, for example hermeneutical doctrines of religious communities. Though some such principles and rules have been noticed here and there, not much has been done about them. Phenomenologists and literary theorists have had a great deal to say about hermeneutics. But projects of the sort envisaged here would keep general hermeneutical theories far enough in the background to concentrate on their own topic. They would take account of the literatures and teaching practices of diverse communities, even if they concentrated on some one. They would focus on principles and rules for deriving authentic doctrines of a community from its sources. These would come into use whenever a community asks what it ought to teach in a situation of some sort, or in general. Distinctions and insights would be brought to bear on these principles and rules and their uses.

Another topic calling for further investigation is the following. What arguments do teachers of religious communities, taken one by one, advance in support of their doctrines? Arguments advanced in situations where opposed doctrines of other religious communities are confronted would be especially interesting. On this topic much can be learned from Ninian Smart's *Doctrine and Argument in Indian Philosophy* and from his earlier *Reasons and Faiths*.

An investigation might begin with a community's primary doctrines about alien claims. Does the community grant that there may be alien claims which are true or right? Especially, does it grant that there may be doctrines of other religious communities which, though they are alien claims, are true or right? Also, the community's governing doctrines which bear on arguments would be considered. Does the community claim that its authentic doctrines are true or right? Does it hold and teach an extended principle of consistency? What patterns of arguments does it approve?

Then the investigation would concentrate on passages in the literature of the community in which doctrines of other communities are confronted. Are the uses of arguments in these passages consistent with the community's primary doctrines and with its governing doctrines? Other questions about the arguments, and the suppositions and consequences of their uses, would arise as the project unfolds. Also, the door to comparative studies of arguments advanced by teachers of different communities would be open.

Index